Genesis 1–11

Genesis 1–11

Its Literary Coherence and Theological Message

Thomas A. Keiser

WIPF & STOCK · Eugene, Oregon

GENESIS 1–11
Its Literary Coherence and Theological Message

Copyright © 2013 Thomas A. Keiser. All rights reserved. Except for brief quotations in critical publications or reviews, no part of this book may be reproduced in any manner without prior written permission from the publisher. Write: Permissions. Wipf and Stock Publishers, 199 W. 8th Ave., Suite 3, Eugene, OR 97401.

Wipf & Stock
An Imprint of Wipf and Stock Publishers
199 W. 8th Ave., Suite 3
Eugene, OR 97401

www.wipfandstock.com

ISBN 13: 978-1-62564-092-5

Manufactured in the U.S.A.

To my wife, Kris

ורחק מפנינים מכרה

Prov 31:10b

Contents

Foreword by Eugene H. Merrill / ix
Acknowledgments / xi
Abbreviations / xii

1   Introduction / 1
2   The Unity of Gen 1–11 / 14
3   The Work of God: The Theology of Gen 1:1—2:3 / 26
4   Creation in the Hands of Humanity:
    The Theology of Gen 2:4—4:26 / 73
5   Judgment, Deliverance, and Salvation:
    The Theology of Gen 5:1—11:27 / 119
6   Summary and Implications / 144

Bibliography / 161

Foreword

Works on Old Testament biblical theology by evangelical scholars have proliferated in the past 40 years or so along with serious exegetical and literary work covering the full range of biblical revelation. However, the combination of these elements that results in a theology grounded in careful study of the text in its original language—its grammar and syntax, its historical and cultural setting, and its literary genre—is rare indeed. Professor Keiser has undertaken the project at hand with a keen sense of the need to integrate both the painstaking task of discovering what the text says by careful attention to its minutiae of lexical and grammatical data as well as attention to the whole, an inductive process that derives theological meaning from the text within its larger context. More important, he approaches his subject well equipped to "decompose" texts as it were, and then to reassemble them in lucid and logical theological terms that make for both delightfully understandable prose and readily apparent application to life and ministry.

The parameters of his endeavors here are remarkably appropriate for this day and time when evangelicals, in particular, are re-framing or perhaps opening for the first time questions about so-called proto-history, that is, the first eleven chapters of Genesis that for centuries have been considered by scholars of the historical-critical school to have little if any legitimate claim to historical reality. Evangelicals lately have found a way out of the impasse of remaining true to the Bible as God's inerrant revelation on the one hand, and, on the other hand, finding a place within the larger academic community that has for years barred them from engagement because of the literalness with which they have approached biblical texts, particularly those purporting to historicize persons and events of the pre-patriarchal world. This has been done largely by (1) ignoring the plain grammatical and syntactical sense of the passages in question and

Foreword

(2) resorting to literary genre analyses that place these passages outside the realm of historiography into that of allegory, fable, parable, and even myth. Thus, the "Seven-Day Creation," "Adam and Eve," "Tempting Snake," "Noah and the Universal Flood," and "Tower of Babel" stories can be held to be inerrant in their theological intent without the need to insist on such trivia as grammar, syntax, and the perplexing question as to how theology can be based on non-existent events when the texts themselves claim otherwise.

Though Keiser's purpose here is not primarily to address these tangential issues, his arguments for a text-based biblical theology lend themselves to this line of inquiry. In any case, the marriage of sound exegetical method and appropriate theological conclusions drawn from that method give his work unusual applicability; indeed, it may well serve as a paradigm for future endeavors in which exegesis and theology should and must coexist and be mutually informing.

Eugene H. Merrill, PhD
Distinguished Professor of Old Testament Studies (Emeritus)
Dallas Theological Seminary

Acknowledgments

I WOULD LIKE TO express my appreciation to a number of individuals who have significantly contributed to this work. Eugene H. Merrill not only provided leadership and quiet mentorship in my study of Genesis 1—11, but exemplified two traits rarely found together: excellence in scholarship and godly humility. For this example I thank him. I thank Robert B. Chisholm Jr. for his friendship, his continual and relentless pursuit of excellence in exegesis, and his openness to discussing new ideas and unconventional approaches to exegetical problems. I express my appreciation to my daughter, Rebekah Duplisea, who provided numerous hours of editorial assistance, not only regarding presentation, but also in relation to efficiency and effectiveness of communication. Finally, I am very grateful to my Research Assistant and fellow biblical scholar and study partner, Benjamin Davis, without whom this book would never have progressed to the point of publication.

Abbreviations

AB	Anchor Bible
AJT	*American Journal of Theology*
AnBib	Analecta biblica
AOAT	Alter Orient und Altes Testament
AUSS	*Andrews University Seminary Studies*
BA	Biblical Archaeologist
BDB	Brown-Driver-Briggs, *Hebrew and English Lexicon of the Old Testament*
BETL	Bibliotheca ephemeridum theologicarum lovaniensium
Bib	*Biblica*
BSac	*Bibliotheca sacra*
BZAW	Beihefte zur Zeitschrift für die alttestamentliche Wissenschaft
CBQ	*Catholic Biblical Quarterly*
Comm	*Communio*
ConBOT	Coniectanea biblica: Old Testament Series
CTJ	*Calvin Theological Journal*
ERT	*Evangelical Review of Theology*
EvQ	*Evangelical Quarterly*
FB	Forschung zur Bibel
HALOT	*Hebrew and Aramaic Lexicon of the Old Testament*
HSM	Harvard Semitic Monographs
ITC	International Theological Commentary
JAAR	*Journal of the American Academy of Religion*
JAOS	*Journal of the American Oriental Society*

Abbreviations

JATS	*Journal of the Adventist Theological Society*
JBL	*Journal of Biblical Literature*
JBQ	*Jewish Bible Quarterly*
JETS	*Journal of the Evangelical Theological Society*
JOTT	*Journal of Translation and Textlinguistics*
JQR	*Jewish Quarterly Review*
JSOT	*Journal for the Study of the Old Testament*
JSOTSup	Journal for the Study of the Old Testament: Supplement Series
NAC	New American Commentary
NICOT	New International Commentary on the Old Testament
NIDOTTE	New International Dictionary of Old Testament Theology and Exegesis
OBT	Overtures to Biblical Theology
Presb	*Presbyterion*
RB	*Revue biblique*
SBLSP	Society of Biblical Literature Seminar Papers
SNTSMS	Society for New Testament Studies Monograph Series
TDOT	*Theological Dictionary of the Old Testament*
TS	*Theological Studies*
TWOT	*Theological Wordbook of the Old Testament*
TynBul	*Tyndale Bulletin*
VT	*VetusTestamentum*
VTSup	Supplements to Vetus Testamentum
WBC	Word Biblical Commentary
WTJ	*Westminster Theological Journal*
ZAW	*Zeitschrift für die alttestamentliche Wissenschaft*

1

Introduction

ALTHOUGH GEN 1–11, IN whole or in part, has been the focus of an enormous amount of study over the last three hundred years, only relatively recently have treatments of these chapters been particularly related to their potential unity and theological purpose. Throughout the Enlightenment and in the more recent advent of postmodernism, hermeneutical approaches and trends in theological scholarship have driven the treatment of Gen 1–11. Source, form, and tradition criticism focused on these chapters from the perspective of their origins while the philosophical influence of the history of religion school treated the material as mythological presentations by ancient peoples of their history and their perceived reality. During the prominence of the history of religion school, the emphasis was on discontinuity, with discussions of theological concerns focused primarily on ascertaining the perceptions and beliefs of the individuals and communities that generated the writings. Then, following World War I, with changes that resulted in searches for commonalities between the Testaments, a tendency developed either to overlook these early chapters of the Bible or simply relegate them to background information.

In the second half of the twentieth century, developments in biblical studies resulted in an increased concern with literary presentation and authorial intent rather than the earlier historical emphasis.[1] Consequently,

---

1. For purposes of this present study, the expression "authorial intent" will be used to indicate the intended purpose expressed by the final form of the text, without prejudice with regard to whether that final form is the work of a single author or that of one or more redactors.

scholars began to focus more on the creative aspects of text formulation, regardless of original writing or redaction, and their employment for the purpose of conveying an intended message. A natural accompaniment to this increased attention to original intent was a greater consideration and acceptance of a unity of texts in their final form. The effect of these shifts in emphases resulted in a significant increase in treatments of Gen 1–11 from the perspectives of authorial intent and theological content.

Another development of the late twentieth century was the return to consideration of the texts of Scripture within their canonical context. One of the ideas included in this focus was the concept that the Bible was a complete and coherent whole, regardless of whether understood in terms of divine origination or simply a compilation by the community of faith. A second idea involved in the canonical focus was that, regardless of the history of the text and regardless of the possible existence of oral or written sources or traditions, the text in its final form is that which has come down to the present day. The compilation of that text, whether by the Jewish or Christian community, is therefore understood to reflect some type of design, whether of a theological or logical nature.[2]

In spite of this increased emphasis on continuity in theological and biblical studies, even with its frequent application to the Primeval History, there have been virtually no attempts to consider Gen 1–11 as a literary and theological unity presenting a coherent message. This work will attempt to begin filling this void by seeking to identify the message of these chapters through utilization of a literary-theological approach, one that seriously considers authorial intent and a canonical perspective.[3]

Shortcomings of Prior Studies on Genesis 1–11

Unfortunately, in spite of the trend in biblical scholarship which employs a greater consideration of unity in the final form of the text and focuses on authorial intent and theological content, recent studies of Gen 1–11 have failed to recognize and study a theological unity of these chapters. The

---

2. See Clements, who argues that the very existence of a canon argues for the presence of a theology. This is especially true, he asserts, given that the Old Testament is a composite of multiple sources. See Clements, *Old Testament Theology*, 15.

3. Accordingly, this book will interact primarily with studies completed in the late twentieth century and early twenty-first century since the vast majority of works prior to that time were focused on issues other than literary unity with a coherent theological message in a canonical context.

Introduction

following discussion will briefly review considerations of the Primeval History published since the inception of the "new" literary movement. These works will be considered under the categories of exegetical commentaries, theologies, and articles reflecting various combinations of emphases and approaches.

Exegetical Works

With all the work that has been done on Genesis in the latter part of the twentieth century, there are surprisingly few in-depth exegetical commentaries on the book. Those commentaries that have been introduced generally lack a consideration of Gen 1–11 as a coherent whole with unified messages and themes.

Probably the most thorough and respected Genesis commentary of this period is by Claus Westermann.[4] In matters related to the concerns of this present study, his work is unusual in that it treats Gen 1–11 as a unity with an intentional theological significance. The theological function of the Primeval History is understood as a bridge between primeval times and the world of ancient Israel which serves consciously to place Israel's history as the people of God within the universal context of all humanity and the whole of history. Although this treatment by Westermann is particularly helpful when one considers the significance and function of Gen 1–11 for the implied reader (see chapter 6), his consideration of the theology, rather than function of the text, is topical (e.g., crime and punishment, human achievement) and does not address an overall theological message or even consider whether such a message even exists.

Other commentaries appear to treat the Primeval History with even less significance for its theology or theological message than does Westermann's. Hamilton notes the difficulty of "dovetailing" Primeval History with patriarchal history and begins his own explanation of the theology of Genesis with the patriarchal narratives, presenting the beginning chapters as informational prolegomena.[5] Similarly, Wenham understands the Primeval History only as a background to the call of Abraham by disclosing the hopeless plight of mankind and showing how the promises made to the patriarchs fulfill God's original plans for humanity.[6] Ruppert follows

4. Westermann, *Genesis 1–11*.
5. Hamilton, *Genesis 1–17*, 39–52.
6. Wenham, *Genesis 1–15*.

the German emphasis on diachronic studies while Mathews bases his commentary on the *toledot* structure of the book, asserting that chapters 1–11 serve as the preamble to Israel's history with the pivotal episode of the entire book being the election of Abraham.[7]

Four recent commentaries have taken some sort of literary and/or theological approach to Gen 1–11 but have not attempted to identify a coherent theological message. Brodie's work, concentrating on demonstrating a binary/diptych structure to Genesis, seems to be more a compilation of observations than an attempt to ascertain a message. He himself states that its purpose is simply "to give an overall sense of direction."[8] Although very helpful in its attention to both theology and literary structure, Waltke's commentary is, as his preface indicates, a compilation of exegetical notes accompanied by theological reflection. Again, there is no attempt to ascertain an overall theological message.[9] Turner's work represents another narrowly focused approach. He considers the relationship between explicit statements of purpose at the beginning of narrative cycles and the subsequent plot, analyzing whether the plot develops in a manner anticipated by the announcement.[10] Finally, although utilizing a literary-theological approach, Collins's recent commentary is not focused on ascertaining a coherent message of Gen 1–4 but rather considers numerous issues arising in the study of those chapters without necessarily addressing their interrelationships.[11]

In summary, recent commentaries have either not attempted to approach Gen 1–11 in a comprehensive manner with a coherent theological message or have focused on the patriarchal narratives with the Primeval History understood as simply providing information of a background nature.

Theological Studies

Just as in exegetical studies, late twentieth century theological works generally treat Gen 1–11 as simply background material. For example, Walter Kaiser, although noting that Gen 1–11 has rarely been treated with a view

---

7. Ruppert, *Genesis*; and Mathews, *Genesis 1–11*, 54.
8. Brodie, *Genesis as Dialogue*, xiii.
9. Waltke and Fredricks, *Genesis*, 11.
10. Turner, *Genesis*.
11. Collins, *Genesis 1–4*.

Introduction

to its contribution to theology, himself provides a sketchy treatment which concentrates on the divine plan of promise which begins with Abram.[12] The approach of Ralph Smith is topical and introductory and does not lend itself to an exegetical-theological discussion of Gen 1–11.[13] Paul House's theology is based on the perspective that theology, by its very nature and evidenced by its name, is about God.[14] He treats the entire book of Genesis as introductory and reviews it from the perspective of the presentation of God in each section, thus not recognizing any special significance of Gen 1–11. Scobie identifies a limited number of themes in the Primeval History and traces them through the Old and New Testaments, following the ideas of proclamation/promise and fulfillment/consummation. Framing Gen 1–11 according to God's order, God's servant, God's people, and God's way, he deals with the passage topically rather than exegetically.[15] Similarly, Goldingay's work centers on interactions between God and Israel, and is based on perceived significant theological issues rather than upon exegesis of the text.[16]

In the 1980s, however, William J. Dumbrell began to publish works which seriously considered the theological significance of Gen 1–11.[17] For example, he sees creation as so significant that it drives biblical theology, being interwoven not only throughout Scripture but explicitly addressed in the final chapters of the Bible.[18] However, Dumbrell bases his perception of the significance of the Primeval History on the existence of various themes identified in these early chapters of Genesis rather than the acknowledgment of an organized coherent message of the whole.

Thus, recent theologies have generally failed to consider Gen 1–11 as a unity with a coherent message and have rather treated it as either simply

---

12. Kaiser, *Toward an Old Testament Theology*, 71.
13. Smith, *Old Testament Theology*.
14. House, *Old Testament Theology*.
15. Scobie, *The Ways of Our God*.
16. Goldingay, *Old Testament Theology*, vol. 1.
17. Dumbrell initially wrote the following: *Covenant and Creation* and *The End of the Beginning*. More recently he has developed his ideas in "Genesis 2:1–3" and *The Faith of Israel*.
18. More recently Fretheim has written a theology based on creation. However, his approach is more topical than exegetical in that he discusses the theology of biblical creation concepts rather than, as Dumbrell, the foundational nature of the creation account of Gen 1. See Fretheim, *God and World in the Old Testament*.

background information or as a source from which concepts or themes are identified and then developed throughout the Bible.

Articles and Other Limited Studies

Although more limited considerations of Gen 1–11 have taken widely varying tacks covering many different sections of these chapters, there has been an observable trend in these studies. Rather than attempting to ascertain a unified message of Gen 1–11, the earlier works (i.e., 1970s and 1980s) tend to focus on method, often with the explicit statement that the purpose of their study is the demonstration of the usefulness of a specific approach. For example, Fokkelman, Patte and Parker, Smith, and Walsh attempt to demonstrate the usefulness of structural analysis while Boomershine combines structural *and* rhetorical approaches.[19] Meanwhile, in a different vein, both Culley and Wallace attempt to demonstrate narrative methodologies, focusing on action sequences and type scenes while Cohn uses narrative structure together with a canonical perspective.[20] However, in all of these works the primary focus is methodology.

A couple of these methodologically focused articles do, however, focus on understanding the intended message of the text. Smith sees the author's purpose as the presentation of the concepts of blessing and cursing upon which the patriarchal narratives are based.[21] Walsh, utilizing a consideration of type scenes, understands the point of these chapters to be the interaction between the divine and human realm as exhibited in creation and the garden of God.[22] This is the same conclusion at which Cohn arrives, albeit by use of different methodology.[23] Nevertheless, even though

---

19. Fokkelman, *Narrative Art in Genesis*; Patte and Parker, "A Structural Exegesis of Genesis 2 and 3"; Smith, "Structure and Purpose in Genesis 1–11"; Walsh, "Genesis 2:4b–3:24"; and Boomershine, "The Structure of Narrative Rhetoric in Genesis 2–3." It should be mentioned that some of these approaches focus on surface structure, thus relating to authorial intent, while others deal with deep structure and are concerned more with values which lie behind the text (e.g., Patte and Parker).

20. Culley, "Action Sequences in Genesis 2–3"; Wallace, *The Eden Narrative*; and Cohn, "Narrative Structure and Canonical Perspective."

21. Smith, "Structure and Purpose," 307–19.

22. Walsh, "Genesis 2:4b–3:24," 161–77.

23. Cohn, "Narrative Structure and Canonical Perspective," 3–16.

Introduction

considering the theological message of the text, these works fail to consider the Primeval History as a whole.[24]

As time progressed, there was an increasing number of attempts to use literary techniques to discover more about the text itself. Combs considers chapters 1–5 in terms of the tension between the ideas of human labor in the form of the blessing of ruling and the curse of toiling the ground.[25] Trimpe studies the intertextuality of the Primeval History with other Old Testament and extrabiblical material.[26] Benjamin deals with various "Adam and Eve" stories while Stordalen concentrates on garden symbolism, with both authors treating their subjects as involving fundamental questions about life.[27] Other writers deal with specific issues: Galambush with the relationship between significant terms; Hess with matters of genealogies, meanings of personal names, etc.; Tsumura with the earth as unproductive and uninhabitable; van Wolde with matters of the earth; and Wittenberg with the implications of cities.[28] Still other treatments focus on themes: Rudman considers knowledge; Wallace deals with creation; Hauser reviews intimacy and alienation; Kikawada and Quinn propose sin/judgment/mitigation; and Miller suggests various ideas such as the interaction and balance between the divine and human worlds, the correspondence of sin and judgment, and the *adamah* motif.[29]

Some additional works have addressed the theology of the Primeval History without focusing so much on unifying themes. For example, Schwarz considers the theology of Gen 1–11 but concentrates on humanity, Witte focuses on redaction issues, and Froebe on the organization of the

---

24. Only one methodologically focused work, that of Margaret Bratcher, specifically attempts to demonstrate the theological message of the Primeval History as a whole. Unfortunately, her work is very "surface-level" and presents little that is new. She simply restates traditional views, albeit from a literary perspective. See Bratcher, "The Pattern of Sin and Judgment in Genesis 1–11."

25. Combs, "Has YHWH Cursed the Ground?"

26. Trimpe, *Von der Schöpfung bis zur Zerstreuung*.

27. Benjamin, "Stories of Adam and Eve"; Stordalen, *Echoes of Eden*.

28. Galambush, "*'adām* from *'adāmâ*, *'iššâ* from *'îš*'"; Hess, "The Genealogies of Genesis 1–11"; idem, "Genesis 1–2 in its Literary Context"; idem, "Splitting the Adam"; idem, *Studies in the Personal Names of Genesis 1–11*; Tsumura, *The Earth and the Waters*; van Wolde, "The Earth Story"; and Wittenberg, "Alienation and 'Emancipation' from the Earth."

29. Rudman, "A Little Knowledge is a Dangerous Thing"; Wallace, "The Toledot of Adam"; Hauser, "Linguistic and Thematic Links"; idem, "Genesis 2–3"; Kikawada and Quinn, *Before Abraham Was*; Miller, *Genesis 1–11*.

Hebrew Bible around primeval themes.[30] However, even though dealing directly with the theology of Gen 1–11, none are exegetical works designed to ascertain the theological message of the entire section.

In spite of increased focus on the author's intended communication through these chapters, there has been little evidence of concern to consider the intent of more than simply a segment or a limited facet of Gen 1–11. There are, however, some exceptions. Abela considers Genesis (and the Primeval History) in relation to the Primary History, proposing that it is an introduction which formulates the themes that are to be developed throughout that history.[31] Clines specifically inquires into the theological message of Gen 1–11, proposing that the spread of sin dominates this section and includes the themes of (1) creation/un-creation/re-creation, (2) spread of sin/spread of grace, and (3) sin/speech/mitigation/punishment.[32] Forrest argues that the Primeval History is actually the foundation for the law as the necessary means to regulate society.[33] However, these attempts do not properly reflect a theological interpretation of the Primeval History based upon exegesis.

Summary and Analysis

The present state in theological studies of Gen 1–11 is effectively articulated by Johnson T. K. Lim's evaluation of the subject.[34] Lim calls attention to the weaknesses of the traditional critical approaches which are being perceived as inadequate by "an expanding guild of scholars and literary critics."[35] He outlines some of the reasons for these perceptions as follows: (1) scholars have lost sight of the big picture; (2) the compositeness of the text has been overemphasized at the expense of its unity; (3) the role of the author has been underestimated; (4) there has been a tendency toward too easily

---

30. Schwarz, *Die biblische Urgeschichte*; and Froebe, *Der Sonderfall des Menschen und der Sündenfall der Theologie*.

31. Abela, "Is Genesis the Introduction of the Primary History."

32. Clines, "Theme in Genesis 1–11."

33. Forrest, "Paradise Lost Again."

34. Lim, *Grace in the Midst of Judgment*. Lim's work provides a helpful critique of hermeneutical theories, while arguing for a theological approach to the text. However, the actual theological review itself lacks depth and originality, particularly from an exegetical perspective.

35. Ibid., 5–8.

Introduction

emending texts to what they "should" be rather than dealing with them as they are; (5) too many conclusions are based upon hypothetical sources and traditions which can never be validated; and (6) the theological dimensions of the text have been minimized, or relegated to the belief systems of Israel. In discussing various paradigm shifts, including the "new" literary and the canonical approaches which focus on the final form of the text rather than its development, Lim affirms literary treatments but speaks against an approach which places meaning in the reader instead of in the text. He argues for a theological reading which treats the text as literature and locates meaning in the text while allowing for "extra-textual reality," that is, reality beyond the text. He argues that this type of approach recognizes that the Bible is foremost a theological book and should, therefore, be taken up on a theological basis. Although the theological message may not be stated explicitly, there are still "theological voices within the text that are a witness to 'the reality beyond the text'" and which, recognizing its canonical nature, treat it accordingly.[36]

Lim's analysis is confirmed by the foregoing consideration of treatments of Gen 1–11. First and foremost is the tendency to impose themes rather than understand the text based upon its own priorities and foci. Second, there is a paucity of studies which deal with the Primeval History as a unified work with a theological message. Although recent years have seen an increasing attention to the theological ideas presented in these chapters, the tendency has been to identify specific issues or themes rather than an intended message of the section as a whole. Third, there are even fewer works which represent exegetically based theology, using techniques such as discourse, narrative, structural, and rhetorical analyses for the express purpose of focusing on the following: (1) the overall purpose of the author in units and subunits, (2) how units and subunits relate to a broader purpose, and (3) how units and subunits relate to the immediate and canonical contexts. Finally, most comprehensive theologies tend to lay their foundation in texts subsequent to Gen 1–11, treating these early chapters primarily as background information. Even those works which do see some greater significance in this section (e.g., Dumbrell) do not attempt to ascertain the intended theological presentation of the section as a whole. That is, even if important issues are identified in the early chapters, the approach is to pull specific ideas or themes out of the text rather than understand the text as a coherent unit.

36. Ibid., 67–71.

Genesis 1–11

In summary, Gen 1–11 has not been addressed adequately while utilizing the following components: (1) consideration of the entire Primeval History as a coherent whole with a theological message and (2) an exegetically based theological interpretation utilizing all appropriate hermeneutical tools for the purpose of ascertaining authorial intent.

Present Study

This work argues that Gen 1–11 presents a coherent theological message which is effectively identifiable by means of a literary-theological exegesis of the text. Further, it is proposed that the specific message of this section is that humankind must, in unity, demonstrate faith and obedience toward God while functioning as God's representative and expectantly awaiting his full blessing, which will be realized when God restores to its full intended vitality the creation which was corrupted through humanity's failure.

The hermeneutical approach taken in this study is primarily literary-theological. The term "literary-theological" is intended to communicate a study which includes (1) an analysis of the literary features of the text as they contribute to the understanding of original intent, and (2) a treatment of the text which assumes the presence of a theological message and seeks to determine that message.[37] The term "literary features" is understood to include the broader issues of both surface and deep structure as well as the narrower matters of rhetoric (i.e., art of composition for the purpose of communication and persuasion).[38]

One of the reasons for adopting a literary approach is that it is particularly suited for ascertaining authorial intent. Van Wolde describes the relationship between composition and authorial intent as follows: "The generation of a narrative structure of a text is strategic, that is to say the construction of a narrative network is controlled by a strategy, a plan to

---

37. This is the same basic idea as that of Mathews. "The focus is a literary-theological exposition of the text that draws on its compositional features with the aim of detecting what is highlighted by the text itself. Biblical exposition is that which permits the text—both its contents and its shape—to dictate the meaning. The intention of a biblical composition is rarely stated; rather it is to be inferred. Thus we must depend on the grammatical and narrative structure as signposts. Only through the window of the text can we discern the intent of the ancient writer" (Mathews, *Genesis 1–11:26*, 23).

38. Alter describes literary features as "the artful use of language, to the shifting play of ideas, conventions, tone, sound, imagery, syntax, narrative viewpoint, compositional units, etc." See Alter, *The Art of Biblical Narrative*, 12.

Introduction

bring about a certain meaning effect in the reader. The narrative structure, or the arrangement of the elements of meaning in a story, guides the reader in the process of giving meaning to or interpretation of the text."[39] This strategic formulation is seen in features such as the ascription of motives or feelings to characters, particularly when this is done in some cases but not others. It is also evident in the presentation of some actions with minimal detail while others receive extensive treatment. Similarly, drastic shifts in time scale of narrated events are generally purposeful, tending to focus attention on significant matters. Thus, in all of these ways and more, literary features serve to direct the reader toward the message intended by the author.[40]

One particular literary feature that is very important to the present study is the use of speech. The essence of the scene in Hebrew narrative is accomplished through dialogue, joined together by narrative. In fact, narrative sometimes simply functions to reinforce the intended communication of dialogue.[41] Speech sometimes reveals the speakers' intentions and aspirations and, through them, their characteristics. It also serves as a vehicle for the development of the plot.[42] Additionally, speech is used to slow the story's pace, focusing attention and creating the impression that events are taking place before the reader's eyes and thus highlighting the crucial incidents, the crises, climaxes, vital decisions, and central activities.[43] Therefore, the use of speech by an author to draw attention to key issues gives important clues for determining authorial intent.

In view of the scope of material addressed in this study, a great deal of discipline will be exercised in order to remain focused upon the overall

---

39. Van Wolde, *A Semiotic Analysis of Genesis 2–3*, 80.

40. Sasson states that it is an "important task to outline the frameworks of overarching, architectonic structure within Biblical narratives and to seek therein evidence for the theological presuppositions and the hermeneutical perspectives of those redactors who, by gathering the hoary traditions, by sifting from among them those which suited didactic purposes, and by shaping as well as by arranging and welding them in a manner which promoted their ideals, created a compilation of Genesis which approximates our very own." See Sasson, "The 'Tower of Babel,'" 213. For further discussion of the significance of literary approaches in determining theology and authorial intent see Cassuto, *Genesis: From Noah to Abraham*, 2; Childs, *Introduction to the Old Testament as Scripture*, 71–75; Clines, *The Theme of the Pentateuch*, 66, 101; Fishbane, *Biblical Text and Texture*, 8; Ross, *Creation and Blessing*, 34; and Sternberg, *The Poetics of Biblical Narrative*, 9–10.

41. Alter, *The Art of Biblical Narrative*, 63.

42. Bar-Efrat, *Narrative Art in the Bible*, 73, 147.

43. Ibid., 150.

message of the various sections. The importance of this endeavor is affirmed by Walsh:

> When we look for the structure of a literary unit of several chapters or longer we have no choice but to resort to major themes as the principal organizing device. It is essential in doing so not to misconstrue or misrepresent the thematic content of a subunit in order to manufacture an echo. Themes should be central to their subunit, and they should be expressed to the extent possible in vocabulary used in the text itself. This is the point at which subjective judgment is most influential and at the same time most inescapable. The analyst can do little more than present his or her conscientious readings to others in the hope that others' judgment will provide the critical control the text itself does not afford.[44]

Similarly, Thompson remarks that it is important to use the entirety of a large extended narrative in order to reduce the tendency towards arbitrariness and willfulness in interpretation.[45]

In summary, this study will concentrate on literary features of the text for the purpose of identifying the theological message intended by the author. In view of the size of the text being considered, attention will be concentrated on overall structure and themes, avoiding digressions of secondary matters unless they are important to the understanding of the whole. Due to its importance for highlighting key components of narrative, speech will be a special focus.

As an underlying basis for seeking a coherent theological message in Gen 1–11, the unity of those chapters will be established in chapter 2. Next, the creation account (Gen 1:1–2:3) will be considered, focusing on the theology of the presentation and arguing for the characterization of creation as a progressive development of life, presented as God's work in which he chooses to involve humanity. The next chapter will review the garden story and its sequel, the Cain narrative, along with the relationship of the two stories to the preceding presentation of creation. The theological emphasis of these narratives will be identified as the work of humanity and its effect on creation and themselves. The last exegetical section considered will be Gen 5–11 in which the full development of themes introduced in the prior narratives is presented along with a change in God's response. The study

---

44. Walsh, *Style and Structure*, 10.
45. Thompson, *The Origin Tradition of Ancient Israel*, 62.

will conclude with a review of the theological presentation of Gen 1–11 and a discussion of its appropriateness and function for the implied reader.

2

The Unity of Genesis 1–11

A FUNDAMENTAL PRESUPPOSITION IN this book is that Gen 1–11 is a coherent unit. If this were not the case, proposals for an intentional theological message might well be considered groundless. Unfortunately, as the result of many years of diachronically centered biblical studies, the unity of these chapters is anything but a foregone conclusion. However, in spite of the dominance of diachronic studies in the nineteenth and early twentieth centuries, Kikawada and Quinn present the perspective and approach of a growing number of Old Testament scholars when they state, "The evidence commonly used to show that Gen 1–11 is a literary patchwork does in our opinion—when closely examined and put in its proper context—support the view that Gen 1–11 is a literary masterpiece by an author of extraordinary skill and subtlety."[1] Thus, they assert that the very same features of these chapters, which diachronic critics see as indications of distinct sources, actually witness to a skillfully created unity. Although their reference to "an author" may cause discomfort among some, if "author" is taken to include "final redactor" there would be considerable agreement.[2]

---

1. Kikawada and Quinn, *Before Abraham Was*, 83.

2. For example, a growing perspective among diachronic critics is seen in the following statement by Mann: "Although we still cannot say that these myths have been converted into history, we can say that they have been transformed into a kind of 'history-like' narrative. In other words, they are no longer self-contained 'short stories'; they are now the opening chapters of an 'historical novel' and as such they provide the dominant themes which will guide our reading of that 'novel.'" See Mann, *The Book of the Torah*, 11.

The Unity of Genesis 1–11

Unity Acknowledged Implicitly

In spite of the diachronic concerns which for years dominated studies of Gen 1–11, much of that discussion actually implicitly acknowledged some degree of coherency in this section. The validity of this surprising assertion is evidenced in the many suggestions regarding the themes and structures of these early chapters of Genesis. That is, the presumption of structure and theme in Gen 1–11 in and of itself acknowledges some level of unity.

Structure and Themes

Suggestions of thematic or structural design of the Primeval History are numerous.[3] One commonly observed theme is the presentation of cycles of sin-punishment-mitigation.[4] In addition to this pattern, other themes are suggested by scholars. For example, Fishbane notes the following: (1) creation and work in the beginning, after Eden, after the flood, and in the plains of Shinar; (2) symbolism of sacred space and the mountain in Eden, in Ararat, and with the tower; (3) man as gardener and maker, in Adam, Cain, Noah, and the neighbors of Shinar; (4) issues of will, desire, and aggressive rebellion with Eve, Adam, and the serpent, with Cain and the "serpentine" sin, with the sons of God and the daughters of the men, and with the builders of Babel; (5) motif of exile, destruction, and dispersion after the rebellion of Eden, after the murder of Abel, after the evil and violence in the generation of Noah, and after the challenge of the tower builders; (6) geographical orientation in the garden of Eden to the east, with the exile of man to the east of Eden, with the exile of Cain eastward of Eden, and with the movement of peoples from the east to build the tower; and (7) typology of man and time in ten generations from Adam to Noah, the latter receiving

---

3. Although the following list addresses the numerous conceptions of themes throughout Gen 1–11, it is important to note that they are frequently made by diachronic scholars. That is, there is no correlation between perceptions of themes and synchronic approaches.

4. Kikawada and Quinn explain this idea by noting that Gen 1–11 contains three stories with significant similarities: Adam and Eve, Cain and Abel, and Noah and the flood. Each has the same plot. Each has an introductory section in which origins are accounted for and a peaceful setting presented. Each then recounts evil action and God's reaction, which, in turn, generates a human response. Each story has a divine curse followed by a threefold mitigation of that curse. See Kikawada and Quinn, 63. See also Bailey, "Some Literary and Grammatical Aspects," 269; Clines, *The Theme of the Pentateuch*, 61–79; and Dumbrell, *The Faith of Israel*, 29.

15

blessing on a recreated earth, and in ten generations from Noah to Abram, the latter of whom also receives blessing.[5]

Similar to Fishbane's observation of the man as gardener, van Wolde sees a continual presentation of a close connection between the man and the earth in that (1) Gen 1 tells humankind to subdue the earth, (2) the Eden narrative is set within the relationship of the man and the earth, (3) the Cain episode involves relationship with the earth, (4) the flood story centers on the destruction of the earth because of humanity, and (5) Babel deals with humankind upon the face of the whole earth.[6]

Further unifying ideas are suggested by others, such as Miller's three themes: (1) the interaction and balance between the divine and human worlds; (2) the correspondence of sin and judgment; and (3) the *adamah* motif.[7] Toews sees four themes in the first four chapters: (1) God, (2) his word, (3) humanity, and (4) the earth.[8] Smith suggests that the blessing "be fruitful, multiply, and fill the earth" represents a theological pattern, while Dempster argues for the development of the paired themes of geography and genealogy and of dominion and dynasty.[9] Wallace posits the focus of these chapters as "the penetration of the divine realm."[10]

Additional examples of themes could be cited; however, it should be evident from those listed above that structures and themes in the Primeval History are commonly perceived. This perception in and of itself assumes some level of unity of Gen 1–11 in its final form although frequently not acknowledging such explicitly.[11]

---

5. Fishbane, *Biblical Text and Texture*, 38–39.

6. Van Wolde, "The Story of Cain and Abel," 34; idem, "A Text-Semantic Study," 106–7; and idem, *Words Become Worlds*, 19–35.

7. Miller, *Genesis 1–11*, 41.

8. Toews, "Genesis 1–4," 38–52.

9. Smith, "Structure and Purpose"; and Dempster, "Geography and Genealogy, Dominion and Dynasty."

10. Wallace, *The Eden Narrative*, 130–32.

11. Another discussion which frequently occurs regarding the Primeval History and which implicitly argues for some form of unity is the significance of the genealogies. One common idea is that the genealogies, together with a series of intersecting narrative episodes, constitute a conscious structure of Gen 1–11. In this view the genealogies serve to link the narratives and determine the basic movement of the cycles. Thus, once again, in discussions of the genealogies, a final redactive unity of these chapters is an underlying assumption. Cf. Fishbane, *Biblical Text and Texture*, 28; Garrett, *Rethinking Genesis*, 87–124; and Westermann, *Genesis 1–11*, 2, 4.

The Unity of Genesis 1–11

Common Exegetical Observations

In addition to the implied acceptance of some level of unity of Gen 1–11 based on suggestions regarding structure and themes, other common exegetical conclusions argue for such a oneness without consciously affirming it.

Flood Narrative and Creation

Discussions of the flood narrative frequently include observations of explicit references to both the Eden narrative and the Gen 1 creation account, thus implying some level of unity in the opening chapters of Genesis.[12] For example, the flood narrative seems to be highly dependent on the Genesis 1 creation account with both the flood and its subsequent revitalization of the earth presented in terms of creation. This association is evidenced in the following features: (1) the signaling of the activity of the spirit/wind of God upon the watery chaos introducing both Gen 1 and the post-flood re-recreation, (2) the restraint of waters and the appearing of dry land in both accounts, (3) the population of the earth by living creatures and man in both accounts, (4) the presentation of humankind as the *imago Dei* in both accounts, and (5) the conclusion of both accounts with a similar blessing upon humanity.

Flood Narrative and Eden

In addition to its connection with the creation account, the flood story appears to be dependent on the Eden narrative as well in that Noah is presented as a second Adam. The following similarities between the two men attest to this relationship: (1) both are uniquely associated with the image of God, (2) both walk with God, (3) both fail in acts of ingesting the product of the earth, (4) the failure of both results in nakedness being discerned and covered by another, (5) the failure of both results in a curse on others (Adam on mankind, Noah on Canaan), (6) both are closely associated with and interact with animals (Adam names, Noah preserves),

---

12. In a discussion of the significance and relationship of the creation and flood accounts, Rendtorff states: "Er erscheint daher als höchst unwahrscheinlich, daß diese 'priesterlichen' Kapitel je außerhalb des jetzigen Kontextes existiert haben." See Rendtorff, *Kanon Und Theologie*, 126.

(7) the commission to both includes "be fruitful, multiply, rule the earth," (8) both work the ground, (9) both have three named sons, and (10) the sons of both portray the concepts of judgment, hope, and division into the blessed and the cursed.

Noah and both Eden and Creation

Not only do various features of the flood story allude to the two prior narratives, but the characterization of Noah alludes to both passages simultaneously. That is, Noah is associated with Gen 1 via the reference to the *imago Dei* and the blessing of Gen 1:28, while the other allusions to Adam draw from the Eden narrative. Thus, not only does the flood account as a whole relate to two prior sections, but, as a single component, it relates to both simultaneously, demonstrating an even greater coherency.

Adamic Genealogy and the Flood and Eden Narratives

In addition to the parallels between the flood and creation accounts, other commonly noted features argue for a relationship between the flood narrative and the genealogy of Gen 5. For example, only Noah (flood account) and Enoch (genealogy) are presented as walking with God, and both of them receive special deliverance. Additionally, the often discussed etymology of the name Noah establishes a direct connection between the genealogical notation regarding Lamech and the introduction to the flood account.[13] Further, some of these features demonstrate simultaneous allusions to the Eden narrative: Enoch and Noah walking with God seems to allude to Adam and Eve enjoying communion with God in the garden, and the reason given for Noah receiving his name alludes directly to the curse of the Eden narrative, even using similar terminology (עצבון in Gen 3:16, 17; 5:29).

---

13. Although the narrative insert regarding Lamech is often considered a later redaction, the fact that it logically and literarily bridges these two accounts which are obviously of different genre supports the concept of a unity in the final form of the text.

On the matter of the rhetorical function of Noah's name, see, for example, Alter, *Genesis*, 25; Cassuto, *Genesis: From Noah to Abraham*, 289, 303, 307; Fishbane, *Biblical Text and Texture*, 31; Hamilton, *Genesis 1–17*, 259; Hess, *Studies in the Personal Names of Genesis 1–11*, 116–18; Mathews, *Genesis 1–11:26*, 317–18; Sarna, *Genesis*, 44; and Wenham, *Genesis 1–15*, 129.

The Unity of Genesis 1–11

Miscellaneous Connections

There are a variety of other commonly noted features of the Primeval History which implicitly argue for a literary dependency. There is an apparent relationship of *gibborim* and "the name" in two separate characterizations of humanity's filling of the earth (see Gen 6:1–4 with the Nimrod entry of the Table of Nations [Gen 10:8–9], and the rhetoric of the Babel story).[14] The commonly observed similarity between the forms of the genealogy of Adam in chapter 5 and that of Shem in chapter 11 reflects some type of dependency.[15] Additionally, scholars often note that the genealogies of Cain and Adam both contain entries for Enoch and Lamech. What is usually missed is that there is a clear rhetorical play made between them, thus indicating a literary connection.[16]

Summary

Common exegetical observations of Gen 1–11 imply interdependency between sections. The flood story is strongly associated with both the creation account and the Eden narrative while Noah is characterized in terminology which simultaneously alludes to creation and Eden. The fact that scholars frequently refer to these and other features of the Primeval History should make it apparent that, while not using them for this purpose, their observations implicitly support a significant level of dependency between sections. In turn, this interdependency supports the idea of some level of literary unity to Gen 1–11.

---

14. The filling of the earth in both of these sections is often noted. For example, Tomasino argues that Noah's drunkenness presents a new Fall and a new conflict between brothers, resulting in the Flood to Babel being a repeat of the history of creation through the flood. See Tomasino, "History Repeats Itself," 128–30. An additional, albeit more subtle observation which argues for this pattern is the presentation of characters in these chapters. In Genesis 1 and the flood narrative, both dealing with creation, God is the prominent character and humans are secondary. But in the subsequent accounts, i.e., Eden, Cain, and Adam's genealogy, all following Gen 1, and the curse of Canaan, the Table of Nations and Babel, all following the flood, humans take a more prominent role as the filling of the earth is presented.

15. See pages 121–22.

16. The relationship between these entries will be discussed in chapter 5 of this book.

Genesis 1–11

Unity Argued Explicitly

In addition to the *implicit* acknowledgment of some degree of unity to Gen 1–11, a number of scholars, including advocates of both diachronic and synchronic methods, argue *explicitly* for a coherency. For example, Mann states, "Despite the fact that Genesis 1 and 2–3 derive from different authors, in their present juxtaposition these chapters are united by a common concern for the central themes we have delineated. The Pentateuchal narrative is certainly no J or P, nor is it even J and P, for the combination of these two units has created a 'new narrative' that includes but also transcends both units."[17] Ouro argues for linguistic, literary, and thematic parallels between Gen 1 and 3 noting, among other things, an association between Gen 1:28 and 3:16 with the usage of רבה in reference to reproduction and a connection between Gen 1:29–30 and 3:2–3, 6 which deal with vegetation, food/diet, and human attitude.[18] Clines sees "de-creation," i.e., the undoing of the order of creation through sin, presented in chapters 3–6 and thus relating to chapter 1.[19] Cassuto understands Gen 2–3 as an elaboration of Gen 1, developing the relationship between humanity and the earth.[20]

Genesis 1 and 2

Other than discussions of sources in the flood account, probably the highest profile issue related to the unity of the Primeval History deals specifically with Gen 1 and 2 and their character as two separate, and often apparently contradicting, creation accounts. However, perspectives on this issue have been changing. Literary studies by Alter and Hess have suggested that even these two "creation stories" are a cohesive unit with a literary purpose.[21] Additionally, recent observations by both diachronic and synchronic scholars have argued for an intentional relationship between these two accounts. Further, rhetorical features and a Hebrew accenting analysis evidence a conscious unity.

---

17. Mann, *The Book of the Torah*, 18.
18. Ouro, "Linguistic and Thematic Parallels."
19. Clines, "Theme in Genesis 1–11," 495.
20. Cassuto, *Genesis: From Noah to Abraham*, 91–92.
21. E.g., Alter, *The Art of Biblical Narrative*, 141–47; and Hess, "Genesis 1–2 in its Literary Context," 143.

Diachronic Observations

Some scholars who take a diachronic approach to Genesis see order and relationship between Gen 1 and 2. For example, Blenkinsopp asserts that sanctuary symbolism is present in both Gen 1 and the Eden narrative, representing macro-cosmic and micro-cosmic treatments, respectively.[22] Alter argues that the first (P) account is concerned with the cosmic plan of creation and appropriately begins with the primordial abyss, whereas the second (J) account is interested in man as a cultivator and moral agent and thus begins with a lack of vegetation and irrigation.[23] Fretheim, also discussing these chapters from the perspective of sources, asserts that the juxtaposition of the two creation accounts is not haphazard but designed to present an adequate picture of the place of man in the creation.[24]

Synchronic Observations

As would be expected, synchronic scholars also propose rationales supporting the concept of a relationship between the creation accounts. Hess asserts that Gen 1 and 2 should not be considered as two separate creation accounts, arguing that Gen 2 is a specification of Gen 1, moving from the generalized account of the creation of the universe to the specific account of the creation of humanity.[25]

Of particular note is the work of Shea who observes that every major element in the second account is already present in the first, albeit in abbreviated form.[26] Thus, he sees the second account as a recapitulation, with added information, providing a focused view of events which occurred on

---

22. Blenkinsopp, *The Pentateuch*, 62–63.

23. Alter, *The Art of Biblical Narrative*, 141.

24. Fretheim, *Creation, Fall, and Flood*, 70; and, idem, *God and World in the Old Testament*, 33.

25. Hess, *Personal Names of Genesis 1–11*, 161; idem, "Genesis and Ancient Near Eastern Stories of Creation and Flood," 29. Cf. Thompson, *The Origin Tradition of Ancient Israel*, 69.

26. This is significant since there is no reason to expect that two unrelated creation accounts would refer to the same basic material, with one presenting a development of the other. Such a correspondence argues for a conscious relationship. Compare, for example, the Egyptian creation and origin accounts in Pritchard, ed., *Ancient Near Eastern Texts Relating to the Old Testament*, 3–10.

one of the seven days of creation.[27] Shea supports his argument for a relationship between the two accounts by drawing attention to a correlation of both form and major themes. Regarding form, he points out that both accounts begin with preliminary statements about the state of the world prior to God's creative acts (Gen 1:2 ends with a reference to the face of the waters while 2:6 ends with a reference to the face of the ground), and both include poetry dealing with male and female at the end (Gen 1:27, 2:23). With reference to themes, he notes that both accounts present the production of plants by the earth, human dominion over animals, and the presentation of humankind as male and female.[28]

Rhetorical Features

Rhetorical features of the text lead to observations similar to those of Shea. Although a review of Gen 2 reveals that it seems to presume the existence of that which was created in chapter 1, Gen 2 deals particularly with that which appeared on the sixth day of creation, thus evidencing a conscious and focused dependency.[29]

Not only are certain issues of Day 6 dealt with in Gen 2, they are specifically those which are highlighted through the important vehicle of speech:[30] animals, humankind, plants as food, and the relationship between them. Thus, while the structure of the Gen 1 creation account clearly presents humankind as the climax of God's work, Gen 2 takes up the primary features of that specific facet of creation as its own focal point and then provides further development.

One example of the development of Gen 1 in Gen 2 is seen by addressing a question which can be raised when studying the latter chapter. What is the significance of the seemingly meaningless digression regarding the creation of animals? Man is created, placed in the garden, and then God observes that it is not good for man to be alone. Why does God then create animals and bring them to man, if only to find out that they are not suitable companions for him? What is the point of this part of the narrative? The

---

27. Shea, "The Unity of the Creation Account." So also van Wolde, "Profiling Creation as Grace," 20; and Fretheim, *The Pentateuch*, 72–73.

28. Further along these lines, van Wolde observes the common theme of God's activity in terms of creation and separation (van Wolde, *Words Become Worlds*, 41).

29. Cf. Collins, *Genesis 1–4*, 56.

30. Refer to page 11 of this book for the importance of speech in narrative.

answer lies in seeing chapter 2 as the development of the presentation of humanity in chapter 1 as unity in plurality.[31] In response to God's statement that he would make a companion for man, he creates animals. The subsequent failure of animals to function as a suitable companion creates tension and serves to highlight the formation of the woman in a way otherwise not possible. Just as in a movie the failure of what appeared to be the story's resolution creates tension and heightens expectation, the same is the case in narrative. Thus, the formulation of the storyline of chapter 2 focuses attention on the development of that which was introduced in chapter 1, specifically, the creation of male and female as unity in plurality.

In addition to the structure of the storyline, two statements by the man and a follow-up comment by the narrator also demonstrate this connection between Gen 1 and 2. First the man eloquently presents his own analysis regarding the woman: not simply is she suitable, she is "bone of my bone, flesh of my flesh," a characterization alluding to the closest relationship among humanity throughout the Hebrew Scriptures (see Gen 29:14; 37:27; Judg 9:2–3; 2 Sam 5:1; 19:13). He provides additional emphasis by naming her in such a way as to demonstrate the closeness of the relationship with himself (אשה from איש). However, the emphasis on the unity of man and woman does not end there. The narrator adds his own comment that, because of this unity, a man will leave father and mother to be joined to his wife, and they will become one. Thus the textual presentation of the close relationship of the man and woman by both a character and the narrator places emphasis on the unity in plurality of humanity which is first introduced in chapter 1. This formulation appears to represent a conscious development of the creation of humanity in Gen 1.[32]

Not only is the emphasis on unity developed by the storyline structure and statements by the man and the narrator, but the characterization of the animals also develops this idea and does so in a similar manner to that in chapter 1. In the Gen 1 creation account animals are introduced apart from any function or purpose—the only thing in the entire account which is presented this way. Created as earth creatures on the sixth day, they appear to function as a foil for humanity, serving to emphasize the latter's

---

31. See pages 82–84 of this book.

32. So also van Wolde, *Words Become Worlds*, 40. This relationship is even argued from a source perspective. Fretheim asserts that man and woman becoming one flesh in chapter 2 is the acknowledgment on the part of J of man and woman as indissolubly linked and together constituting mankind (Fretheim, *Creation, Fall, and Flood*, 79).

uniqueness.³³ The presentation in Gen 2 seems to operate similarly, in that animals function as a foil for humanity, emphasizing the unity of male and female human beings.

Even the curious and often overlooked matter of food demonstrates a conscious relationship between the two accounts. For example, עשׂב and עץ are the two items which God gives to man as food in Gen 1:29 and are the same two items which appear as food in chapter 2. In the garden man has the privilege of eating from the trees (עץ, Gen 2:16), but, banished from Eden, by the sweat of his brow he must eat the herb of the field (עשׂב, Gen 3:18–19). Although it is somewhat curious that, in the grand scope of the creation of all things, Gen 1 addresses what humankind would eat, these very two items end up playing an important role in the Eden narrative.³⁴

Hebrew Accenting Analysis

The developmental relationship between Gen 1 and 2 discussed above has also been observed from an entirely different perspective. Lode, using discourse analysis with an emphasis on the significance of Hebrew accenting, concludes that the second creation account consciously builds off the first. Without consideration of literary or theological schemes, he argues based on accenting that, in Gen 1, the discourse structure presents creation as a progression culminating in the creation of humankind. Gen 2 picks up that topic and further develops it, which, he asserts, is a type of presentation expected in Hebrew discourse structure. That is, clarity is commonly achieved by the presentation of complex situations through repetition from different points of view. Thus, he concludes, the two creation accounts should be considered as a unit with the oft noted "differences" expected in view of the typical Hebrew approach.³⁵

Summary

For many years biblical scholarship, without any explicit assertions to this effect, has implicitly acknowledged that the Primeval History is

---

33. See pages 62–66 of this book.

34. This particular feature actually argues for a construction of the creation account with the knowledge of the content of the Eden narrative, and which is consciously formulated in a manner which sets up that narrative. Cf. Gowan, *From Eden to Babel*, 43–44.

35. Lode, "The Two Creation Stories in Genesis Chapters 1 to 3."

characterized by some level of coherency. This acknowledgment has been evident in attempts to identify structure and themes in these chapters as well as in the observation of relationships between various sections. Recently both diachronic and synchronic scholars have explicitly argued, from varying perspectives, for a unity in the Primeval History. The foregoing discussion of the rhetorical strategy in Gen 1–2 also argues for a direct and conscious unity within the Primeval History, as does Lode's study of Hebrew accenting. Thus, there seems to be a more than ample basis for a synthetic approach to these chapters which assumes a literary and theological unity.

3

The Work of God
The Theology of Gen 1:1—2:3

Introduction

THE CREATION ACCOUNT OF Gen 1 is one of the most discussed sections of the Bible, thanks in part to debates regarding source criticism, creationism, and other matters. Although there is extensive agreement on detailed exegetical issues, there seems to be little consensus regarding the overall purpose and significance of the account. One of the probable reasons for this phenomenon is the lack of attention paid to a well-considered methodological approach. A review of commentaries and articles on Gen 1 reveals that a variety of hermeneutical approaches have been taken with little overt treatment of the matter. On specific issues, such as the debate over whether "day" (יוֹם) in Gen 1 refers to a literal twenty-four hour period, there is a great deal of discussion of literal versus figurative meaning.[1] However, these arguments rarely, if ever, are applied to the matter of an appropriate and consistent hermeneutic for the *entire* creation account, and, therefore, inconsistencies tend to result.[2] For example, the

---

1. For a sampling of these issues and their associated debates, see Youngblood, *The Genesis Debate*.

2. One notable exception to this situation is the work of Walton, who argues convincingly for a non-literal approach, while suggesting a cosmological treatment. A principle difference between Walton's work and that suggested here is that his focus seems to be upon the rejection of the imposition of modern scientific models than upon ascertaining a theological method from the account's literary presentation. See Walton, *The Lost World of Genesis 1*, and *Genesis 1 as Ancient Cosmology*.

The Work of God

same author may take a literal approach to the matter of the definition of the term "day," but assume language of accommodation is used with reference to "waters above." Or, a literal approach may be taken with the statement that God made the firmament while a metaphorical interpretation is applied to the announcement that "the earth brought forth."

The treatment of the creation account in this book will attempt to maintain a consistent hermeneutic, namely, an exegetical-theological approach.[3] In this regard, the impressive literary character of the creation account will be a matter of special focus since literary creativity is generally functional rather than simply aesthetic, used for the purpose of intentionally focusing the reader on the primary message and themes.

Since literary approaches commonly employ structure as an indication of authorial intent, that feature will be one focus of this study. A creative presentation also frequently uses nuanced terminology in order to communicate theological ideas. Therefore, the matter of "figural representation" will also be taken into account. Wells describes this concept as follows:

> Figural representation is a simple concept. It is the basic recognition that the biblical authors employ images or figures familiar to their readers (animals, objects, people, institutions, events from the past, etc.) to present their eschatological messages. . . . Of course, figural representation is not limited to the employment of familiar objects and institutions. An author often employs real historical events familiar to the reader as figures representing past, present or future realities. This kind of figuration is a way of seeing one event by looking at another. That is, an author articulates a correlation or nexus between two real events for the purpose of illuminating one by means of the other. . . . Figural representation is therefore not to be confused with typological interpretations, which approach the matter of figuration from a variety of reader-oriented perspectives that aim at finding meaning in texts or events. Over against these approaches, intertextual figural representation is not a method of interpretation brought to the text but a method of composition within the text. In short, figural representation is not something that a reader of a text does; it is what an author does. To focus on figural representation, therefore, is to recognize that the authors of biblical texts are not merely recording the events and people about

---

3. As evidenced by the lack of corresponding studies, this approach is unusual for Genesis 1. For an outline of the hermeneutical approach taken in this present study see pages 10–12 of this book.

> which they write but are reflecting upon them. *As a matter of literary strategy, they employ them for particular thematic purposes.... Figural representation is not something that a reader of a text does; it is what an author has done. It is a compositional technique, not an interpretive one.*[4]

This concept becomes even more significant for those who see the Bible as divinely inspired. For them, figural representation is not only arguable on the basis of intertextuality relating to human authors, but even more so because of divine authorship. That is, throughout the process of the inspiration and compilation of the Scriptures, it is anticipated that God would use figures in consistent patterns. However, whether considered simply in terms of intertextuality or on the basis of divine inspiration, an exegete must investigate potential consistencies in figural representation in addition to his usual efforts to recognize biblical patterns of morphological, grammatical, or syntactical constructions.

In summary, the following study will attempt to apply a consistent hermeneutical approach which focuses on authorial intent as evidenced in the literary presentation. Special attention will be paid to structure for the purpose of determining emphases and to figural representation for clues regarding the theological message.

Literary Presentation

Structure

The structure of the Gen 1 creation account is a widely recognized feature. Some of the structures commonly identified include the seven day form, the paneling of two sets of three days, the word-fulfillment motif, and repetition. In the following discussion these patterns as well as some

---

4. Wells, "Figural Representation and Canonical Unity," 113–15, emphasis added. One must not make too much of Well's discussion of figural representation as applied in the context of eschatology. First, a review of his argument reveals that it is as applicable to narrative as to eschatology. Second, and even more significant for the purposes of this present study, he specifically discusses figural representation in various parts of Gen 1–11 considering this section to be eschatological. Thus his discussion of figural representation is explicitly applicable to the subject of this present study, with the emphasis herein being its conscious utilization as a compositional technique. For additional perspectives on Genesis as eschatology see Gage, *The Gospel of Genesis*, 7–15; and Gunkel and Zimmern, *Schöpfung und Chaos in Urzeit und Endzeit*, 369.

The Work of God

others will be considered along with their implications for understanding the passage as a whole.

Seven Day Structure

The seven day structure is the most obvious feature demonstrating the literary creativity of this account.[5] Not only is the account presented in a seven day fashion, but it is presented as a unit with a clear and definite focus, rather than simply seven separate and unrelated acts. On this matter, Westermann notes that the narrative of chapter 1 is not presented as a story with a tension, reaching a climax and then resolving. Rather, it is "characterized by its onward, irresistible, and majestic flow."[6] Fishbane agrees with this position, arguing that the pattern of the presentation of each day sets up the distinctiveness of the seventh day.[7] Hart develops this idea further by giving the following reasons for understanding the seventh day as the goal of creation: (1) there has been a gradual ascent toward the creation of human beings, with the triple "and God said," the double "God saw that it was good," and the presentation of his image; (2) God blessed the seventh day—only the seventh day; (3) the reoccurrence in 2:1–3 of the key words of 1:1—"heaven and earth," "God," and "create"; and (4) three seven-word sentences each containing the phrase "the seventh day."[8] Thus, Hart concludes that, although one must look at the week as a whole, the content and meaning of the seventh day permeates the entire week.

Further support for the idea of dramatic significance to the seven day pattern, moving toward the goal of the seventh, is provided by Sarna. He states that the ascending order of a "six-plus-one" literary pattern dictates the seventh day as the "momentous climax," with humankind being the pinnacle of creation, although the central issue is the work of God.[9] Wallace agrees, adding that the absence in the seventh day of "evening and morning," verbs of action, and indicators of time all focus attention on this day

---

5. One might respond to this statement with the claim that the seven day structure is not literary, but rather simply factual. That is, creation in seven days is not a literary tool but simply reflects the historical timing of creation. However, if one holds to a literal seven day creation, he must still ask why God chose to complete it in this manner.

6. Westermann, *Genesis 1–11*, 80.

7. Fishbane, *Biblical Text and Texture*, 11.

8. Hart, "Genesis 1:1–2:3 as a Prologue."

9. Sarna, *Genesis*, 14.

which is "a new type of period when the completion of creation leads into an ongoing period of blessing by God."[10] Additional support for this approach is offered by Dumbrell who sees this day as special in that it belongs to God alone and is the context in which the remainder of history occurs.[11] All of these perspectives are in line with Westermann who asserts that the creation week is not presented as a progression of six days ending in a sabbath (a succession of six independent days leading to a seventh day of rest), but rather as a chronological unity which is a whole because of its goal.[12]

A comparison of each day's narrative structure also demonstrates a steady escalation. Although each day contains a variety of components, a comparative analysis of those components reveals a crescendoing presentation. The first day of creation is very succinct, comprising God's speaking followed by a narrative which briefly states that (1) what God spoke happened, and that (2) God evaluated, separated, and named. The second day presents a definite change in this pattern, including God's statement followed by a narrative which, instead of simply stating that it happened, also adds that God *made* what he had already *spoken* into being. Thus, whereas Day 1 presents a very succinct account, Day 2 is lengthened through repetition. Day 3 provides even further escalation by presenting two creation acts, the first presented in a manner similar to that of Day 1 (succinct), and the second like that of Day 2 (lengthened through repetition). The account of Day 4 represents a new pattern, comprising God's speech followed, this time, by *two* repetitious narrative statements (God made, God set). Day 5 supplies further intensity by including God speaking, followed by a repetitive narrative about God making, and then presenting a new component, namely, God speaking again, albeit this time in blessing. The crescendoing effect peaks in Day 6 with an expanded presentation of two creative acts. The first act is presented with a pattern similar to that appearing in Day 2 and in the second act of Day 3, namely God speaking followed by a repetitious statement that God made what he had already spoken into being. The *second* creative act of Day 6 provides the most literarily developed one, comprising God's speech followed by the narrative statement that he made and then by two more accounts of God speaking, once in blessing and once in direct address. Thus the gradual increase in the complexity of the literary

---

10. Wallace, "Rest for the Earth," 50, 54.

11. Dumbrell, "Genesis 2:1–3," 220.

12. Westermann, *Genesis 1–11*, 90, 170. Cf. Smelik, "The Creation of the Sabbath (Gen. 1:1–2:3)," 9–12.

components of each successive day of creation further develops the idea that the Gen 1 account progresses to a climax.

Another factor which appears to support the idea of escalation throughout the creation account is the use of the term ברא ("create"). This verb, particularly its use in Gen 1, has been the subject of much discussion. Whereas some argue that its usage in comparison to other terms (e.g., עשה) is significant,[13] others assert interchangeability in the terms.[14] Those who assert a special significance to the utilization of ברא note that it is used in the creation account only when something entirely new is created: it is used in verse 1 with reference to the heavens and earth, in verse 21 with reference to living creatures, and finally in verse 27 regarding humankind. A review of the structure of the creation account tends to support the position that the term is used intentionally in a distinctive manner. In the creation days following the first usage of the term (Days 1–4), the components of each account include one occurrence of God's speech. In the day that the second usage occurs (Day 5), the creation of living creatures, a second incidence of God's speech occurs, namely, blessing. In the day which includes the final occurrence of the word (Day 6), God's speech occurs three times. Further, in addition to this increased number of God's speeches appearing in correlation to the use of ברא ("create"), the content of his speech escalates in accordance with the number of occurrences. Initially, God's speech is limited to the subject of that which is created. However, when living creatures are made, the second incidence of speech includes a blessing. Corresponding to the final usage of the term, God's speech comprises that which is to be created, a blessing, and then a direct address to that which is created. Thus, the structure of the creation account supports the idea that the term ברא ("create") is used to indicate new and more highly developed forms of created entities and thus further exemplifies the literary structure of the entire account as a progressive development to a goal.

The progressive development of the creation account is even further demonstrated by the development of life forms. Life is first introduced in Day 3 with the production of plant life on the earth. The lexical emphasis of that account seems to be on the potential for reproduction. First, the specific term דשא ("sprout") and the manner in which it is used in God's speech seem to emphasize production. Not only does the verb itself include

---

13. E.g., Anderson, *From Creation to New Creation*, 8; Martin, "Male and Female He Created Them," 248; Rooker, "Genesis 1:1–3," 21; and Sarna, *Genesis*, 5.

14. E.g., Westermann, *Genesis 1–11*, 86–87.

the nuance of abundant productivity,[15] but the combined usage of the verb along with its nominal form provides further emphasis.[16] In addition, the redundant use of the terms "fruit" and "seed" in the following narrative component clearly places an emphasis on productivity. Similarly, the introduction of the second life form, living creatures, includes an emphasis on productivity with the blessing to be fruitful and multiply.[17] However, in this latter case there is not simply *potential* for productivity as seen in the presence of seed, but God apparently grants the ability to living creatures to reproduce at will. The final and most developed life form, humankind, is not only granted the ability to reproduce at will, but is also explicitly placed over the other two forms of life (dominion over creatures and freedom to use plant life for food). Thus, once again the creation account seems to present a clear progression toward the goal of Day 7.

From the foregoing discussion it becomes evident that the overall seven day structure of the creation account is intentionally presented as a steadily crescendoing progression to a goal. Thus, each feature of the creation account must be considered in conscious view of its contribution to the forward progression, resulting in the realization of that final goal.[18]

---

15. See Koehler and Baumgartner, *The Hebrew and Aramaic Lexicon of the Old Testament*, 233.

16. Waltke and O'Connor, *IBHS*, 584, §35.3.1.b.

17. If Mulzac is correct, then further emphasis is created by the use of hendiadys. See Mulzac, "Genesis 9:1–7," 67, 69–70.

18. The presentation of creation in a seven day pattern, especially given the significance of the number seven in the ancient Near East, is significant. Citing Pritchard, *Ancient Near Eastern Texts Relating to the Old Testament*, 904, Waltke notes that ancient Near Eastern literature provides numerous examples of the use of the seventh day as the climax of a significant event, and indicates completeness. See Waltke and Fredricks, *Genesis*, 71. Although one might argue that the seven day structure may be art for art's sake, given the significance of the number seven in the ancient Near East, the original audience would certainly perceive the implications of the number rather than simply admire the artistry involved. Accordingly, both Sarna and Cassuto argue that the number seven emphasizes the basic ideas of design, completion, and perfection. In this regard, Cassuto proposes that the number is used in this account with the same significance with which it occurs in Akkadian and Ugaritic literature. He notes the following: (1) there are seven paragraphs, each corresponding to a day; (2) there is a sevenfold repetition of each of the nouns in verse 1, each representing basic concepts (אלהים, ארץ, שמים); (3) there are ten utterances divided into two groups of seven divine fiats, and three pronouncements which emphasize concern for man's welfare (with three being the number of emphasis); (4) the terms "light" and "day" occur seven times in the first paragraph; (5) "light" occurs seven times in the fourth paragraph; (6) "water" is mentioned seven times in paragraphs 2 and 3; (7) "It was good" occurs seven times; (8) the first verse has seven words; (9) the

The Work of God

Paneling Structure

Another significant structure commonly identified in Gen 1 is the paneling pattern of two sets of three days. Hamilton's presentation of the structure is typical.

Day 1—one work (light)	Day 4—one work (lights)
Day 2—one work (firmament)	Day 5—one work (birds, fish)
Day 3—two works (earth, vegetation)	Day 6—two works (animals, man)

He notes that double work, in both cases, is reinforced by a double evaluation.[19] Unfortunately, proposals of a paneling structure are not particularly helpful in assessing the theological significance of the creation account. Not only is there no consensus on the exact nature of the correlation between panels, but many of the suggestions are more related to the previously discussed progressive movement of the account than to the paneling structure itself.[20]

In spite of the lack of consensus regarding the detailed relationship of the proposed panels, there is a well-known suggestion made regarding

---

second verse has fourteen words; (10) in the seventh paragraph (the seventh day) there are three sentences, each with seven words, and the middle expression is "the seventh day"; and (11) the seventh paragraph contains thirty-five words. See Cassuto, *Genesis: From Noah to Abraham*, 13–15. Sarna observes that the opening proclamation contains seven words; the description of the primeval chaos is presented in seven times two words; there are seven literary units seven times featuring the divine fiat and divine approval; and the culmination of creation is in a seventh day (Sarna, *Genesis*, 4).

19. Hamilton, *Genesis 1–17*, 125.

20. There are various perspectives regarding the presence and significance of a paneling pattern. Fishbane proposes that the first three days present creation in general terms, and the next three present the details of those features which affect the habitat of human beings, while Hamilton understands the panels to move from generalization to particularization (Fishbane, *Biblical Text and Texture*, 10; and Hamilton, *Genesis 1–17*, 117). Waltke suggests that the second set of panels presents the inhabitants ruling over the spheres in which they have been placed and which were created in the first panel, with each triad progressing from heaven to the earth, presenting a consistent escalation of activity and freedom (Waltke and Fredricks, *Genesis*, 57–58; so also Cassuto, *Genesis: From Noah to Abraham*, 42; and Sarna, *Genesis*, 4). Still another perspective is that there is a movement from inorganic matter, to the lowest forms of organic life, to living creatures, and then to humankind (Sarna, *Genesis*, 4). Walsh discusses some of these observations regarding the paneling structure and sees an intensification from immobile to mobile, which, he asserts, is probably symbolic of a movement from non-living to living and from mysterious to familiar. See Walsh, *Style and Structure in Biblical Hebrew Narrative*, 36–38.

their overall relationship. That overall relationship is often understood in terms of the two panels mirroring the opening verses of the account in that what was formless and void is now formed and filled.[21] Unfortunately, this idea suffers from both the weakness of the argument that תהו ובהו means "formless and void," and the idea that each day of the second panel represents the filling of the corresponding day of the first panel.[22] First, there is insufficient evidence to conclude that the expression תהו ובהו presents the two distinct ideas of "formless" and "void."[23] Second, a close scrutiny of the two panels reveals that the proposed relationship simply does not exist. If the idea of filling that which was formed was valid, then Day 4 would correspond to Day 2 rather than Day 1, since it was the firmament (Day 2) that was filled by the light bearers (Day 4).[24] There are also problems with the idea that Day 5 presents the filling of that which was formed in Day 2. Although Day 5 presents the "filling" (i.e., populating) of the waters, these waters preexisted the beginning of God's creative work. However, if one were to associate the "waters below" with a specific day, it would be Day

---

21. E.g., Fields, *Unformed and Unfilled*.

22. For examples of those who understand the two panels to be related by the concepts of forming and filling see Dorsey, *The Literary Structure of the Old Testament*, 49; and Waltke and Fredricks, *Genesis*, 57.

23. Although there is little discussion of the words in isolation, there are many opinions regarding the meaning of the combined expression תהו ובהו. Unfortunately, many of the commentaries seem to derive the meaning from the presumed sense of Gen 1:2 rather than first understanding the meaning of the expression and then interpreting Gen 1:2 accordingly, usually as referencing chaos. See, for example, Bush, *Notes on Genesis*, vol. 1, 28; Cassuto, *Genesis: From Noah to Abraham*, 22; Sarna, *Genesis*, 6; and von Rad, *Genesis*, 49. Tsumura takes a different approach, offering a more in-depth consideration of the combined expression than usually found. See Tsumura, *The Earth and the Waters in Genesis 1 and 2*. He proposes that the combined expression is related to the Ugaritic *nabalkutu* and refers to the unproductiveness of the earth. He asserts that the expression תהו ובהו has a similar meaning and refers to a state of aridness or unproductiveness (Jer 4:23) or desolation in the sense of uninhabitable (Isa 34:11). His conclusion is that the phrase has nothing to do with chaos and simply means "emptiness," referring to the earth as an unproductive and uninhabited place. The purpose for such an expression is to present the earth as "not yet" the earth with which the original audience was familiar. Since Tsumura's work, this view seems to be developing into the consensus position, e.g., Dumbrell, *The Faith of Israel*, 14; Habel, "Geophany: The Earth Story in Genesis 1," 38–39; Hamilton, *Genesis 1–17*, 108–9; Lim, "Explication of an Exegetical Enigma in Genesis 1:1–3," 309; Ouro, "The Earth of Genesis 1:2: Abiotic or Chaotic? Part 1"; Sailhamer, *The Pentateuch as Narrative*, 85; and Waltke and Fredricks, *Genesis*, 59.

24. Although there is a clear connection between Day 1 and Day 4, the latter presents the "objectification" of that which was created in Day 1 rather than its filling.

The Work of God

3 since that is when they were named. Although one might suggest a correlation between Days 2 and 5 in that the birds fill the firmament, the birds are actually presented as flying "on the face" of the sky and over the earth and then as multiplying on the earth, thus introducing them in as much an association with the earth as with the heavens.[25] So no matter which way it is considered, the correlation of Day 5 to Day 2 is not as expected in a formed-filled structure.

Therefore, although a paneling structure is commonly proposed, the correlation of the suggested panels continues to evade clear identification. Therefore, it would seem appropriate to forego drawing any interpretive conclusions from this type of structure, if not abandoning the idea entirely.

Repetition

There is a great deal of repetition present in the creation account, whether in ideas or in wording. This repetition is peculiarly both regular and irregular, leading to diverse conclusions regarding its significance. Some observations of regular patterns are as follows: (1) repetition of a word-fulfillment motif, (2) repetition of the phrase "God saw that it was good," and (3) the enumeration at the end of each day, "there was evening and morning, Day x." Some, like Fishbane, see this repetition as indicative of order. He states, "With respect to Gen 1:1–2:4a, the formality of its sequences, the repetition of its key words, and the serialization of its contents combine to produce several theological meanings: that Elohim, alone, 'at the beginning,' created a good, ordered world; that He 'separated' and hierarchically ordered the primordial mass into a 'good' pattern; that the created world of nature is, as a result, a harmony; and that Elohim is Omnipotent and without rival."[26] Others, however, with varying perspectives on significance, note that the patterns are less than perfect (e.g., eight creative acts in six days). For example, Fretheim suggests that "the diverse images, the less than perfect symmetry, with the call to subdue the earth, convey a sense that this creative order is not forever fixed, but is still in the process of becoming."[27] Still others, observing that there are repeated questions regarding the fact that the number of created works do not correspond with the number of

---

25. The fowl fly over (עַל) the earth, on the face of (עַל פְּנֵי), not *in* (בְּ, as used in Day 4), the firmament.

26. Fishbane, *Biblical Text and Texture*, 8.

27. Fretheim, *The Pentateuch*, 73.

Genesis 1–11

days of creation, assert that it is impossible to make orderly sense of the entire situation.[28]

In view of the varying perspectives regarding the repetition in the text and its simultaneous symmetry and asymmetry, the following discussion will review some of these features and consider their significance for understanding the account.

Word-Fulfillment

In popular discussion of the passage or in comparisons to extrabiblical creation accounts, it is common to encounter emphases placed on the word-fulfillment pattern of Gen 1.[29] However, commentaries frequently note the inconsistency of the text in this regard. That is, although each day begins with God saying "let x happen," the text does not always present it as happening simply by virtue of God speaking.[30] In the first, third, fourth, and sixth days, God spoke and it happened. In contrast, in the second and fifth days he spoke but then made or created.

Day 1	God said, "Let there be light"	God spoke, and it happened (there was light)
Day 2	God said, "Let there be a firmament, let it divide"	God spoke but then made, after which it happened (it was so)
Day 3	God said, "Let there be a firmament, let it divide"	God spoke, and it happened (it was so)
	God said, "Let there be a firmament, let it divide"	God spoke, and it happened (it was so)
Day 4	God said, "Let there be lights"	God spoke, and it happened (it was so)
Day 5	God said, "Let the waters swarm, let fowls fly"	God spoke and then created[A]
Day 6	God said, "Let the earth bring forth"	God spoke, and it happened (it was so)
	God said, "Let us"	God spoke, and it happened (it was so)

A. "It was so" (καὶ ἐγένετο οὕτως) occurs in the Greek text, but is probably a textual harmonization. See Hendel, T*he Text of Genesis 1–11*, 20–21.

28. See Turner, *Genesis*, 20; and Westermann, *Genesis 1–11*, 88–89.

29. For word-fulfillment proposals, see, for example, Amit, *Reading Biblical Narratives*, 114; and Mann, *The Book of the Torah*, 18.

30. God's initial statement always begins with a jussive, which, with the exception of the last occurrence, is taken as performative.

The Work of God

At times there are attempts to ascribe significance to this inconsistency, but not only is there no consensus, there is not even a trend.[31] In the absence of an apparent consistency and any clear explanation for that absence, it is probably best to treat the matter as stylistic variation and that probably for the purpose of creating a crescendoing progression throughout the account.[32]

Third Party Generation

Related to the word-fulfillment idea is the commonly observed phenomenon that sometimes God himself creates while at other times he seems to act through a mediating entity. For example, in the first, second, and fourth days God is the one who creates while in the third, fifth, and sixth days mediating entities are presented as the source of that which appears on the scene.[33] Brown proposes that the commands expressed by linking the jussive verb with its object is a device used only in Gen 1 and presents God transferring productive power to the object.[34] He concludes that this device is utilized to emphasize God as the creative speaker while highlighting the active roles of the earth and the seas in creation.

In spite of such suggestions, one should probably not make too much of the third party issue (e.g., the earth bringing forth). One notices that in Day 5 the waters swarm, but fowls fly. The waters swarming seems to be creation whereas, if taken literally, the fowls flying seems to be the presentation

---

31. For example, Combs notes that in the creation of light, God spoke and it happened, which he sees as distinctly different from the rest of creation where God speaks but has to make in order for his will to be accomplished. For Combs, the pattern of divergence between God's speeches and the response to them argues for a literary strategy intended by the author to teach that, in the reporting of God's speech and actions, there is an ongoing process of interpretation which is characterized by perplexity. He proposes that the fact that not everything responded as did the light, there are implications for the meaning of "it was good." See Combs, "Has Yhwh Cursed the Ground?," 270–71. Sailhamer, on the other hand, asserts that it is not a lack of internal consistency but rather the presentation of "reader-oriented comments" which clarifies issues for the reader. He sees this type of reading of the creation story as accounting for duplications and, more importantly, focusing on what is perceived as the author's chief interest in the events which he is recounting. See Sailhamer, *The Pentateuch as Narrative*, 90–91.

32. Similarly, Westermann, *Genesis 1–11*, 134–35.

33. This phenomenon is further complicated by the fact that, in the fourth and sixth days, God is said to create following the presentation of a word-fulfillment pattern.

34. Brown, "Divine Act and the Art of Persuasion in Genesis 1."

of the *function* of creatures which already exist rather than their creation. Additionally, although the waters swarming seems to be generation by a third party, the text proceeds to state that God created those creatures (v. 21), thus presenting a potential contradiction.

There are further complications in an analysis of third party production. In Day 4 God says "let the earth sprout sprouts," and it happened, thus presenting the earth as the generating entity; however, in Day 6 God said "let the earth bring forth living creatures," again presenting the earth as the generating entity, but this time *he* created them. In view of this lack of consistency, and even potential contradiction if taken too literally, perhaps this phenomenon is best taken as simply another example of stylistic variation and likely for purposes of formulating the overall progression.[35]

Day X

An obvious pattern of the creation account, albeit one with confusing inconsistencies, is the concluding phrase "and there was evening and morning, Day x." The two subjects of discussion on this topic concern the inconsistent use of the article throughout the account and the reason for the use of a cardinal number in Day 1.

Although each of these matters has defied explanation over the years, several scholars have recently provided a great deal of help on these issues. On the matter of the cardinal versus the ordinal in verse 1, Steinmann has effectively refuted a common approach which argues that it is simply a cardinal number being used as an ordinal.[36] Through a study of the use of cardinals as ordinals, he demonstrates that cardinals are used as ordinals only in the enumeration of the days of a month, the reign of a king, or in a list of countables, none of which applies to the creation account. He proceeds to propose that the cardinal, used in conjunction with the presentation of evening and morning as "a day," is necessary since the term "day" has already been used in reference to light in contrast to darkness. Thus, the expression is used to define what a day is, namely, a time period which encompasses both the time of daylight and the time of darkness, including the transitions (evening and morning). He further proposes that this approach explains the lack of articles on the second through the fifth days in that they were not, for example, "the" second day but "a" second day, that is, a second

---

35. Similarly, Westermann, *Genesis 1–11*, 137, 42.

36. Steinmann, "אחד as an Ordinal Number and the Meaning of Genesis 1:5."

time period of day, darkness, evening and morning. The inclusion of the article in Day 6 signals the climax of the creation period—the culminating day—while its inclusion in the seventh day presents that day as special.

Steinmann's approach is very similar to that taken by Sterchi.[37] Arguing on the basis of syntax, Sterchi asserts that the term "day" is not a chronological presentation, but rather a literary one. He makes the following observations: (1) "day" does not have the article except for possibly Day 7; (2) the article does not appear on the numbers either, except for Days 6 and 7; and (3) a cardinal number is used for Day 1, but ordinals for the rest. The pattern is standard in that each occurrence of "day" is followed directly by its number. Based on the use of the article he concludes: (1) Day 1 can be either definite or indefinite; (2) Days 2 through 5 are probably indefinite; and (3) Days 6 and 7 are probably definite. Genesis 1:5 should be "one day" rather than either "Day 1" or "the first day," with the sequence being "one day," "a second day," "a third day," etc.

The observations and conclusions of Sterchi and Steinmann reflect those arrived at independently by this writer. The cardinal number in Day 1 is used to define a period of time which involves a cycle from light to darkness back to light ("there was evening and morning, i.e., one day"). The following ordinals without the articles on "day" reflect further occurrences of cycles ("there was evening and morning," i.e., a second day). The introduction of the article on Day 6 points to the significance of that day, which, as will be discussed, is confirmed by the usage of other literary techniques.[38] Finally, the double use of the article on the seventh day, conspicuously coupled with the absence of a cycle (evening and morning), effectively presents the final day as both the goal and the cessation of cycles, i.e., the final permanent situation.[39] The identification of "day" as a cycle will be further developed throughout this chapter. However, the introduction of the cycles, mounting to a presentation of the sixth day as particularly significant, followed by attaining the goal of the seventh, validates the previous suggestion that the creation account is presented as a unit which focuses attention on the goal of the final day.

---

37. Sterchi, "Does Genesis 1 Provide a Chronological Sequence?"

38. So also Cassuto, *Genesis: From Noah to Abraham*, 60; and Waltke and Fredricks, *Genesis*, 67.

39. Scobie understands the creation account as based upon cycles, although he does not develop any associated theology. See Scobie, *The Ways of Our God*, 152.

Genesis 1–11

Repetitious Statements

In view of the foregoing discussion, particularly in reference to the crescendoing structure of the creation account, it appears that repetitious statements are commonly used for the purpose of both creating that sense of progression and focusing attention on content. For example, in Day 1 God said "Let there be light," and there *was* light. There is no repetition in this succinct account. However, in Day 2, following God's saying "Let there be an expanse," which, based on the prior day's account, should cause the reader to assume that it was therefore accomplished, the narrator adds the statement that God created the expanse, followed by the further redundancy, "It was so." Thus he uses repetition to both expand the account as well as repeat the content, thereby focusing attention.[40] Similar usages of this technique continue throughout the account, reemphasizing important content while simultaneously building the crescendo.[41]

Significance of God's Speech

One matter which is addressed inadequately in discussions of the creation account is the relative significance of reported speech included in the narrative in comparison to the narrative itself. As Alter puts it, "Spoken language is the substratum of everything human and divine that transpires in the Bible, and the Hebrew tendency to transpose what is pre-verbal or nonverbal into speech is finally a technique for getting at the essence of things."[42] That is, the essence of the scene in Hebrew narrative is accomplished through dialogue, joined together by narrative. Moreover, direct speech represents the primary instrument used in narration for revealing the varied and nuanced relationships of characters to the actions in which they are implicated.

If speech in narrative is so significant, more attention should be paid to its role in Gen 1. Although the significance of God's speech is sometimes noted, it is generally limited to the assertion that the creation account

---

40. This repetition in narratival statements to confirm what is already implied in speech is a common literary convention used to focus attention on what was said in the speech. See Alter, *The Art of Biblical Narrative*, 76–77.

41. Cf. Day 3 part 2, and especially Day 4.

42. Alter, *The Art of Biblical Narrative*, 70.

comprises God's speeches joined by narrative.⁴³ However, if the creation account is an account of God's speech joined by narrative, and speech is the primary instrument used in Hebrew narrative for identifying the essence of things, then the determination of the significance of each day, as well as that of the account as a whole, should focus on the content and form of that speech.

In view of the significance of speech in narrative, particular attention will be paid throughout this chapter to God's speech, with the assumption that it contains the principal emphasis of each particular day. However, a consideration of all the speeches together gives clues as to the focus of the creation account as a whole, namely, the goal of Day 7. For example, almost every time God's speech is presented it is with jussives and frequently includes statements of function and/or purpose along with the concept of separation. As a result, the entire account is structured in such a way that the creation is presented in terms of God's purpose, featured as a crescendoing effect in the progression of speech in the respective days.⁴⁴

Day 1: simple jussive
Day 2: simple jussive with function (separation)
Day 3:
  Part 1: complex jussive (implied function, separation)
  Part 2: simple jussive, with elaboration (productivity and separation)
Day 4: simple jussive with complex purpose (separation and light)
Day 5: complex jussive (implied character, i.e., movement)
    blessing (reproduction)
Day 6:
  Part 1: simple jussive (separation)
  Part 2: cohortative (intention) with function
    blessing (reproduction, command, function)
    direct address (provision of sustenance)

God's speech becomes more complex in each day of creation. At first, his statements move from simple to complex. Then, there is the introduction of blessing added to the simple jussives. Finally, in the last creative act of the sixth day, generally recognized as the climax of creation, God's speech

---

43. E.g., Fishbane, *Biblical Text and Texture*, 7; Hamilton, *Genesis 1–17*, 119; and Waltke and Fredricks, *Genesis*, 56.

44. Sailhamer asserts that even the usage of the term בראשית carries the thought of a starting point of a specific period which is marked by an end. Therefore he sees the introductory terminology itself indicating that God has a plan and purpose in mind, i.e., an end. See Sailhamer, *The Pentateuch as Narrative*, 83; idem, *Genesis Unbound*, 38–45.

becomes even more developed. Whereas in all other days his statements present the introduction of a new entity, in Day 6 he speaks of intention and purpose prior to introducing that entity. Then, following the blessing, for the first time God's speech includes direct address to that which he has created.[45] Thus, a consideration of the manner in which God's speech is presented throughout the account reaffirms the implication of other structural clues that the creation account should be understood in terms of a progressive development, building and crescendoing to the climax of the creation of humankind, thus reaching the goal of the sabbath.[46]

Summary

This review of the literary presentation of the creation account has resulted in the conclusion that multiple strategies have been employed in order to portray the record as a crescendoing progression to a climax (Day 6) and a goal (Day 7). The seven day structure presents a progression which focuses attention on the seventh day. The introduction of days as cycles, leading to the presentation of the sixth day as especially significant, followed by Day 7, characterizes the creation account as a unit which focuses attention on the goal of the sabbath. Even reported speech and various forms of repetition are utilized in a way which highlights this progressive development to an end. Thus, the creation account appears to be consciously structured in a manner which presents a steady and mounting progression towards the climax of the creation of humankind, thus reaching the goal of the sabbath.[47]

---

45. It is possible to understand God's blessing to the animals as direct address. However, even if this is the case, God's addressing humankind is of a different nature. While the blessing neither implies nor requires understanding on the part of those blessed, the statement to humankind is presented as communication. Cf. Sarna, *Genesis*, 13; and Waltke and Fredricks, *Genesis*, 67.

46. As Bird observes, even at the grammatical and lexical level the culminating act of creation is indicated by a shift in the word of announcement from intransitive verbal forms or verbs of generation to an active-transitive verb, and from third to first person speech. See Bird, "'Male and Female He Created Them,'" 346.

47. Landy sees this ordered progression in a closed structure as so dominant that it clearly sets creation apart. See Landy, *Paradoxes of Paradise*, 188.

Theological Exegesis

A very critical component of a theological exegesis of the creation account in Gen 1 is the understanding of verses 1–2. Therefore, these introductory verses will be discussed at length, followed by an overview of each day of creation. The goal throughout is to ascertain the intended theological message by paying close attention to literary clues and figural representations.

Introduction (Gen 1:1–2)

The introductory verses of this chapter have generated a great deal of discussion. It is interesting to note that, at least intuitively, biblical scholars understand these verses to contain a significant amount of important theological information. This observation is evidenced by the fact that much of the discussion focuses on the theological implications of the various alternatives. For example, do these verses imply a former creation which was previously marred, presumably by the fall of Satan? Do these verses present creation *ex nihilo*? Do they deny creation *ex nihilo*? Did God create evil? Thus, although this chapter is not usually approached with a conscious theological focus, the result is nonetheless a theological discussion. Furthermore, the results of that discussion tend to drive the treatment of the entire creation account. Therefore, due to their importance, these verses must be considered at length, particularly in terms of the theological foundation which they lay.

Temporal Clause or Summary

One of the most commonly discussed issues in the introductory section is the nature of the first verse. Hamilton summarizes the possibilities as follows: (1) the first word is in an absolute state, functioning independently, and all of verse 1 is an independent clause and a complete sentence ("In the beginning God created . . . "); (2) the first word is an indeterminate noun used as a relative temporal designation ("Initially, God created . . . "); (3) the first word is in the construct state, and the first verse is a temporal clause subordinated to verse 2 ("When God began to create . . . "); (4) the first word is in the construct state, and the first verse is a temporal clause subordinated to verse 3, with verse 2 a parenthesis ("When God began to create the heavens and the earth, the earth being without form and void . . .,

God said ... "). A review of the critical discussion on this matter demostrates the truth of an assertion made by both Hamilton and Westermann: Hebrew syntax is not sufficient to resolve the situation since competent Hebraists take different positions.[48] The position taken in this study is one of the predominant views, namely, that verse one presents a summary statement.[49] That is, "In the beginning God created the heavens and the earth" is a statement which summarizes all of the following material through Gen 2:3. It is important to note that, however this verse is understood, it does not seem to affect the theological message of the creation account as argued in this work.

Formless and Void

Regardless of the position taken on the nature of verse one, verse two describes the state of the earth at the time the creative activity presented by the remainder of the account begins. The fact that the condition of creation is explicitly stated, with three clauses utilized in that presentation, implies that it is significant to the account. Therefore, it is important to understand the description properly.

The first statement is that the earth was תהו ובהו, "formless and void" according to the traditional interpretation. A common understanding of the expression is that it presents chaos. Although the term "chaos" may be accurate in one sense, it is probably best to understand the Hebrew expression as indicating a state which is unproductive and uninhabitable, that is, unfit for life.[50]

This nuance of the phrase תהו ובהו is important to an understanding of the overall presentation of creation. Varying perspectives on the expression have resulted in seemingly endless debate regarding whether God created evil, whether creation was *ex nihilo*, whether a gap exists between the first two verses, etc. Although these questions may be valid concerns, the primary question in exegeting this passage is whether or not they reflect

---

48. Hamilton, *Genesis 1–17*, 103–8; and Westermann, *Genesis 1–11*, 78. So also Lim who proposes that one's presuppositional view of God comes into play in this discussion. See Lim, "Explication of an Exegetical Enigma in Genesis 1:1–3," 306.

49. Cf. Dumbrell, *The End of the Beginning*, 172; idem, *The Faith of Israel*, 13; Fretheim, *Creation, Fall, and Flood*, 51; idem, *The Pentateuch*, 73; Hamilton, *Genesis 1–17*, 117; Thompson, *The Origin Tradition of Ancient Israel*, 69; Waltke, "Creation Account in Gen 1:1–3," 222–28; and Westermann, *Genesis 1–11*, 94.

50. See footnote 23, page 34.

The Work of God

the concerns of the original author. The literary formulation of the text, along with the meaning of the expression תהו ובהו, seems to indicate that the emphasis is not on these questions, but rather upon God converting that which is unproductive and uninhabitable into a creation flourishing with life.

Darkness

The term "darkness" is another expression whose meaning seems to be assumed apart from any thorough investigation. However, as with תהו ובהו, its meaning is critical to understanding the presentation of creation in Gen 1.

A common perception of this term is that its figural representation expresses evil in some form and derives from the popular notion that darkness in Scripture is associated with evil. For example, Provan states, "Darkness is a uniformly negative phenomenon in the Bible."[51] Applying that perspective to Gen 1, Fretheim asserts that darkness is presented as a malevolent power over creation, while Cassuto proposes that in Day 1 of creation the text specifically states that the light was good in order to disallow the thought that the darkness was also good.[52] However, a study of the biblical usage of the term seems to reveal a different connotation.

The Hebrew word for darkness (חשך) commonly occurs in the Bible in contrast to light. It means "a state in which one cannot see" with several nuances: (1) inability to function (Exod 10:21–23; Job 19:8; 22:11; Ps 35:6; Isa 59:9); (2) that which hides or obscures, literally or figuratively (Job 12:22; 24:16; 34:22; 37:19; 38:2; Ps 139:11; Isa 29:18; 45:19; 49:9); (3) a covering around God (Deut 4:11; 2 Sam 22:12; Ps 18:12); and (4) a metaphor pertaining to the obscurity of death (Job 10:21; 12:22; 17:13). It does not always seem to be negative in and of itself, but rather simply that which precludes clarity (e.g., Isa 45:3, 7).[53] That is, although the general connotation of obscuring is negative rather than positive, the emphasis seems to be on the character of hiddenness rather than on morality. Thus, any negative nuance is connected more with the result on humankind than any inherent moral quality in the darkness itself. In the New Testament, the

---

51. Provan, "Creation and Holistic Ministry," 295.

52. Fretheim, *Creation, Fall, and Flood*, 57; and Cassuto, *Genesis: From Noah to Abraham*, 26.

53. The same connotation seems to be attached to חשך, "darkness" (Gen 15:12; Pss 18:12; 82:5; 139:12; Isa 8:22; 50:10).

Genesis 1–11

Greek term for darkness (σκότος) seems to carry the same basic meaning as חשך, namely, that which obscures (e.g., John 3:19; 12:35; Acts 13:11; 1 Cor 4:5). Sometimes it is associated with that which carries a negative connotation, as with reference to a place of banishment (e.g., Matt 22:13; 25:30; Jude 1:13), and sometimes with moral evil, as in the powers of this world ("power" or "works" of darkness as in Luke 22:53 and Eph 5:11). However, in both cases it still carries the basic meaning of that which obscures sight. The New Testament "outer darkness" is similar to the Old Testament usage of darkness with reference to Sheol, the place about which little to nothing is known (see Job 33:28, 30 where the grave is contrasted with light among the living).[54]

Although no commentaries were found which specifically discuss the biblical usage of this term, several scholars agree with this conclusion as it relates to Gen 1. Habel states that there is nothing negative about the darkness. It is simply the condition which hides the presence of several components of the primordial domain, namely, Elohim, the waters, and the earth.[55] Waltke states that darkness is simply the opposite of light (see Exod 15:8; Prov 2:13).[56] While noting that the term is often a symbol of evil, misfortune, death, and oblivion (see Isa 5:20, 30; 8:22; 9:1; Nah 1:8; Zeph 1:15; Ps 88:11–13; Job 10:20–22; 17:12–13; Lam 3:2; Eccl 6:4), Sarna asserts that here it simply seems to be the absence of light.[57] Bush takes the same position.[58]

Thus, just as in the case of תהו ובהו, the negative connotation frequently associated with חשך is probably not the correct biblical figural representation. Rather, the term seems to simply connote the absence of light, indicating obscurity.[59] The theological implications of this will be discussed

---

54. These findings are supported by Hamilton's suggestion that in light of Ps 18:12 darkness has both a benign and sinister nuance in the Bible. The sinister nuance is connected with its being the opposite of light, while it is at times benign in that it can be protective (Hamilton, *Genesis 1–17*, 109 fn. 20). Cf. Harris, Archer, and Waltke, *TWOT*, §769; VanGemeren, ed., *NIDOTTE*, §3124.

55. Habel, "Geophany," 36.

56. Waltke and Fredricks, *Genesis*, 60.

57. Sarna, *Genesis*, 6.

58. Bush, *Genesis*, 29.

59. Contra Freedman, who states that the Bible regards darkness as substantial matter, rather than the absence of light. See Freedman, "רוח אלהים–and a Wind from God," 13. Even if Freedman is correct, the figural representation of darkness as that which obscures is not changed.

The Work of God

later, but at this point it is sufficient to note that darkness does not address the moral character of the pre-creation state, but rather describes that with which the creative activity of God began. In view of the figural representation of תהו ובהו, and darkness, that pre-creation state is presented as unsuitable for life and enshrouded in obscurity.[60]

The Deep

The term תהום has generated a great deal of discussion regarding a relationship between the biblical and extrabiblical creation accounts (e.g., Tiamat and combat with the sea).[61] In the past, this term, along with תנינים ("dragons," "sea monsters") was understood as one of the strongest evidences for a correlation between these stories. However, more recent scholarship, with the benefit of more developed comparative language studies, is beginning to reject the former position. Hamilton argues against תהום having any connection to Tiamat since "any relationship is blurred beyond recognition" by their differences.[62] Westermann discusses the uses of תהום in the Old Testament and observes that it usually occurs apart from personification and appears in creation contexts without any mythical reference.[63] Tsumura goes into great depth on this term and studies its etymology. He first argues that there is no basis for understanding the term in the context of a de-personification of a divine name which alludes back to Tiamat's primeval battle. He argues that, although the Hebrew term is related etymologically to Akkadian and Ugaritic, it is simply a reflection of a common Semitic term and is best understood as a common noun. In fact, all of its cognates are best understood simply as common nouns.[64] After considerable discussion Tsumura concludes that there is no Canaanite mythological

---

60. Breytenbach connects the principles of obscurity and unsuitability for life when he argues that in Semitic languages there is an apparent connection between the terms for light and vegetation, as well as darkness and drought. See Breytenbach, "The Connection between the Concepts of Darkness and Drought as well as Light and Vegetation."

61. Cf. Harris, Archer, and Waltke, eds., *TWOT*, §2495a; VanGemeren, ed., *NIDOTTE*, §9333.

62. Hamilton, *Genesis 1–17*, 111. So also Westermann, *Genesis 1–11*, 104–5.

63. Westermann, *Genesis 1–11*, 104–5.

64. Tsumura, *Earth and Waters in Genesis 1 and 2*, 52–56. Both Tsumura and Westermann argue that the absence of the article on the common noun is not a valid basis for arguing personification (Tsumura, *Earth and Waters in Genesis 1 and 2*, 57; Westermann, *Genesis 1–11*, 104–5).

background to Gen 1:2 and that, therefore, the text does not reference *Chaoskampf*.[65] Rather, he asserts, תהום is better understood in conjunction with ארץ ("earth") as a hyponymous word pair. That is, "earth" is to "the deep" as "fruit" is to "the apple," with "the deep" referring to the ocean as part of the earth in the expression of verse 1 "heavens and earth." The hyponymous word pair "earth-deep" is described as not yet productive and inhabited, and without light.[66] This lack of any mythical allusion is asserted by other scholars as well.[67]

The earlier popularity of understanding תהום as an allusion to Tiamat has engendered a strong negative connotation to the term. However, if it is true that there is no allusion to the mythical character, then this connotation must be reconsidered. A study of the biblical usage of תהום reveals that it is used as follows: (1) in contrast to the heavens (שמים, as in Gen 49:25; Ps 107:26; Prov 8:27–28); (2) in contrast to dry land (Exod 15:8; Ps 106:9); (3) as a source of water (Ps 78:15; Ezek 31:15), whether in the land (Deut 8:7; 33:13) or even in the sea (Job 38:16); (4) in parallel with "sea" (ים, as in Job 28:14; 38:16; Ps 33:7); (5) in contrast to mountains (Ps 36:7; Hab 3:10); and (6) in parallel with "waters" (מים, as in Pss 77:17; 104:6; Ezek 26:19). Thus, the term is consistently used in relationship to the three spheres presented in the creation account: heavens, earth, and sea.

A study of the figural representation of the sphere of the sea, when used in a metaphorical sense, reveals that it is used primarily in connection with that which is hidden, unknown, and out of reach.[68] Therefore, the term in Gen 1 probably refers to nothing other than the deep or waters of the deep, tending to reinforce the image created by the term darkness by reiterating the concept of obscurity.[69]

---

65. Tsumura, *Earth and Waters in Genesis 1 and 2*, 65.

66. Ibid., 163.

67. Fretheim, *Creation, Fall, and Flood*, 356; Habel, "Geophany," 42; Ouro, "The Earth of Genesis 1:2: Abiotic or Chaotic? Part 1"; and van Wolde, "The Story of Cain and Abel," 25.

68. Deut 30:13; 2 Sam 22:16; Job 11:9; 28:14; 36:30; 38:16; Pss 65:5; 68:22; 77:19; 139:9; Amos 9:3; Mic 7:19. In ways associated with this connotation it also alludes to movement and turmoil (Job 26:12; 41:31; Ps 65:7; Jas 1:6; Jude 1:13), noise (Ps 93:4; Isa 5:30; 17:12; 51:15; Jer 6:23; 31:35; 50:42), and that which must be restrained (Pss 106:9; 114:3–5; Prov 8:29; Jer 5:22; Nah 1:4).

69. Even though the primary nuance in Gen 1 is to waters, in subsequent texts it does sometimes carry a negative nuance, just as חשך. Again, the phenomenon may be due to its natural character or possibly due to mythical associations.

The Work of God

The Spirit of God or a Mighty Wind?

The referent of רוח אלהים has generated much discussion, with the issue being whether the expression should be understood as "a mighty wind" or "the Spirit of God." As Waltke points out, a good argument can be made for either "Spirit" or "wind."[70] Those who argue for "mighty wind" present the following rationale: (1) Gen 1:2c begins with a nominal clause, but, if it were in contrast to 2a–b, one would expect a *wayyiqtol*;[71] (2) Gen 1:2c seems to be in parallel with 2b; (3) the structure of Gen 1 seems to indicate that the process of creation does not begin until v. 3; (4) there is no mention of רוח in the following verses, suggesting it has nothing to do with creation; (5) when רוח and מים occur in association with each other, the common connection is between wind and waters (see Gen 1:2; 7:18; Exod 32:20; Job 5:10; 24:18; 26:10; Eccl 11:1; Isa 18:2; 19:8; Hos 10:7). On the other hand, those arguing for "Spirit of God" note the following: (1) when רוח occurs in genitive construction with אלהים (or Yahweh), it always refers to some activity or aspect of the deity; (2) the word אלהים is used thirty-five times in the creation story, thirty-four of which clearly refer to God; (3) the analogy of Deut 32:11 argues for "Spirit of God" (God likened to an eagle hovering over the nest of her young); (4) parallels between creation and the tabernacle in Exodus argue for "Spirit of God" in that both are the Spirit's work (Gen 2:2; Exod 31:5)[72]; (5) of the eighteen occurrences of this phrase in the Old Testament, it never means anything like "mighty wind," and (6) a comparison between the biblical usages of רוח אלהים and דבר אלהים (Job 26:13; Pss 33:6; 104:30; Isa 34:16; 40:13), both exuding creative and life-giving power, is more consistent with Deity than with the physical wind.[73] Waltke's conclusion is probably correct when he argues that, due to context, the expression is probably best understood as "Spirit of God." If the term

---

70. Waltke and Fredricks, *Genesis*, 60.
71. See Childs, *Myth and Reality in the Old Testament*, 34.
72. Sailhamer, *The Pentateuch as Narrative*, 87.
73. Freedman, "רוח אלהים–and a Wind from God," 13. This comparison of the word of God with the Spirit of God may be further supported by the context. Habel comments that in the early verses of Gen 1 God is first introduced in connection with his Spirit, and then his word. He references Ps 33:6 where the word and breath are alternative images to express the presence of God as a creating power. Elohim, hidden as spirit/breath, is now revealed as word. See Habel, "Geophany," 40.

referred to wind, it would have to be understood as operating within the firmament which was not created until the second day.[74]

A proposal by DeRoche on the significance of "Spirit of God" in this verse may be helpful. He attempts to resolve the problem of the meaning of the term by considering it in Exod 14:21 and Gen 8:1.[75] In these two cases as well as in Gen 1, the Lord sends a רוח against a body of water.[76] He proposes that in each context the term רוח is part of the terminology of cosmogony and, more specifically, announces creative activity. Some items of which to take note are as follows: (1) in Exodus the verb בקע is used, which although not associated with creation, appears in other passages which describe Yahweh's control over the waters (e.g., Isa 63:12; Job 26:8; Gen 7:11); (2) the land which appears in the flood and the exodus is referred to using the term יבש (Gen 8:7, 14; Exod 14:16), which is the same term used to describe the land appearing in Gen 1:10; (3) in Exodus, the people's going into the sea is referred to as going into the midst of waters, the same expression used of the primeval seas in Gen 1:6; (4) all examples are understood as an act of creation; and (5) Exod 15:8–10 make a cosmogonic presentation. DeRoche's conclusion is that רוח אלהים alludes to the impending creative power of God, expressing his control over the cosmos and his ability to impose his will upon it. It should be noted that this conclusion coincides with Hamilton's and Habel's view outlined above, but argued from a completely different perspective, namely, that the Spirit of God's "hovering" presents the idea of anticipation prior to God's divine creative intervention.[77]

---

74. Waltke and Fredricks, *Genesis*, 60. However, in personal communication Chisholm has suggested that this discussion may represent a false dichotomy in that the Spirit is associated with wind elsewhere (e.g., Ezek 37:5–10). See Chisholm, *Handbook on the Prophets*, 233.

75. DeRoche, "The *Rûaḥ 'Ĕlōhîm* in Gen 1:2c." Similarly, Löning and Zenger, *To Begin with, God Created*, 19.

Wyatt's discussion tends to support the idea that the reference to the Spirit of God implies God's impending activity when he argues that darkness should be understood, at least in part, as the primeval dwelling place of God, and that 1:2 represents the beginning of a theophany. See Wyatt, "The Darkness of Genesis I.2."

76. So also Sailhamer, *The Pentateuch as Narrative*, 91.

77. For a similar conclusion from still another perspective, see Perry, "A Poetics of Absence," 3–11.

Hovering

Although there is consensus regarding the essential meaning of the participle מרחפת ("hovering"), there is some debate over the exact nuance of the term, which, in turn, is generally dependent upon one's perception of רוח אלהים. Von Rad sees it as meaning "vibrate," "tremble," "move," "stir," and belonging to a description of chaos.[78] Cassuto understands the basic verb (רחף) to mean "hover" in the sense of Deut 32:11, namely, the protection of a parent for a young bird which cannot care for itself.[79] Sarna asserts that the basic idea is that of motion, which is the essential element in change and originates with God's dynamic presence.[80] In the context of Gen 1, Hamilton argues from Ugaritic passages and Deut 32:11 that the term is best associated with "spirit" rather than "wind" and understands that the Spirit is superintending the situation of formlessness prior to specific creation.[81] So also, Ouro asserts that רחף is an activity carried out by a living being.[82] In addition, Habel sees the Spirit of God hovering as presenting anticipation which is fulfilled by the end of the creation week.[83] Thus, the perception of the exact nuance of "hovering" is more connected with one's position on רוח אלהים than on the meaning of the term itself.

Face of the Waters

According to Cassuto, "face of the waters" is another term for "the deep," corresponding by parallelism, as well as terminology, to "the face of the deep."[84] Similarly, Westermann asserts that "upon the face of the deep" and "upon the face of the waters" have the same meaning and are simply two phrases which describe what is over the surface of the deep, namely, the Spirit of God (רוח אלהים) and darkness.[85] A review of the biblical use of the term מים ("waters") reveals that it is commonly used as another term for, or is the same concept as, "sea" (ים), which in turn supports Cassuto's and

---

78. Von Rad, *Genesis*, 47.
79. Cassuto, *Genesis: From Noah to Abraham*, 25.
80. Sarna, *Genesis*, 7.
81. Hamilton, *Genesis 1-17*, 115–16.
82. Ouro, "The Earth of Genesis 1:2: Abiotic or Chaotic? Part 3," 64–65.
83. Habel, "Geophany," 44.
84. Cassuto, *Genesis: From Noah to Abraham*, 27.
85. Westermann, *Genesis 1-11*, 106.

Westermann's position.[86] Therefore, in view of the conclusion that "waters" are essentially the same as "the deep," Habel appears to be correct when he states that there is nothing negative about the waters, no indication in the text that they are foreboding or threatening.[87] They simply cover the earth, helping to render it invisible and uninhabitable.

Synthesis

There has been a tendency to understand the introductory verses of the creation account as presenting a morally negative condition. This tendency has been closely associated with the idea that the passage alludes to the mythical Tiamat; however, as discussed above, the passage is probably best understood apart from any mythical allusions. In addition, the above studies on the terminology utilized in verse two fail to indicate the presence of anything which is inherently morally negative. Rather, the beginning verses of the creation account present a pre-creative state which is unproductive and uninhabitable, and which is characterized by obscurity. However, it also is presented as a state which faces the impending creative activity of the Spirit of God.[88] Thus, the introductory verses set up the account's overall

---

86. Cf. Pss 33:7; 46:4; 69:1–2, 14–15; 74:13; 77:16, 19; 78:13; 93:4; 104:3, 6; 136:6; 144:7; 148:4; Prov 8:29; 30:4; Isa 11:9; 17:12–13; 18:2; 19:5; 28:2; 40:12; 43:16; 51:10; 57:20; 51:55; Ezek 1:24; 26:19; 27:26, 34; 31:4, 15; 43:2; 47:8; Amos 5:8; 9:6; Jonah 2:5; Hab 2:14; 3:15; Rev 1:15; 14:2; 19:6.

87. Habel, "Geophany," 37. In personal communication, Chisholm has noted that the singular form ים is not used, commenting that if the narrator had wanted to associate the waters with chaos/evil he probably would have used that term rather than מים, תהום, and ימים.

88. In an interesting and somewhat related approach, Wyatt sees Gen 1:2 as a type of theophany. He reviews the poetic parallelism of verse 2 which he considers a tricolon with synonymous parallelism of the second two cola. The structure of ab, acb, with the two b's being synonymous, implies that the two a's (i.e., "darkness," "Spirit of God") correspond in some way. (Although he notes that one could argue that they are contrasting [i.e., conjunction translated "but"] or that רוח refers to wind, he prefers to see them as synonymous in some respect.) Affirming that "darkness" must not be understood in simply negative terms, he refers to Ps 18:12 (cf. also 2 Sam 22:12) which "makes darkness the locus of the invisibility, and therefore perhaps of the spiritual essence, of the deity." He notes that the passage in Psalms links darkness with the waters as the extraterrestrial location of God, while Deut 4:11, 23 use darkness in the context of a theophany, the medium for the divine voice. Thus he sees divine glory issuing forth out of darkness.

Wyatt further supports his proposition from additional features of the parallelism of verse two. He notes that, while the first colon is a monocolon, it demonstrates a "peculiarly intimate relationship with the first stich of the bicolon." The verb "to be" of the first

The Work of God

emphasis on life by describing a lifeless situation upon which the Spirit of God is about to act.

The Days of Creation

The nature of the presentation of the successive days of creation is significant for the theological understanding of the account. The following discussion will consider each day and the fundamental concepts which are included. Although various other themes are also introduced, it will be seen that the focus of the creation account is on the progressive development of life.

Day 1

The emphasis of the first day of creation is on light. Even though separation and naming also occur in Day 1, the content of God's speech shows that light is the focus. The figural representation of light throughout the Bible is well-known and is associated with manifestation (e.g., Eph 5:13).[89]

On the first day of creation God not only creates light, but he also separates that light from darkness, naming both. The light he calls "day" and the darkness he calls "night." Therefore, the first thing God does with

---

colon may be seen as doing double duty, filling in the absence of a verb in the second colon. Thus, since the second and third cola cannot be separated, verse 2 may actually be a tricolon of abc, ac, adc. The first colon equates a and c, but also implies the equating of a and c in the second and third cola. This results in a chiastic structure (supported, he asserts, by the assonance of the gutturals) which emphasizes the central theme, namely, darkness over the face of the deep. He sees this emphasis of the chiasmus as reinforced by the absence of a copula in the second colon. Thus, he sees this verse as the initial stages of the manifestation of the deity, describing three stages: (1) the improbable condition of chaos in which it is to occur; (2) an inchoate medium of revelation, namely, the darkness; and (3) the spirit of God intuited rather than seen traversing waters as yet unordered. See Nicolas Wyatt, "The Darkness of Genesis I.2," 543–54.

89. Gowan adds an interesting idea when he asserts that light is symbolic, representing the presence of God himself in the world, and portending the experience of life. See Gowan, *From Eden to Babel*, 22. As will be discussed, a clear and progressively intense focus on life is presented throughout the remainder of the creation account.

Although Gowan's suggestion that light represents God in the world may appear to contradict Wyatt's assertion that God is even in the darkness (fn. 88), there need not be a discrepancy. According to Wyatt, darkness is the locus of invisibility of the deity, and that out of which he speaks in theophany. Thus, the hiddenness (i.e., transcendence) of God may be found in the darkness while the revelation of God (immanence) is found in the light.

the pre-creative state is to shed light on that which was previously obscured; however, he does not completely eliminate darkness, but rather controls it by "putting it into its place" (i.e., "separation") and naming it.

Even though the focus of this day is on the creation of light, it is still important to consider the nuances of separation and naming, both of which are commonly understood to present the exercise of God's dominion.[90] Separation does not mean to pull apart, but rather to assign to each part its respective sphere.[91] Thus, separation focuses on God's authoritative intentions as he reveals, distinguishes, and assigns. Naming complements the idea of separation by clearly designating what has been separated according to God's purposes.[92]

---

90. According to Waltke, the term בדל denotes both separation of that which does not go together as well as separation of tasks. For example, light and darkness do not go together and have separate tasks. See Waltke and Fredricks, *Genesis*, 61. Similarly, Sarna understands it as indicating differentiation (Sarna, *Genesis*, 7).

91. Hamilton, *Genesis 1–17*, 119; and Sarna, *Genesis*, 7.

92. The concept of naming in the Primeval History seems to have far more to do with designation than with determination and authority. (So also Fretheim, *The Pentateuch*, 74.) The overall presentation of Gen 1 including naming in the context of God's authority commonly results in the uniting of these two concepts (e.g., Sarna, *Genesis*, 7; Westermann, *Genesis 1–11*, 114). Naming follows creation and separation and seems to directly correspond to those things. However, in the Eden narrative, naming by Adam is presented in a different manner. In that passage there is no specific mention of separation prior to naming nor is there any concept of creation by the one who names. That is, there is no idea of bringing into being, separation, and then naming as is the case in the creation account. Instead, the man simply recognizes the pre-existent distinction/separation ("each according to their kind") which had been created by God and designated accordingly. This association of naming with recognition and designation rather than determination in the Eden narrative warrants a reconsideration of its usage in the creation account in that it may have the same nuance there as well. In Gen 1 the portrayal of authority is clearly presented in God's creation and separation, things which cannot be accomplished by any other than God himself. Naming, however, may simply denote God's recognition of the clear distinction between the things which he has created and distinguished (separated). Of course, God's naming is authoritative, but perhaps only such because of who is naming rather than because of the nuance of naming itself. Therefore the significance of naming may be better understood as designation for the purpose of communication to others what has been recognized about the nature and character of something rather than any type of authoritative determination of that nature and character. In the case of creation God labels what he has created and separated, providing further clarification of his work, all authoritative because of who he is and what he is doing. In the case of the man in Eden, naming is the recognition of the distinctions among what God has created and separated. Thus, it seems that naming carries the idea of designation rather than determination and is related to authority only insofar as the one naming has a place of authority. (Cf. Ruth 4:17 where the town women named but probably had no authority.)

The Work of God

The first day of creation ends in a very interesting fashion, but, because of familiarity, it is often overlooked. The narrator states: "And there was evening and morning, Day one." Unfortunately there tends to be a great deal of discussion about literal twenty-four hour days and whether a day should be understood as beginning in the evening or in the morning; however, these discussions seem to miss the point of the text.[93] One must ask, given the context where only light and darkness exist along with the watery mass, with each assigned its place, what is the significance of the introduction of the terms "evening" and "morning"? Since these words are terms of transition,[94] they introduce a new concept into the narrative, namely the movement from the light to the darkness and back to the light again.[95] As discussed previously, this movement from light to darkness back to light again, coupled with the use of a cardinal number, introduces the idea of a cycle.[96] The overall seven-day literary structure of the creation account, rather than, for example, seven separate acts, argues for some intended significance to this concept since these cycles repeat each successive day but disappear on Day 7. By presenting a transition between light and darkness, rather than destruction of darkness, these cycles represent the first negative feature of creation in the sense that even though God is moving things from darkness and obscurity, these conditions still remain and periodically dominate—that is, until Day 7.

In summary, the presentation of the first day of creation introduces the following: (1) light, (2) separation of light and darkness, (3) naming of light and darkness, and (4) a transition from light to darkness back to light again. Understood with a theological focus, this day presents God's creative activity beginning by shedding light, that is, revealing and exposing things

---

93. There is no intent here to argue for or against whether God's creative activity was accomplished in six literal twenty-four hour days, but rather to recognize that this is not the primary idea or most natural informed reading of the text. Any attempt to argue otherwise must confront the difficulty presented by the fact that the word "day" is used in three senses in 1:1–2:4: (1) evening and morning taken together; (2) light as opposed to darkness; and (3) the sense of "when" in collocation with a preposition (2:4). So also Dumbrell, *The Faith of Israel*, 15.

94. Cf. McCabe, "A Defense of Literal Days in the Creation Week," 106–9, 14; Sarna, *Genesis*, 8; VanGemeren, *NIDOTTE*, §1332.

95. See also Kline, who argues that evening and morning must be understood figuratively since the celestial objects which regulate the day were not yet created. See Kline, "Because It Had Not Rained," 156.

96. See pages 38–39.

Genesis 1–11

as they really are.[97] He then creates a clear demarcation between that which reveals and that which hides, assigning to each its place and function. Finally, as a statement of fact rather than God's creative activity, a "shadow" is cast by the observation of a cycle, a transition from the light to the darkness and back to the light again.[98] Given the nature of transition and the figural representations of light and darkness, the presentation of a cycle creates tension and anticipation in the reader regarding the final outcome. Although God has begun to expose things as they really are, darkness still exists, and there appears to be a periodic swing in the balance of power between the two.[99]

Day 2

The second day of creation involves the introduction of an expanse. God's speech focuses attention on both the expanse and its purpose for existence as a separation between waters. Although the referent of "firmament" is frequently discussed, and that from various perspectives,[100] perhaps it is best to understand it by its presentation in the text itself rather than based upon perspectives of either cosmology or abstract impressions. When introduced, the firmament is described in terms of its function, namely, sepa-

---

97. A study of the scriptural usages of the term light demonstrates that it is presented as that which reveals, especially when used in an abstract sense (cf. Pss 90:8; 119:105; 139:11; Mark 4:22; Luke 8:17; 12:3; John 3:20–21; 11:9–10; 12:35–36; 1 Cor 4:5; Eph 5:13). It is associated with salvation (Pss 27:1; 44:3; Isa 49:6; Acts 13:47; 26:18); with life (Job 33:30; Pss 36:9; 56:13; John 1:4; 8:12; 2 Tim 1:10); with knowledge (Ps 119:130; Prov 6:23; Dan 2:22; 5:11, 14; Luke 2:32; 2 Cor 4:6); and with justice (Ps 37:6; Isa 51:4; 59:9; Hos 6:5; Mic 7:9; Zeph 3:5). Similarly, Sarna understands light in the Bible as a symbol of life (e.g., Pss 49:20; 56:14; Job 3:16; 33:30), joy (Job 30:26; Ps 97:11; Isa 60:20), justice (Hos 6:3; Mic 7:8; Zeph 3:5; Ps 87:6) and deliverance (Job 33:28; Isa 9:1; Pss 27:1; 97:11). Sarna, *Genesis*, 7, 353.

98. Bonhoeffer suggests that this cycling indicates theologically that beyond a literal day there are times of wakening and times of slumber in nature, in history, and in the nations. See Bonhoeffer, *Schöpfung und Fall*, 45.

99. It is important to note that this characterization of a cycle affects only light. This implies that it is not a matter of reality, but rather the clarity or obscurity of that reality.

100. For example, Cassuto understands the firmament to be what we call heaven (Cassuto, *Genesis: From Noah to Abraham*, 31). Waltke states that it seems to be the atmosphere of the sky, which is spoken of elsewhere as being hard as a mirror (Job 37:18) and like a canopy (Isa 40:22). He also sees it as the source of rain (Waltke and Fredricks, *Genesis*, 62; cf. Provan, "Creation and Holistic Ministry," 296; and Westermann, *Genesis 1–11*, 116.)

rating between the waters above and the waters beneath. Since, as discussed above, the figural representation of the waters is that which is hidden from man in obscurity, the introduction of a firmament has the effect of distinguishing between the obscurity above and that below. The implications of this phenomenon are particularly striking when additionally noting that it is only the waters below that are named. Thus, from man's perspective, the waters above remain in unnamed obscurity and out of reach, while the waters below, although obscure, are somewhat accessible and identifiable (i.e., named).[101]

Considering the second day theologically, obscurity is divided into two segments, namely, one which is defined and somewhat accessible to humankind and one which remains as obscure as ever. Therefore, it seems that the presentation creates a distinction between an obscurity which is somewhat accessible to humankind and that which remains completely beyond him. As is commonly noted, the second day does not include the statement "it was good," which is understandable in that it does not include any further development in the sense of revelation or production. Rather, it simply distinguishes, for future reference, that which is within the purview of humankind from that which remains hidden and completely inaccessible.[102]

Day 3

The third day of creation presents, for the first time, two creative acts, namely, the appearance of the earth and its productivity.

---

101. This idea is supported by Hamilton who observes the distinction between the collocation of the prepositions בין x ל x (v. 6) and בין x בין y (v. 7). He proposes that the first combination, which appears thirty times, versus 126 for the latter, is used consistently to draw a distinction which refers to unspecified classes. When the waters are general classes, the first is used, but once two specific sets are created, the other is used. That is, the waters above are presented as separate and distinct from the waters below, and should be understood accordingly. See Hamilton, *Genesis 1–17*, 122.

102. This feature becomes relevant in the Eden Narrative when mankind attempts to move beyond boundaries established by God.

Genesis 1–11

Appearance of the Earth

The appearance of the earth is presented in a manner which contrasts it to the waters in that it is called "the dry" (היבשה).[103] In fact, it seems that the waters are restricted for the express purpose of "the dry" appearing.[104] Therefore, the issue is not the appearance of the earth, *per se*, but the contrast between that which is dry and that which is wet. In view of the prior discussion of the pre-creative state, the significance of this contrast is the introduction of that which is suitable for life.[105] This conclusion is supported by the fact that the appearance of dry conditions is inseparably linked with the introduction of life.

Vegetation

The presentation of vegetation is probably not a threefold classification of דשא (sprouts), עשב (herbage), and עץ (trees), but rather twofold, with דשא and its verb referring to vegetation in general.[106] Thus, the command means "let the earth be covered with a fresh green mantle of verdure"[107] and introduces the basic idea of the earth being productive.[108] The idea of production

---

103. The term is used in the Bible primarily in the context of creation and the Exodus, with the latter being an allusion to the former (cf. Gen 1:9, 10; Exod 4:9; 14:16, 22, 29; 15:19; Josh 4:22; Neh 9:11; Ps 66:6; Isa 44:3; Jonah 1:9, 13; 2:11). Only in Exod 4:9 and Jonah 1:13; 2:11 is it not used in one of these contexts. However, in both of these cases it is used in direct contrast to water.

104. יקוו המים מתחת השמים אל מקום אחד ותראה היבשה is probably best taken as a volitive sequence presenting purpose. That is, the water gathering to one place is for the purpose of the dry land appearing. Although syntactically the clauses could be conjunctive instead of subordinate, the physical action seems to imply a subordinate relationship. This conclusion is further supported by the continual emphasis on purpose throughout the creation account.

105. Of course, this idea assumes that life is presented from the human standpoint. As Westermann states, acts of creation are not concerned with mere existence of the world, but rather the world as related to human existence (Westermann, *Genesis 1–11*, 121).

106. The correctness of this view is attested by the fact that in vv. 29–30 only two categories are mentioned. So also Cassuto, *Genesis: From Noah to Abraham*, 40; Hamilton, *Genesis 1–17*, 126; Sarna, *Genesis*, 9; and Westermann, *Genesis 1–11*, 79, 124.

107. Cassuto, *Genesis: From Noah to Abraham*, 40.

108. The term דשא seems to be generally associated with the ground in the context of fruitfulness and production (Gen 1:11[2x], 12; Deut 32:2; 2 Sam 23:4; 2 Kgs 19:26; Job 6:5; 38:27; Pss 23:2; 37:2; Prov 27:25; Isa 15:6; 37:27; 66:14; Jer 14:5; Joel 2:22). So also

is further reinforced by the repetition in both speech and narrative of the terms "fruit" (פרי) and "seed" (זרע), the product and means of production, respectively.

There is further emphasis placed on productivity with the repetition of "according to their kind."[109] However, the way in which it is presented indicates that productivity is not indiscriminate. The concept of separation continues here, but now not with just God separating, but also with creation bringing forth according to its kind, that is, maintaining that separation.

Synthesis

The two basic concepts introduced in Day 3 are an environment suitable for life and productivity, along with a continued emphasis on separation.[110] After God acts on the pre-creative state by creating light and separating between waters, he brings forth "the dry" by setting a boundary for the waters. In addition, he names the separation between the waters as well as the waters below and the dry land. From a theological perspective, the creation account first presents the revelation of things as they really are, namely, unproductive, uninhabitable, and hidden in obscurity. Next, order is initiated by relegating each sphere to its own particular place, followed by the introduction of life in the newly-formed, orderly environment.

---

ibid., 41; and Hamilton, *Genesis 1–17*, 126.

109. So also Hamilton, *Genesis 1–17*, 126.

110. There is no mention of the purpose of vegetation, thus indicating that the issue at this point is the general division among plants rather than their relationship to humankind, although the latter turns out to be their true significance (Westermann, *Genesis 1–11*, 125). Cf. Day 6.

Day 4

Day 4 presents the creation of celestial light bearers. Even though the presentation itself is long, God's speech indicates that the emphasis is on function.[111] This emphasis is demonstrated further in the following narrative as the concept of function is mentioned two additional times.

Although, in one form or another, the function of the light bearers continues to emphasize the idea of separation and order, the concept of rule is introduced for the first time.[112] In this regard it is significant that the lights were created for the express purpose of being the vehicles by which something that God had already created (Day 1) was maintained, namely, to divide between day and night and to provide light.[113] This connection seems to support Westermann's suggestion that the idea of rule here is an abstract concept indicating prominence or dominance,[114] although Habel's terminology is probably more suitable in that he sees the connotation as one of regulation.[115] Thus, although light and division between day and night already existed, God created entities for the purpose of representing and regulating that distinction.[116]

---

111. Discussions of Day 4 often involve the issue of polemics, with the "two great lights" understood as an expression alluding to pagan deities. For example, Hamilton proposes that the reason the unusual terminology is used for the sun and moon is the avoidance of utilizing the names of pagan deities (Hamilton, *Genesis 1–17*, 127), while Waltke proposes that, instead of ruling humankind, in the biblical account they serve him (Waltke and Fredricks, *Genesis*, 62–63). Westermann understands the obvious repetition in Day 4 as further polemicizing in that the author is attempting to portray "in every possible way his thesis that the sun and the moon are creatures and nothing more" (Westermann, *Genesis 1–11*, 127). However, as previously discussed, there is little solid basis for considering the creation account in terms of polemics against pagan mythology. Habel makes an interesting, and probably correct, suggestion that the reference to the sun and the moon as the greater and lesser lights, avoiding reference to their names, focuses attention on their *function* rather than being a polemic (Habel, "Geophany," 44).

112. It is not clear how to understand the phrase ויהיו לאתת ולמועדים ולימים ושנים. Westermann is probably correct in his approach. He asserts that "days and years" are to be understood as one unit since the preposition ל is not repeated. Unlike others, he does not see a specific reference to cultic and non-cultic dates, but rather to continuous, extended time and fixed determined dates, i.e., the calendar. Thus, the term "signs" takes on the broader all-inclusive meaning, and could be interpreted "Let them be for signs, and indeed for..." See Westermann, *Genesis 1–11*, 130.

113. The same term for "divide" (בדל) is used in both days.

114. Westermann, *Genesis 1–11*, 131–32.

115. Habel, "Geophany," 44.

116. So also Levenson, *Creation and the Persistence of Evil*, 123.

Considering the account of this day theologically, the concept of rule is introduced in conjunction with the concept of representation, in terms of regulation, of that which already existed. Thus, the important precedent of delegation is introduced, foreshadowing what will occur in Day 6.

Day 5

The focus of the fifth day of creation is revealed by God's speech and its narrative follow-up. Whereas in each of the prior days God's speech dealt directly with the introduction of an entity (e.g., "let there be light," "let there be an expanse," "let the dry appear," "let the earth sprout sprouts"), this time his statement addresses the *activity* of a new entity rather than its creation (i.e., "let the waters swarm," "let fowls fly"). This activity-focused presentation is further emphasized by repetition in terminology, i.e., "let the waters *swarm* with *swarms*" (ישרצו המים שרץ), and "let *flying things fly*" (ועוף יעופף).[117] Then, even more emphasis on activity is presented in the following narrative with the expression "all creatures, the living and *the moving*" (כל נפש החיה הרמשת).

Not only is there an emphasis on activity in Day 5, but the structure of progression and intensification in the presentation closely associates that activity with the creation of a new life form.[118] However, as previously discussed, this new life is presented in the context of mobility and freedom of movement, thus representing a distinct development and progression of complexity in the creative process.

Although not presented as the central emphasis of this new entity, the blessing added to this day continues and develops the idea of productivity which was introduced in Day 4. However, whereas plant life contained only the potential for reproduction, evidenced in the possession of seed, living creatures are blessed with the ability to reproduce at will.[119] Thus, Day 5 develops the idea of creation in terms of life by introducing more developed creatures which possess the freedom both to move and to reproduce at will.

---

117. Cassuto asserts that the use of the *Polel* of עוף instead of the *Qal* indicates flying about in all directions rather than simply flying, which would further emphasize activity (Cassuto, *Genesis: From Noah to Abraham*, 48).

118. See pages 33–35.

119. Westermann asserts that ברך represents a continuous power rather than maintenance of a state (Westermann, *Genesis 1–11*, 161).

Another feature possibly presented in Day 5 is the relationship between the introduction of dominion and representation of Day 4 and the development of life. As mentioned above, Day 4 introduces the concepts of dominion and representation, probably foreshadowing Day 6. However, the fact that life is further developed immediately following their introduction may also foreshadow the conjoining of the creation of the highest form of life, humankind, with his function as God's representative in creation.

Day 6

Land Animals: A Foil

Day 6 begins with the creation of living creatures which populate the dry ground. Since living creatures had already been created, one would not expect another introduction of the same life-form, albeit in a different environment. Accordingly, the key indicator of emphasis, namely, God's speech, does not follow the pattern of Day 5 saying, "Let the earth crawl with crawling things," or anything similar, which would focus on the same characteristics presented in the previous day. He does not even say simply, "Let the earth bring forth living creatures." Rather, he says "Let the earth bring forth living creatures *according to their kind*" (תוצא הארץ נפש חיה למינה). This presentation introduces a different emphasis in that the qualification "according to their kind" presents a type of limitation. This limitation in reproduction did not occur in God's speech when sea creatures and birds were formed. Although it was, in fact, presented with the introduction of living creatures in Day 5, the fact that the restriction appears in the narrative section indicates that it is a secondary issue. However, its inclusion in Day 6 in God's speech, and that in connection with the same level of life, brings this limitation to the forefront.

This presentation of land creatures with a focus on limitation serves to anticipate literarily another land creature who will soon appear, one who is completely different. Given the creation account's consistent presentation of a continual escalation in the complexity and development of life, the obvious question arising in the mind of the attentive reader is why living creatures are introduced in one day, but then land animals, representing the same level of life form, are introduced in the next day of creation. The tension created by this question is further developed by a characterization which occurs only here, namely, creation without any statement of either purpose or function.[120] This creative presentation of the sixth day, including a second introduction of living creatures, albeit this time on land, with an emphasis on boundaries and apart from any statement of purpose or function, serves as a literary device which highlights the land creature who is about to be created, and upon whom God's attention is specially focused.

Humankind: The Climax

The entire creation account has been building to the point now reached, namely, the creation of humankind. As discussed above, in multiple ways the structure of the account has created a crescendo, building to the climax of man's creation. God's speech also draws special attention to this act of creation in that, for the first time, it includes a statement of purpose *prior* to the act. Additionally, the activity of Day 6, beginning with the presentation of land animals as a foil for humankind, further highlights this climactic event.[121] Even the grammar and content of the event itself demonstrate that this creative act is the climax of creation. At the grammatical level, there is a shift in the word of announcement from third to first person speech and from intransitive verbal forms or verbs of generation to an active-transitive verb.[122] Additionally, the content highlights the creation of humankind in that not only is a purpose given prior to their creation, but it is associated with God himself, representing a significant change in the characterization of his work throughout this account. A further highlighting by the content is seen in the inclusion of poetry in the midst of a narrative presentation (v. 27), which is a convention literarily attesting to its special importance by ensuring that the reader grasps the significance.[123]

---

120. Although it may be noted that in Day 3 plant life is not introduced with a purpose or function, this information appears in Day 6 (i.e., food). This delay is probably best understood as a literary device which creates a void and thus anticipation which is then resolved in connection with the creation of humankind. However, no purpose or function of land creatures is ever given.

121. The granting of עשב and עץ for food to humankind, while animals were only given עשב further develops a contrast between the two, and will be picked up later in the Eden narrative.

122. Bird, "'Male and Female He Created Them,'" 346.

123. So also Cassuto, *Genesis: From Noah to Abraham*, 57; and Waltke and Fredricks, *Genesis*, 67. Walsh's analysis of this poem, if correct, even further highlights its significance. He suggests that 1:27–28a is a chiastic quatrain, rather than three poetic lines as usually suggested.

    A   And God created humankind in his image

Image of God

The idea that the creation of humankind is the crowning point of the creation account is seldom, if ever, debated; however, there seems to be no limit to the books and articles written on the subject of humanity's creation in the image and likeness of God.[124] Unfortunately, one significant feature that is missed in most of these discussions is the fact that the creation of humankind in the image of God appears in conjunction with the simultaneous presentation of both Elohim and humankind with both singular and plural terminology.[125] Throughout the creation account, third person masculine

---

    B In the image of God he created it.
    B' Male and female he created them
    A' And God blessed them

In discussing the significance of this construction, he argues that it not only emphasizes the creation of humankind, but also presents various clues regarding its nature. "In Hebrew the 'A' subunits begin with the verb of the sentence, representing the normal Hebrew word order. The paronomasia of ויברא ('he created') with ויברך ('he blessed') suggests that the creation of humankind is not to be understood as a simple, neutral cosmogonic event, but as salvific. The 'B' subunits use unusual word order to emphasize the first phrases in each line—'in the image of God' and 'male and female' are coordinated. Neither gender is the image of God alone, but in their diversity and complementarity they are." See Walsh, *Style and Structure in Biblical Hebrew Narrative*, 106.

124. For a comprehensive discussion of a century of scholarly discussion regarding image, see Jónsson, *The Image of God*.

125. The referent of the "us" in Gen 1:26 has experienced a proliferation of interpretations accompanied by a lack of consensus. The usual suggestions made regarding the referent of the plural are as follows:

1. Fragment of a myth: This view holds that the text is a remnant of an earlier story from which the editor has not removed all pagan elements. In this case the reference is to multiple gods, including the one speaking.

2. Address to creation: Occasionally, one will encounter the suggestion that God is speaking to creation, specifically, the earth.

3. Address to the heavenly court: This view notes other biblical references to a heavenly court, and understands the plural as spoken by God, referring to the entire court, including himself.

4. Plural of majesty: This view suggests that the plural corresponds to the plural of majesty usually associated with nouns, e.g., *elohim*.

5. Self-deliberation or self-summons: Based upon examples such as Isa 6:8; 2 Sam 24:14, this view understands the plural to be a colloquialism of some sort, expressed in the plural but referring to the individual.

6. Duality within the Godhead: This view of the plural is that it represents some type of duality within the Godhead. For example Barth sees an I-Thou relationship within the Godhead, while Clines suggests that it references the Spirit of

singular verbs describe God's actions, clearly presenting him in the singular. But, when the divine plural appears, associating both singularity and plurality with Elohim, it occurs along with the presentation of humanity as both singular and plural ("Let *us* [Deity, plural] create *man* [humanity, singular] ... so that *they* [humanity, plural] ... " [v. 26], and "*God* [Deity, singular] created *man* [humanity, singular] in *his* [Deity, singular] own image, in the image of God [Deity, singular] created *he* [Deity, singular] *him* [humanity, singular], male and female [humanity, plural] created *he* [Deity, singular] *them* [humanity, plural]" [v. 27]). This simultaneous introduction of both Deity and humanity in both singular and plural terminology in the context which presents man as the image of God provides a strong indication that there is a connection between the two.

Not only are divine and human singular-plurals mentioned together, but the latter is characterized in terms of "male and female." When this feature is mentioned in *imago Dei* discussions, the expression "male and female" is frequently understood to represent community. Even though this idea is probably implicit in the presentation of the idea of "unity in plurality," that is likely not its only nuance. A review of the expression זכר ונקבה ("male and female"), occurring only in Gen 1:27; 5:2; 6:19; 7:3, 9, 16, reveals that the context is always one of reproduction. Therefore, it is probably best to understand humankind's introduction as "male and female" as community in the context of generation of life. It is of note that the divine plural is introduced with a similar nuance. That is, the transition from singular to plural with reference to God is also made in the context of the generation of life ("let us make man"). Thus, not only are both the divine and human

---

God who has already appeared in 1:2.

The position assumed in this study is that it refers to some type of plurality within the Godhead. (See also Barth, *The Doctrine of Creation*, 60; and Clines, "The Image of God in Man.") Although a full discussion of this matter is beyond the scope of this work, it seems that the strongest positions on the subject are plurality within the Godhead and an address to the heavenly court. A problem with the latter perspective is that there is no biblical precedent for an abrupt switch from a singular to a plural within a narrative where the identity of the plural referent is either not obvious or not explicitly stated (based on a review of 557 occurrences of 1cp imperfects). Therefore, the abrupt change within the narrative from a singular reference to a plural minimizes the possibility of the divine plural alluding to the divine council. That is, since there is no precedent for such an abrupt change apart from an indication of the referent, the absence of the introduction of a new referent in the context of Gen 1 is probably best understood as indicating that the same referent is in view—the one who was previously and subsequently referenced in the singular.

singular-plurals introduced together, they are both presented in connection with the same concept, namely, generation of life.[126] Additionally, in both cases, the life generated is associated with the one who generates that life. God creates humanity "in his image," while male and female humans reproduce human beings. Thus, the narrative presentation continues to focus on the progression of creation in terms of the development of life. That which is unproductive and unsuitable for life ends up, through God's creative activity, full of life and vitality, even with life which in some way reflects God himself.

It is appropriate at this juncture to caution the reader against inferring something from the foregoing discussion which is probably not intended by the narrative presentation. That is, the connection of the image of God with male and female human beings should not be taken as an indication that the narrative presents God as male and female in any way. Such an understanding would be to confuse tenor and vehicle, making the subject like the image instead of vice versa.

Dominion and Rule

Regardless of the exact nuance of humankind as the image of God, it is widely accepted that it is associated with the idea of representation.[127] This

---

126. So also Fretheim, *God and World in the Old Testament*, 49–50. Man in the image of God, corresponding to animals after their kind, also implies a relational connotation and one which involves generation of life. See *Dominion and Rule* below. Cf. van Wolde, *Stories of the Beginning*, 24.

127. Hart discusses this expression noting that "image" (צלם) occurs seventeen times, with ten referencing a physical image, two comparing man to a shadow, and five pertaining to man being in the image of God (Gen 1:26, 27; 5:3; 9:6). He asserts that the functional interpretation has become the majority view (i.e., the view that image is related to function rather than ontology, with function being representation). He sums up the image concept as follows: "Man is appointed king over creation, responsible to God the ultimate king, and as such expected to manage and develop and care for creation." See Hart, "Genesis 1:1–2:3," 324. Cf. Anderson, *Creation to New Creation*, 7, 15; Clines, "The Image of God in Man," 101; Dumbrell, *The End of the Beginning*, 175–76; idem, *The Faith of Israel*, 16; Fretheim, *The Pentateuch*, 75; Habel, "Geophany," 46; von Rad, *Genesis*, 57, 61; Waltke and Fredricks, *Genesis*, 65–66; and Westermann, *Genesis 1–11*, 146. On the matter of the term "likeness" (דמות), Bird expresses what seems to be a growing sentiment, namely, that the construction in v. 26 must be understood as one complex idea including creation in God's image-likeness for the purpose of dominion. That is, nature and design is directly related to function and position, and it is difficult to distinguish between the various facets. See Bird, "'Male and Female He Created Them,'" 338–39. Cf.

The Work of God

idea is supported by the syntax of the Hebrew construction which indicates God's intention to create man in his image and likeness for the purpose of ruling.[128] This idea is further supported by the change in terminology used with reference to living creatures. Whereas the other land creatures were made according to their kind, man was made in the image of God (Gen 1:21, 24, 25). Literarily, this characterization sets him apart as uniquely suited to fulfill his special purpose.[129]

Although רדה does not engender much debate, the term כבש ("subdue") is a different matter, carrying significant theological implications for how one understands the creation account. It is frequently noted that the Hebrew term כבש ("subdue") suggests coercive power and a display of force. Unfortunately, the tendency of the few scholars who even discuss the matter is to evade this connotation without providing any real justification for that slight.[130] However, the implications of this term are far greater than indicated by this lack of discussion. The utilization of כבש implies that the earth needs to be subdued, thus logically creating the impression that something within creation requires such action.[131] But this notion goes against

---

Hart, "Genesis 1:1—2:3," 321.

128. As is commonly noted, the imperfect with a conjunctive *waw* following a cohortative usually indicates purpose/result (e.g., Waltke and O'Connor, *IBHS*, 529, §32.2.2).

129. Although there is wide agreement on the overall meaning of "ruling" (רדה), various nuances are suggested. Hart connects the term with "managing" (cf. 1 Kgs 5:4), while Hamilton sees it as reflecting royal language relating to compassionate, rather than exploitative, rule (e.g., rule as the servant). In a similar vein, Provan understands ruling as the presentation of government, especially royal government (cf. 1 Kgs 4:24; Ps 19:14; Isa 14:2). The subsequent narrative may give clues regarding the nuance of this term in that God brings animals to Adam for naming and to Noah for protection. See Hart, "Genesis 1:1—2:3," 322–23; Hamilton, *Genesis 1–17*, 138; and Provan, "Creation and Holistic Ministry," 297.

130. For example, although noting that the term generally suggests violence or a display of force, Hamilton does not want to take it in this manner, but offers no real support (Hamilton, *Genesis 1–17*, 139–40). Sarna states that the verbs used express coercive power, but argues against the allocation of exploitive rights (Sarna, *Genesis*, 12). Habel, on the other hand, noting the connotation of the term as harsh control and forceful subjugation, relegates the matter to a literary device which presents an internal conflict or tension (Habel, "Geophany," 46–47). A proposal which seems to mesh well with the scope of this paper is that subduing the earth deals with humanity extending the boundaries of Eden throughout the earth. See Beale, "Eden, the Temple, and the Church's Mission in the New Creation," 10; Dumbrell, "Genesis 2:1–17," 57–59; and Walton, *Genesis*, 186.

131. Thus Provan, who, understanding this as language of military conquest (cf. Num 32:22, 29; Josh 18:1), and the association of "dominion" with royal government, proposes that creation (as represented by ארץ) is not some benevolent entity anxious to embrace,

Genesis 1–11

the nearly universal presupposition that God's creation was perfect in the sense of being unimprovable or finished; however, the characterization of creation is not as something which is unimprovable and finished, but rather as still requiring further action or development.[132] Thus, as Fretheim asserts, "subdue" refers to a continuation of creation in the sense of bringing order out of disorder (see 2:5, 15; 3:23).[133]

In view of the foregoing discussion, and given God's pronouncement of creation as "very good," it must be *the situation* which is being referenced rather than the product itself.[134] That is, that which is very good is the creation of the physical world, plants, animals, etc., coupled with the placement of everything under the dominion of man for the purpose of man doing his (man's) work.[135]

Summary

As evidenced in the structure of the entire account, Day 6 presents the climax of God's creation. Within the day itself, the content and structure point to humankind as the crowning act. Humankind is introduced as the highest form of life and one which represents God. Thus, the culmination of creation results in the transformation of that which was uninhabitable

---

but rather something which must be conquered as a king conquers and subdues (Provan, "Creation and Holistic Ministry," 297–98).

132. Similarly, Barth asserts that creation was not completed simply because it was concluded (Barth, *The Doctrine of Creation*, 176). Dumbrell sees this in terms of God's rest indicating his final intention for the New Creation to emerge from this beginning (Dumbrell, *The Faith of Israel*, 19). See also Fretheim, *The Pentateuch*, 73.

133 Fretheim, *God and the World*, 44. Cf. Brodie who asserts that "subduing" involves development. See Brodie, *Genesis as Dialogue*, 136.

134. Along these lines, Fretheim implies that "good" does not mean perfect or static or in no need of development, but rather "appropriate for God's intended purposes" (Fretheim, *The Pentateuch*, 74). So also Dumbrell, *The Faith of Israel*, 117.

135. In a discussion of Day 7, Hart asserts that the use of the word מלאכה for what God did on the sixth day is surprising since it is the usual word for human work, especially since one of the emphases is on the uniqueness of creation as God's work. He proposes that the reason for the use of this word is to emphasize the correspondence between God's work and man's and suggests that the content of the creation narrative clears the ground for man's work because a good God has made a good world. Similarly, Ansell understands filling and subduing as a call for man to finish God's creative work by bringing the whole world to its divine fulfillment. See Ansell, "The Call of Wisdom/the Voice of the Serpent," 39; and Hart, "Genesis 1:1–2:3," 316.

The Work of God

and unsuitable for life into a vibrant creation, full of life, and in which God himself now lives and continues his work, albeit through his representative.

Day 7

As was discussed under the subject of structure, the seventh day presents the goal of the entire creation account. With the climax being reached in the creation of humankind in Day 6, the goal of creation has now been achieved, and God's work can cease.[136] However, this characterization is not only seen in the seven-day structure, but also in an analysis of discourse features which emphasize accent indicators. In his study of the importance of Hebrew accenting for discourse analysis, Lode concludes that although humanity's appearance is the apex of creation, it is only a "local peak" with the focus of the entire discourse being the rest, blessing, and sanctification of the seventh day.[137] Thus, even the seventh day is formulated in a manner that manifests both the climax of the entire account (the creation of humankind) and its goal (rest for God).

Also of note is that humankind, although receiving dominion as the "crown" of creation, is not given any special place in Day 7. This feature ensures that the focus of the account remains on God. Not only is God the only actor throughout, the account concludes with the focus on him.[138] Thus, the creation account must be understood as God's activity, reflecting his purposes, albeit including humanity in the achievement of his goals.

Summary

Literary Presentation

As evidenced in the overall structure of the section, the creation account presents a crescendoing progression of God's creative work. The

---

136. E.g., Cassuto, *Genesis: From Noah to Abraham*, 63; Dumbrell, "Genesis 2:1–17," 54; Sarna, *Genesis*, 15; and Westermann, *Genesis 1–11*, 89.

137. He states: "The formal marker is the advanced position of the temporal phrase 'on the seventh day' before the object and before a nuclear adverbial phrase in 3:2, and the repetition of the seventh day as object in the two following main clauses, and as fronted adverbial phrase in the subordinate KI-clause. As far as I have seen, such advanced temporal phrases in Genesis and Exodus occur only on discourse or paragraph climaxes." See Lode, "The Two Creation Stories in Genesis Chapters 1 to 3," 31.

138. Wallace, "Rest for the Earth," 53.

presentation of the entire work in terms of life and vitality is set up by the characterization of the pre-creative state and then developed by the crescendoing progression of creation itself. The initial activity with reference to the pre-creative state was to reveal things by shedding light. Then, after things were revealed, order and boundaries were established, creating an environment suitable for life. Next, life and productivity were introduced by creating increasingly higher life forms, associated with increasing freedom to move and reproduce at will. Finally, the crown of creation was presented with the fashioning of humankind in God's image and for the purpose of representing him in that creation. With this final act, a perfect and complete situation is achieved, and God ceases his creative activity.

The significance of humankind is seen in the fact that God has not just performed creative work, but has chosen to include humanity as his representative in that work. Meanwhile, the successive presentation of light, separation, introduction of life, dominion, and representation, followed by further development of life, may well foreshadow the intended effect of humanity's rule, namely, the spread of life and vitality. This suggestion is supported by the presentation of the image of God in a manner which associates it with generation of life.

Interestingly, the characterization of creation is not entirely positive. Potential problems are foreshadowed by the introduction of cycles between light and darkness rather than continuous light, as well as the idea that the earth needs to be subdued. However, in contrast to the cloud over creation which results from these matters, the pronouncement "very good" in Day 6 and the cessation of cycles in Day 7 seem to portray everything in a very positive light. Thus, the creation account is presented with a tension. Day 6 ends with unresolved issues, Day 7 implies their resolution, and the nature of the transition between these two characterizations is left unaddressed.[139]

The idea of a tension is also evident when one considers the rhetorical impact of the presentation on the implied readers. As those reading it for the first time and without having yet been exposed to subsequent chapters, the dramatic disconnect between the utopic portrayal of creation and their own present existence as humans in a fallen world must have been "attention-getting" to say the least. The tension would be heightened even more in view of the fact that the account portrays the utopia of creation as being

---

139. Actually, it is the resolution of this tension which the body of Scripture seems to address.

under the dominion of humanity—those who, according to the experience of the audience, now suffer and struggle to eke out survival.

The existence of this tension has recently been observed by several scholars. McBride states, "The crucial question of how iconic humankind will manifest, extend, or imitate the sovereignty of God within the cosmic temple is left open. What remains intentionally ill-defined or unresolved here will unfold as the plot of the Pentateuch's genealogical narrative."[140] Goldingay also notes a tension resulting from the command to subdue earth. He states:

> It gave its key players a demanding task of mastering a world that had a mind of its own. It left them naked and not ashamed, yet commissioned to look after an orchard with that negatively sacramental tree bearing deadly fruit. Now they find themselves under pressure from within nature and from heaven itself, and the consequences are devastating for the entire future of humanity. The story from Eden to Babel comprises a narrative analysis of what went wrong with humanity in its relationship with God, in people's relationships with their spouses, their siblings, their parents and their children, and in the lives of communities, nations and cities, generating the characteristics we still experience.[141]

Although it is beyond the scope of this present work to validate, this tension seems to be developed in subsequent biblical texts, continuing throughout the Bible until resolved in the final pages of the Book of Revelation.[142]

Theological Implications

There are a wide variety of proposals regarding the theological significance of the creation account. For example, Cassuto suggests that the purpose of the creation presentation is to teach that "the whole world and all that it contains were created by the word of the One God, according to His will, which operates without restraint," thus reflecting an approach similar to that of Waltke, who sees it as presenting God as creator.[143] Anderson takes

---

140. McBride., "Divine Protocol: Genesis 1:1–2:3 as Prologue to the Pentateuch," 17.

141. Goldingay, *Israel's Gospel*, 131.

142. If this proposition is valid, then an eschatological character may be seen within Genesis and particularly within the Primeval History.

143. Cassuto, *Genesis: From Noah to Abraham*, 7; and Waltke and Fredricks, *Genesis*, 78.

a human focus arguing that "the intention is not to define the essence of humanity or the essence of God, but rather to indicate the task of human beings and their relationship to God."[144] Habel, on the other hand, while agreeing with Anderson's view that the issue is not about God, asserts that the main subject is the earth, rather than man.[145] Tsumura adopts a different approach arguing that the concern of the narrative is life, while Westermann, taking a more critical than theological track, understands the creation account as part of the entire Primeval History which addresses the origin of the present state of the world.[146] Smelik argues that the account is not about the creation of the universe or the origin of species, but rather the creation of the Sabbath.[147] Regardless of the varying views, the one consensus seems to be that, as Waltke asserts, the narrative has been clearly crafted around theological concerns.[148]

Based on the consideration of the creation account in *this* study, those theological concerns seem to focus on several issues which, in turn, have obvious implications. The beauty, greatness, and perfection of God's creation are presented in terms of the fullness and vitality of life. Although it is seen as entirely his work and based on his valuations, he chooses to include humanity, his representative, who, in some manner, reflects God's own life, in the completion of his divinely ordained role.[149] However, the entire account is left with a tension which seems directly to involve humanity and the faithful completion of his responsibilities.

---

144. Anderson, *Creation to New Creation*, 33.

145. Habel, "Geophany," 34–48.

146. Tsumura, *Earth and Waters in Genesis 1 and 2*, 42–43; and Westermann, *Genesis 1–11*, 4.

147. Smelik, "The Creation of the Sabbath (Gen. 1:1–2:3)," 9–12.

148. Waltke and Fredricks, *Genesis*, 78.

149. Similarly, Mann sees the primary theme as God's perfectly ordered creation, and the secondary theme as man's responsibility, turning into irresponsibility and the disorder of creation (Mann, *The Book of the Torah*, 14).

4

Creation in the Hands of Humanity
The Theology of Gen 2:4—4:26

Introduction

THE CREATION ACCOUNT PRESENTS God's transformation of that which was unsuitable for life into a vibrant and living creation. Throughout the narrative there is a presentation of a progressive escalation of life, eventually placed into the hands of a living creature who is in the image of God; however, the account also introduces tension through both the explicit characterization of the earth as that which must be subdued and its portrayal as something very distinct from the personal experience of the audience. Thus, the account in Gen 1 introduces God's creation of all things with the emphasis on life, placed under humanity, while simultaneously foreshadowing ill in a subtle manner. It is this foreshadowing which is addressed in the Eden narrative and the story of Cain.

It is very difficult to enter into a discussion of Gen 2–4 in a manner which circumvents the readers' preconceived notions about the text.[1] Rightfully so, these chapters have been the focus of endless discussion and debate and have been approached from every conceivable angle. The result has been that virtually everyone interested in biblical matters, whether believer or skeptic, has considered the story at length, formulating at least some preferred perspective. However, regardless of the numerous ways

---

1. Trible states, "This engagement is both intimate and explosive, since everybody knows the story and everybody has fixed ideas about it. Familiarity breeds stereotypes, mistakes and, yes, contempt." See Trible, *God and the Rhetoric of Sexuality*, 72.

in which this narrative can be considered, the one topic which remains a critical issue in most discussions is the question of how to understand "the knowledge of good and evil."[2] The disobedience of the man and his wife involves eating from the tree of the knowledge of good and evil, which first produces immediate effects on them personally and is then followed by the Lord's judgment. The understanding of what is happening throughout this process, and hence the message of the story, is directly related to the meaning one ascribes to "the knowledge of good and evil."

---

2. The legitimacy of this focus is evidenced in the numerous analyses of the structure of these chapters. No matter how one fine-tunes the narrative structure, the sin and its consequences are generally understood as the focus of the Eden narrative. For example, Walsh proposes the following concentric pattern.

    a   man established in the garden (2:4b–17)
        b   all characters, regarding relationships (2:18–25)
            c   eating from the tree, three statements (3:1–5)
                d   Man and woman eating (3:6–8)
            c'   eating from the tree, three questions and answers (3:9–13)
        b'   all characters, regarding relationships (3:14–19)
    a'   man exiled from the garden (3:22–24)

See Walsh, "Genesis 2:4b–3:24," 161–77. Dorsey proposes a similar structure:

    a   creation of man: happy situation with earth, garden
        b   creation of woman: happy situation with man
            c   serpent: tempts woman
                d   sin and God's uncovering
            c'   punishment of serpent: spoiled relationship with woman
        b'   punishment of woman: spoiled relationship with man
    a'   punishment of man: spoiled relationship with earth, garden

See Dorsey, *The Literary Structure of the Old Testament*, 50. Another variation is presented by Ouro.

    a   placement of man in the garden of Eden (2:5–15)
        b   divine commandment and organization of human life (2:16–25)
            c   disobedience of humans in the Garden of Eden (3:1–7)
        b'   divine judgment and reorganization of human life (3:8–21)
    a'   expulsion of man from the garden of Eden (3:22–24)

See Ouro, "The Garden of Eden Account: The Chiastic Structure of Genesis 2–3," 224. As observed by these scholars and others, there is undoubtedly some type of concentric pattern in the presentation of the garden narrative and one which focuses on the Fall.

Knowledge of Good and Evil

This question of the meaning of "the knowledge of good and evil" has been approached from many different perspectives. A review of numerous discussions of this issue indicates that these various approaches can be categorized as either theological or exegetical.[3] The theological approaches, whether biblical or philosophical, tend to approach the question from outside the text, using an understanding of broader issues such as anthropology or theology; however, it is an approach which deals with the text's own presentation which is best suited to reveal the original authorial intent. Therefore, the following discussion will utilize an exegetical approach and make a suggestion regarding the intended meaning of "the knowledge of good and evil."

In view of the emphasis placed in recent years on literary composition, many exegetical approaches concentrate on literary techniques such as narrative, discourse, and semiotic analyses. Other discussions tend to consider terminology used in the narrative, deriving meaning intertextually from other biblical usages; however, seldom, if ever, is the terminological approach taken, and then validated from the perspective of the literary presentation. This type of an approach, which provides a "double check" to one's conclusions, will be utilized in the following discussion.

Terminology

Throughout the Bible, the expression "good and evil" seems frequently, if not always, to be set in a context which involves a clear differentiation between these two terms which generally function as representation of opposite polarities. Moreover, there is usually a clear distinction between these two polarities with an emphasis on discerning and maintaining that distinction.[4]

Although one might be tempted to ascertain the meaning of the knowledge of good and evil by considering those two terms alone, Westermann rightfully argues that the entire expression, "the knowledge of good and evil," should be considered, rather than the separate parts, since it is

---

3. For a review of various common perspectives, see Westermann, *Genesis 1–11*, 2–45.

4. Cf. Lev 27:10, 12, 14, 33; 2 Sam 14:17; 19:26; 1 Kgs 3:9; Pss 34:14; 36:4; 37:27; 52:3; Prov 14:22; 31:12; Isa 5:20; 7:15, 16; Amos 5:14, 15.

the meaning of the combination which is at issue.[5] A review of "good and evil" in conjunction with "knowing" reveals only eight occurrences in the Bible, with only four outside the garden narrative (Deut 1:39; 2 Sam 19:36; Isa 7:15–16). In Isaiah the issue is not good and evil, *per se*, but rather the ability to choose appropriately between the two. It is presented in a context in which being able to discern properly between the two is associated with maturity. A similar nuance occurs in the Samuel passage in which Barzillai cites his inability to discern between good and evil as an example of the potential for his becoming a burden to David. His self-presentation as a potential burden is in sharp contrast to his only other appearance in the biblical narrative in which he provides provisions to David and his companions. Thus, his self-portrayal characterizes him in a dependency role, unable to function as a responsible, independent individual. In Deuteronomy, the lack of knowledge of good and evil is associated with the vulnerability and dependence of children. Thus, the combinations of "good and evil" with "knowing" outside of the Eden narrative are always associated with the issue of maturity and, specifically, with whether one is dependent or independent.

This association of the knowledge of good and evil with maturity and the consideration of dependence versus independence is supported by extrabiblical evidence as well. The Rule of the Congregation (1QSa 1.16–11) states: "And this is the rule for all the armies of the congregation, for all native Israelites. From his youth they shall educate him . . . during ten years he will be counted amongst the boys. At the age of twenty years he will transfer to those enrolled to enter the lot amongst his family and join the holy community. He shall not approach a woman to know her through carnal intercourse until he is fully twenty years old, when he knows good and evil."[6]

From the foregoing review of the concept of knowing good and evil, it appears that it is an expression which refers to the matter of maturity and specifically addresses the issue of dependence versus independence. There is little to no association in these contexts with the identification of what is good and what is evil, but rather the matter of discernment between the two. Therefore, based on the consideration of terminology, discussions which focus on the *content* of the knowledge the couple acquired are probably

---

5. Westermann, *Genesis 1–11*, 241.
6. Martínez, *The Dead Sea Scrolls Translated*, 126.

Creation in the Hands of Humanity

misplaced.[7] Rather, the focus of the investigation of what the expression means in this narrative should probably be on the matter of dependence versus independence, evidenced in discernment between good and evil, rather than on *what* the couple came to know.[8]

Literary Issues

From the perspective of the story itself and as evidenced by other discussions of the problem, a satisfactory solution to the matter at hand must adequately address (1) God's statement, "Man has become like one of us, to know good and evil," and (2) the narrator's usage of, and the characters' reactions to, the matter of nakedness. Both of these issues are commonly discussed in regards to the meaning of "the knowledge of good and evil," but seldom, if ever, is there any attempt to argue for a particular meaning of the expression from a perspective that adequately deals with these concerns. However, the following discussion will attempt to achieve that standard by testing the foregoing conclusion, reached on the basis of terminology, against the issues related to the literary presentation of the story. It will be seen that not only does the literary perspective correspond to the terminological study, but it will also shed light on the thrust of the narrative as a whole.

"Like One of Us"

In view of God's statement in Gen 3:22, which seems to verify the serpent's assertion in 3:5, any conception of the meaning of "the knowledge of good and evil" must deal with the manner in which such knowledge made man like God and/or the gods. The relationship between verses 5 and 22 seems to require that the one's knowing good and evil are the same in both cases; however, the primary question is the identity of the referent, i.e., the ones

---

7. Common suggestions regarding content include morality, sexual knowledge, complete rather than partial knowledge, and divine knowledge. The idea that content is not the issue is possibly reaffirmed by the persistent inability of scholars, no matter how much the matter is studied and discussed, to arrive at a consensus. That failure is probably because a question is being asked of the text which it was not intended to answer.

8. The widespread consensus of biblical scholarship is that the terms "good and evil" refer to that which is beneficial and detrimental rather than to morality.

who know good and evil. Some important information on this question is revealed in consideration of the use of Elohim in the Eden narrative.

Throughout this account the narrator always uses the expression "Yahweh Elohim" when referring to Deity; however, in the dialogue between the serpent and the woman, the reported speech of the characters employs the term Elohim.[9] In the serpent's initial question posed to the woman (3:1), he alludes to God's speech, which the narrator presents as from "Yahweh Elohim" in 2:16–17. In view of this allusion to 2:16–17, the serpent's use of "Elohim" clearly refers to God. The woman, in her response, references the same speech of God and also refers to him as Elohim (3:3). In view of the content of the dialogue, the next usage of "Elohim," which occurs in the serpent's response which disparages God's intentions, must also be understood as a reference to God. The final and only other use of the term "Elohim" in this passage is made by the serpent with reference to humankind becoming like Elohim, knowing good and evil. Since every other usage of "Elohim" in this dialogue clearly refers to God, it may be argued that this final one is best understood in the same way. The fact that the usage of "Elohim" without Yahweh in the Eden narrative is unusual, being restricted to one conversation, renders it unlikely that the term would have multiple referents in this limited context.

However, possibly contradicting the foregoing conclusion is the fact that the last statement of the serpent uses ידע in both a singular and plural sense and both in connection with "Elohim." First, he states, "God knows" (ידע אלהים), and gives the content of that knowledge in terms of their being like God/gods, knowing good and evil (... כאלהים ידעי ...). This switch from a singular to a plural participle may argue for a change in referent despite the previous consistent referents of "Elohim."

Another possible problem with the conclusion that "knowing good and evil" refers to God is a syntactical observation made by Chisholm. He notes that in the collocation of an equative verb followed by the preposition

---

9. Although from a theological perspective one might understand the omission of "Yahweh" as a hint that the God-man relationship is in jeopardy, its occurrence solely within the conversation of characters argues against it. If the *narrator* utilized "Elohim" it might indicate an intended signal to the reader. However, its occurrence in the speech of characters and not followed up in the narrative comments argues for its significance lying in the perspective of those characters. It seems unlikely that the serpent would omit "Yahweh" because his temptation of the woman was jeopardizing the human-divine relationship. However, it may well indicate a purposeful avoidance of that relationship on the part of the serpent and a lack of conscious sensitivity on the part of the woman of the privileged relationship existing between humanity and God.

כ followed by a noun followed by an adjective or participle, the adjective and/or participle is usually attributive, modifying the noun, rather than substantival, modifying the subject of the verb.[10] This usual construction would argue for taking the plural participle ידעי as modifying אלהים. Chisholm concludes that the participle would therefore refer to a plural noun, and hence אלהים would refer to the heavenly council rather than God. Chisholm does note, however, that "the predicative understanding ('you will be, like God, knowers of good and evil') is possible (see Gen 27:23), but very rare."[11]

In spite of these potential difficulties, the conclusion that "knowing good and evil" refers to God still seems to be the best option. First, as Chisholm notes, the expression has syntactical precedence for understanding it as referring to the man and woman rather than "Elohim." Second, as noted in the discussion of Gen 1 (see pages 64–66 of this book), the divine plural in 1:26 is introduced along with plurality in humanity, simultaneously introducing divine plurality and singularity with human plurality and singularity in a context in which humanity is presented as the image of God. Although beyond the scope of this present study to validate, the position taken here is that the reference is to some type of plurality in the Godhead.[12] If this understanding of the divine plural in Gen 1 is valid, then Chisholm's syntactical observations that the participle probably refers to a plural noun could be taken to indicate another presentation of some type of plurality in God, rather than a reference to the heavenly council. It could also explain the shift in verb from singular to plural. Third, there is no clear reference thus far in the context of Genesis to the existence of angelic beings. From a narrative perspective it seems unlikely that heavenly beings and their capabilities would be assumed in the absence of any prior introduction. Thus, the arguments in favor of understanding "Elohim" as a reference to angelic beings are not conclusive and could even be interpreted as supporting a singular-plural reference to God. Therefore, it is the opinion of this writer that the knowledge of good and evil is best understood as a capacity attributed to God and not the angelic beings of the heavenly council. This position is further supported by the presentation of God in Gen 1 as the one with ultimate, independent discernment, which the foregoing lexical

10. Chisholm, *From Exegesis to Exposition*, 68.
11. Ibid.
12. So also Clines, "The Image of God in Man," 63–69.

discussion indicated is the intended nuance of the knowledge of good and evil.

If knowing good and evil is something which is initially attributed only to God, and then acquired by humankind, it must be understood in a manner which makes sense in both cases. At times this issue is ignored, such as with the suggestion that it refers to the full knowledge which God has, or, alternatively, to sexual knowledge. However, neither of these suggestions makes sense of the text since humankind is never presented as knowing as God does, nor is God presented in a way which would indicate that his knowledge relates to sexual matters.

A possibility which may make sense when applied to both God and humankind is that the knowledge of good and evil is the acquisition of awareness of morality in contrast to innocence. However, the problem with this approach is that it conflicts with the terminological study which indicates that the knowledge of good and evil is related to independence in discernment rather than content. Additionally, it does not correspond to the scholarly consensus which understands "good" and "evil" as referring to that which is beneficial or detrimental, rather than to morality.

Unlike other suggestions, the idea that knowing good and evil refers to independence in discerning between the two makes good sense when applied to both God and humanity. Not only is God uniquely capable of discernment, but this attribute appears to be a major theme throughout the creation account which, in turn, serves as the basis for the Eden narrative. Not only is God the one who creates, but in the creative process he continually divides, separates, and names. Further, he introduces different forms of life and declares that they will reproduce according to their kind, thus setting up a situation in which his differentiation is maintained. Additionally, as the creator, God is portrayed as completely independent in his discernment. All of these features portray God (Elohim) as the one with ultimate discernment, especially in references to the discernment of what is "good."[13] Thus, the conception of the knowledge of good and evil proposed above not only makes sense as applied to Deity, but it corresponds very well with the theme and presentation of the prior narrative.

The knowledge of good and evil as *independence* in discerning between the two also makes sense when applied to humanity. Not only is the concept understandable, but it corresponds especially well with the themes and emphases of the Eden narrative. First, the man is already a discerning

---

13. Good (טוב) is probably implied in contrast to evil (רעה).

being when introduced in the first part of Gen 2. The characterization of trees as pleasant to the sight and good for food (2:9) is certainly presented in relationship to man and, therefore, implies his ability to discern. Further, his naming of the animals entails discernment, as does his inability to find a suitable companion. Finally, his reaction to God's creation of the woman represents evaluation on his part. Therefore, man is already presented as being capable of discernment, and discernment even appears to be a special characterization of him. But since the text already portrays the man as a discerning being in multiple ways, what then changes when he acquires the knowledge of good and evil? The probable answer is that he takes to himself the right to independently make judgments concerning what is beneficial and detrimental. All the examples of his evaluating things prior to eating from the forbidden tree involve situations which were presented to him by God in a context in which God wanted his evaluation. Eating of the tree was something quite different in that he took the position of one who could independently distinguish for himself. This independence is what occurs when a child becomes an independent adult and is exactly what the study of the terminology of knowing good and evil was determined to mean.

The suggestion that the knowledge of good and evil represents independence in judging what is beneficial or detrimental also corresponds to terminology used in the narrative of the temptation. In his summary statement regarding the reason for the woman eating the fruit (3:6), the narrator refers to the tree as desirable for making one wise (שכל). The usage of this term in the summary statement, especially since it is from the narrator rather than a character, probably indicates that wisdom is an appropriate description of what was attained through eating of the tree of the knowledge of good and evil. Since an apt description of wisdom is the autonomous ability to discern what is beneficial and detrimental (see Prov 1:1–7), the usage of שכל seems to support the conclusion reached above. Of potential significance in this regard is the fact that this term is only used two other times in the Pentateuch, the literary and chronological context of the canonical presentation of this expression (see Deut 29:8; 32:29). In the latter of those occurrences שכל is used in connection with knowing what is beneficial and detrimental.

From the foregoing discussion, it is evident that the knowledge of good and evil as independence in discerning for oneself is consistent with the presentation of the narrative of both God and man as having that knowledge. Further, it not only corresponds with that particular feature, but fits extremely well with the themes, emphases, and terminology of the Eden narrative.

Nakedness

The characterization of nakedness in the Eden narrative is another significant issue in the question of the meaning of "the knowledge of good and evil." How is nakedness portrayed in the narrative? Is it good or bad? If it is bad, why were the man and the woman not only created naked, but their lack of shame regarding their nakedness characterized in a positive light? On the other hand, if nakedness is neutral or even good, why did the knowledge of good and evil have the immediate effect of shame on the part of the primeval couple? In order to address these questions, an adequate assessment of the knowledge of good and evil must explain both the manner in which nakedness is portrayed by the narrator and the response of the couple.

The tendency in answering this question is, once again, to consider various options regarding the content of the couple's newly acquired knowledge; however, since the expression is not used elsewhere in relation to content, there is no precedent for understanding the expression in this way.[14] On the other hand, the idea that it involves independence in discernment seems to adequately deal with these issues.

In order to understand the way nakedness is used in the Eden narrative one must be aware of the significance of the emphasis placed on unity in plurality in both this account and that of creation. Day 6 of creation focuses on the unity in plurality of humankind while presenting their creation in terms of God's image and likeness. The Eden narrative then takes up the creation of Day 6 and further develops it in a manner which places a strong emphasis on that unity in plurality of humanity. First, animals are introduced as a foil for the woman, highlighting man's lack of a companion in a manner which creates anticipation. Second, the response of the man himself comprises two separate statements, which focus directly on her suitability for him and their close connection. Finally, the narrator adds emphasis with a poetic statement concerning their oneness although they are two separate beings. The closing comment regarding nakedness and

---

14. Although shame is associated by some with sexuality, Wambacq argues that throughout the Hebrew Bible the two are not related. See Descamps, de Halleux, and Rigaux, eds., *Mélanges bibliques*, 547–56.

Creation in the Hands of Humanity

lack of shame finalizes this presentation of unity in plurality and serves to epitomize the oneness of the couple, while simultaneously foreshadowing future problems in this unity through the wordplay of "naked" (ערומים) with the "craftiness" (ערום) of the serpent. Thus, nakedness is portrayed in positive light and in a context which focuses on the unity of the man and woman.

This positive presentation of nakedness seems to convert into a negative characterization when it becomes a source of shame; however, it is not the portrayal of nakedness which is the issue, but rather the loss of the unity between the man and woman. Bonhoeffer seems to have assessed accurately the situation when he comments on the significance of the principle of unity in plurality in humankind. He proposes that sexuality expresses two complementary sides, namely, that of being an individual and that of being one with the other, and that it is nothing but the ultimate possible realization of belonging to each other.[15] In accordance with this idea of oneness though separate individuals, he asserts that shame arises only out of the knowledge of humankind's dividedness and even one's own dividedness.[16] That is, shame results from one's perception of individuality. Nakedness is not the problem; rather, the problem comes from the realization of self as distinct and separate from others.

Bonhoeffer is not alone in this perspective. In speaking of the nakedness of the primeval couple, Gowan remarks that "it speaks of a condition which does not exist in our world, of people without awareness of themselves as autonomous units over against other selves, but living in communion with another without the need for defenses—and clothes are our first line of defense."[17] He proceeds to describe the introduction of shame by stating, "In their fall they become self-conscious, aware of themselves in a new way, as autonomous beings over against other selves."[18]

Although only considering the aspect of shame in nakedness, Hauser and Fretheim take positions similar to that presented above. Hauser, citing Gen 42:9, 12; Isa 20; Ezek 16:22, 39; 23:22–35; and Hosea 2, sees nakedness as being laid bare before the world, made open and vulnerable, with one's innermost self-exposed.[19] Fretheim, referring to Jer 13:22–26, states that

15. Bonhoeffer, *Schöpfung und Fall*, 100.
16. Ibid., 101.
17. Gowan, *From Eden to Babel*, 50.
18. Ibid., 55.
19. Hauser, "Genesis 2–3: The Theme of Intimacy and Alienation," 388.

the shame of nakedness has nothing to do with sexual awareness, as is often asserted. The fact that it is not primarily a physical concern is demonstrated in 3:10 in which the man says that he hid because he was naked, although he had clothed himself already. Bodily shame is here a way of expressing what is felt by man. It suggests the idea of being unmasked, exposed.[20] Of course, this sense of exposure, as noted by Bonhoeffer, requires awareness of self as distinct from and differentiated from others. It is the transition from complete absorption in oneness to awareness and concern for self as an individual which precipitates shame. It is not the nakedness itself.

This perspective on nakedness in the Eden narrative meshes well with the suggestion that the knowledge of good and evil concerns independence in discernment. If nakedness is a portrayal of complete openness, the lack of shame in that nakedness results from a lack of awareness of self as an entity separate from others, thus epitomizing the narrative's emphasis on the unity of humankind. The acquisition of the knowledge of good and evil as the willful grasping of independence in discernment of that which is beneficial or detrimental ushers the couple into a state of awareness and concern for individuality, and hence shame when exposed.

Not only does this idea of the knowledge of good and evil adequately explain the portrayal of nakedness in the story, but it highlights the narrative concern with the loss of the unity of humanity. This emphasis is then further developed by the initial reaction of the couple after they ate, as well as the judgment of God. Both the man and woman divert blame away from themselves when confronted by God, with the man even blaming the one whom he previously saw as part of himself. Then, God's judgment focuses on the future conflict between the two people, with the woman seeking to dominate the man while he subjugates her. This entire presentation revolves around a particular act, namely, attaining the knowledge of good and evil, while presenting the consequence in terms of lack of unity.

Therefore, understanding the attainment of the knowledge of good and evil as taking to oneself the right to independently assess for oneself what is beneficial and detrimental explains the portrayal of nakedness and fits very well the thrust of the entire story.

---

20. Fretheim, *Creation, Fall, and Flood*, 85.

Summary

In summary, a study of the terminology and collocation of the expression "the knowledge of good and evil" implies that it does not address content, but rather the ability to independently assess what is personally beneficial or detrimental.[21] A review of some features in the story directly associated with this knowledge reveals that this understanding not only answers common interpretive problems, but also meshes well with the presentation of the story. Finally, a review of the manner in which the narrative as a whole is presented demonstrates that the background, the temptation, and the effects of attaining knowledge are all formulated in such a way that emphasizes this understanding of the expression.

---

21. This perspective of the knowledge of good and evil is along the lines of those made by a number of scholars. Hamilton suggests that the knowledge of good and evil involves moral autonomy in that it includes both morality and the individual personal autonomous assessment of that morality. See Hamilton, *Genesis 1–17*, 165. Dumbrell sees it as the exercise of moral autonomy which is reserved for God alone. Wisdom comes from God alone (e.g., Solomon in 1 Kgs 3:28) and by eating the fruit man was intruding into God's realm. See Dumbrell, *The End of the Beginning*, 179; idem, *The Faith of Israel*, 23; idem, *Covenant and Creation*, 38. White understands knowledge of good and evil as referencing no specific content, "but rather an inner subjective relation to knowledge itself which poses the human being as its ultimate judge." According to White, Adam's disobedience shifts his mode of existence from one whose meaning is derived from response to God to that which is derived from self, from knowledge of good and evil, i.e., being autonomous. See White, *Narration and Discourse in the Book of Genesis*, 119–22. Clark argues that "good and evil" does not refer to omniscience, or even knowledge, but rather "man takes upon himself the responsibility of trying apart from God to determine whether something is good for himself or not. It is not that man has no knowledge before and gains knowledge, or that to know good and evil means to experience evil in addition to good. Rather, man himself declares what is good. He does what is good in his own eyes rather than what is good in the eyes of God." See Clark, "A Legal Background to the Yahwist's Use of 'Good and Evil' in Genesis 2–3," 277. "Knowing good and evil," according to Fretheim, probably refers to discretion. The sin of humankind was taking that discretion to himself, that is, making his own decisions as to what is ultimately best. In this way he becomes like God himself and is autonomous. See Fretheim, *Creation, Fall, and Flood*, 77. Similarly, Wittenberg thinks it is the ability to determine what is good and beneficial or evil for oneself, with the emphasis being on the act of knowing. See Wittenberg, "Alienation and 'Emancipation' from the Earth: The Earth Story in Genesis 4," in *The Earth Story in Genesis*, 108. For other scholars who argue similarly, see Ansell, "The Call of Wisdom / The Voice of the Serpent," 40; Borgman, *Genesis: The Story We Haven't Heard*, 28–29; Gonzales, *Where Sin Abounds*, 36, 52; Trible, *God and the Rhetoric of Sexuality*, 115; van Wolde, *A Semiotic Analysis of Genesis 2–3*, 143; and idem, *Words Become Worlds*, 37–38.

Genesis 1–11

Structure

A variety of features of the text indicate that Gen 2:4–4:26 should be treated as a unit. Genesis 2:4 is widely recognized as a major transition, as indicated by the following: (1) the introduction of the *toledot* structure;[22] (2) the declaration of 2:1–3 that the creation presented in chapter 1 is complete; (3) the change in narrative style from a formal, poetic style, and seven day structure to a story-type presentation; (4) a change in the narrative stance from omniscience to observation;[23] (5) a change in the name of God from Elohim to Yahweh Elohim; (6) a shift in perspective from outside the earth looking in, to a specific locality on the earth;[24] and (7) the introduction of humans as active participants.[25] The end of chapter 4 is clearly presented as another major break by the change in form from narrative to genealogy and by the introduction of another *toledot* in 5:1. Thus, the boundaries of this section are clearly marked.

The general inner structure of these chapters is widely agreed upon as well, with Gen 2–3 seen as one section and chapter 4 as a second. In addition, structural parallels *between* these sections are frequently noted. For example, Hauser observes the following correspondences: (1) the principal characters are introduced in terms of their functions, (2) each episode presents two characters given life at the same time and in harmony with one another, (3) each episode includes a word of warning prior to the respective

---

22 Although there is much discussion concerning whether the *toledot* statement of 2:4a concludes the creation account or begins the Eden narrative, the fact that the *toledots* clearly serve as the beginning of sections throughout the remainder of Genesis argues convincingly that it must be taken the same way here. In addition, the observation of both Walsh and Kempf with reference to the tight organizational structure of 2:4 further argues that 2:4a should not be separated from 2:4b. They note the following chiastic structure within this verse:

    A   These are the generations of *the heavens*
        B   and *the earth*
            C   *when they were created*
            C'   *in the day when Yahweh God made*
        B'   *the earth*
    A'   and *the heavens*

See Kempf, "Introducing the Garden of Eden," 39; and Walsh, *Style and Structure in Biblical Hebrew Narrative*, 187.

23. Stordalen, *Echoes of Eden*, 216.

24. Cf. Hess, "Genesis and Ancient Near Eastern Stories of Creation and Flood: An Introduction," 28.

25. Cf. Dorsey, *Literary Structure of the Old Testament*, 49.

Creation in the Hands of Humanity

sins, (4) the characters are confronted by God, who exposes their sin by posing leading questions, (5) God pronounces sentence, (6) the characters are driven away from their original context, (7) the characters are separated from God, and (8) the characters dwell east of Eden.[26] Similarly, but more theologically focused, Smith notes the following parallels: (1) decision/command of the Lord, (2) temptation, (3) sin, (4) sin's result, (5) investigation, (6) excuses/denials, (7) accusations, (8) pronouncement of judgment, (9) recognition of the judgment as righteous by the sinner, (10) mitigation, and (11) notice of execution of judgment.[27] This presentation of parallelism indicates that the two episodes must be understood as two parts of the same section, and, therefore, related in overall scope. The nature of this relationship will become evident throughout the following discussion as these chapters will first be considered separately, then together, followed by a consideration of theological implications.

Humanity's Failure to Rule: The Theology of Gen 2–3

Since Gen 2–3 is presented as a story, the following discussion will survey the account by focusing on the narrative presentation. The story begins with a heading, indicating the initiation of a major section, followed by an extensive set-up of the climactic event, and then the event itself along with its resolution.

Heading (2:4a)

The *toledot* statement in 2:4a not only functions as a marker of a major division, but it also gives a clue to the significance of this entire section. Although there is little debate regarding the meaning of the other *toledots* in Genesis, this particular one is discussed a great deal, particularly because of its connection with the heavens and earth instead of with a person.

---

26. Hauser, "Linguistic and Thematic Links between Genesis 4:1–16 and Genesis 2–3," 297–305.

27. Smith, "Structure and Purpose in Genesis 1–11," 314. Still another theologically focused comparison is offered by Dumbrell: (1) people introduced in terms of their function; (2) harmony between two people disrupted by sin; (3) actors warned of consequences prior to their sin; (4) characters confronted by God after their sin; (5) God pronounces sentence; (6) characters driven away from their original context; (7) separation from God as a result of sin; and (8) both end up east of Eden (Dumbrell, *The Faith of Israel*, 24).

However, given its function as a section heading and its basic meaning applying to that which issues forth, its use here introduces an account of what happened to the heavens and the earth that were just introduced in the preceding passage.[28]

Of particular significance to this accounting of what happened with the heavens and earth is the fact that Gen 2 appears to develop specifically the presentation of Day 6 of creation.[29] First, everything presumed to already exist as the Eden account begins has already been explicitly introduced in the first five days of creation. Then, the account specifically takes up the creation of Day 6, focusing on the themes of that day, albeit from a different perspective. Just as Day 6 highlights the role of man in God's creation, the account of Gen 2 develops that concept, bringing it even further to the forefront of the reader's attention.[30] And, as is indicated by the heading, the story presents what happened with the earth and the heavens, albeit expressing it in the context of humanity's function as God's representative.[31]

---

28. On this matter, Willeson comments as follows: "In line with these usages it is reasonable to interpret Gen 2:4, 'These are the *toledot* of heaven and earth,' as meaning, not the coming of heaven and earth into existence, but the events that followed the establishment of heaven and earth. Thus the verse is correctly placed as introducing the detailed account of the creation and fall of man." See Harris, Archer, and Waltke, eds., *Theological Wordbook of the Old Testament*, §867g. Although Willeson is probably correct in his basic idea, a somewhat better translation is offered by Woudstra, namely, "this is what came forth from, this is what became of, the heaven and earth." See Woudstra, "The *Toledot* of the Book of Genesis and their Redemptive-Historical Significance," 187. This nuance is not only consistent with the utilization of the term elsewhere, but is also meaningful for understanding the following narrative. See also Blenkinsopp, *The Pentateuch*, 60; and Garrett, *Rethinking Genesis*, 95.

29. Although Gen 2 develops Day 6 of creation it must not be understood as referring *only* to Day 6. For example, the birds are created on Day 5 but are included in the presentation of chapter 2. The point is that the themes and concerns of Day 6 and their development are the focus of this account.

30. See chapter 2 for further treatment of the relationship between the two "creation accounts."

31. The reversal of the order of "heavens" and "earth" also functions to indicate that the subject introduced is man's impact on creation. That is, it is now presented with the prominence given to man's sphere of influence, namely, the earth.

Set-up

The set-up of the climactic event (2:4b–25) is very extensive and creatively highlights the key themes of the narrative. It includes an introduction of the creation of the man and his environment, an unexpected problem, and a resolution, all of which develop key issues and set up the Fall.

Introduction

The first section of the narrative (2:4b–7) presents the background of the story,[32] and, in accordance with a common literary technique, features several deficiencies which provide the context in which the narrative is played out.[33] The opening of a discourse can function as a setting, a preliminary incident, an introduction, or a combination of the foregoing.[34] Although it can also serve as indication of the direction and theme of the subsequent narrative, that is probably not the case here.[35] As Kempf notes, although the climax and resolution usually fulfill the lack, it does not mean that the plot is determined by the lack; rather, the lack is simply the context in which the plot is developed.[36] In view of the fact that the development of the story as a whole focuses on humanity's sin and its *multiple* consequences, rather than solely the matter of cultivation, the lack expressed in Gen 2–3 is probably best taken as the context, rather than the determiner, of the plot.[37]

---

32. The main line of the narrative begins with a *wayyiqtol* beginning verse seven ("The Lord God formed man") preceded by a temporal clause indicating the context of man's creation. Temporal references in an infinitive construction and/or prepositional phrase often begin a paragraph or episode. See Andersen, *The Sentence in Biblical Hebrew*, 86; Collins, *Genesis 1–4*, 102–3; Kempf, "Introducing the Garden of Eden," 40; and Westermann, *Genesis 1–11*, 198.
33. Cf. Ouro, "The Garden of Eden Account," 223.
34. Kempf, "Introducing the Garden of Eden," 44.
35. Contra Stordalen, "Man, Soil, Garden," 8–10.
36. Kempf, "Introducing the Garden of Eden," 48–49.
37. This position harmonizes with the common idea that Gen 2–3 is an etiology. For example, Herion argues that the curse has become an etiology for the hard work of raising crops while Fishbane proposes that the text presents the origination of evil, raising the question of who is responsible. See Herion, "Why God Rejected Cain's Offering: The Obvious Answer," 54; and Fishbane, *Biblical Text and Texture*, 22. Regardless of its exact nature, these chapters may well be etiological in that they present a condition of things prior to that which was known and experienced by the original audience.

Genesis 1–11

The initial presentation of a lack does more, however, than simply provide a context. It also provides clues regarding how the story will end, namely, with the resolution of the deficiencies. The narrative begins with no growth of shrubs and plants due to no man to cultivate the soil and a lack of water. However, water is immediately introduced along with the explanation that it watered the ground, thus resolving the one deficiency. Therefore, the reader is signaled to pay close attention to the matter of humanity and his role as a cultivator. As will be discussed below, the creation of this expectation serves to heighten tension and increase interest when the actual story begins to lead in a completely different direction.

Creation and Placement of the Man

The main storyline begins by presenting the formation of the man and continues steadily, recounting the events leading up to the significant event of the first speech.

Man's Creation

The story begins with the statement that God formed the man from the dust of the ground and then placed him in the garden. Both the order of the presentation and the lengthy discussion of the garden portray that placement as a special privilege and blessing.

First the order of presentation indicates that the man is the primary subject, followed immediately by his placement in the garden. If the garden were the primary subject then one would expect that its planting would have been presented prior to the formation of man. Further, if the *character* of the garden were the primary issue, then one would anticipate a full description of the garden as soon as it was introduced. However, the primary subject is indicated by the initial presentation of man followed immediately by his placement in the garden. Only then is the nature of that placement fully developed.

The man's placement in the garden is also portrayed as a blessing. In the context of a lack of vegetation, partially due to the absence of mankind, the man is formed. But, surprisingly, in view of this introduction in terms of a deficiency, the man does not provide the resolution by beginning to work the ground; rather, he is placed into a special environment which requires minimal work and does not even involve working with the ground.[38]

This unexpected development serves also to heighten the interest of the reader. By the introduction presented in terms of a deficiency, the reader would anticipate movement toward the resolution of that deficiency; however, the placement of the man in a completely different environment serves to pique interest.

The Utopia of the Garden

Woven into the narrative presentation of the creation of the man, the extensive description of the garden is clearly presented in terms of paradise.[39] Although this fact is always noted and fully discussed in treatments of this story, too often the *fact* of the utopic environment is emphasized to the detriment of the manner in which it is presented. That is, Eden as paradise is not as significant as why it was so paradisaical, since this latter issue is very important for understanding the implications of the story as a whole.

The first thing mentioned in the description of the garden is the presence of fruit trees. Their presentation as part of the mainline of the story signals that trees are to be understood as especially significant.[40] This perception is further attested by a contrast between the presentation of food in Day 6 of creation and the introduction to the Eden narrative. In the sixth day of creation, the narrator utilizes the focusing medium of speech to introduce both cultivated grains and trees as sources for humankind's food.[41] Then the Eden narrative begins with a reference only to cultivated grains, noting their lack due in part to the absence of humankind. But, instead of the expected presentation of man's creation and cultivation of these plants, he is placed into a garden of trees. This construction serves to set

---

38. Eden is presented as an orchard. Thus, the man's function in keeping the garden was horticultural rather than agricultural. So also Stordalen, "Man, Soil, Garden," 16; and Strus, "Gn 2,4b–3,24. Structure et décodage du message," 452.

39. The term "paradise" is used here and throughout in its generic sense as a place of ideal beauty, loveliness, and delight.

40. The introduction of trees is part of the *wayyiqtol* series, while the description of the rivers occurs in an extensive disjunctive background section (vv. 10–14).

41. Scholarly consensus is that שיח refers to wild plants and shrubs and עשב refers to cultivated grains. See, for example, Futato, "Because It Had Not Rained," 2–10; Hamilton, *Genesis 1–17*, 154; Mathews, *Genesis 1–11:26*, 194; Stordalen, "Man, Soil, Garden," 19; and Westermann, *Genesis 1–11*, 199.

up a contrast between the two sources of food introduced in the creation account. This contrast is enhanced by the implied association of grains with man's arduous labor (i.e., not existing because of no human beings and then existing because of hard work [see Gen 3:18–19]), while trees are presented as good for food apart from any reference to laborious work.[42]

Of further interest with regard to the trees is that Gen 2 explicitly describes them as desirable (נחמד) for seeing and good (טוב) for eating.[43] Since the assumed subject of the desiring and the judge of the tasting is the human being, the narrator is establishing the subjective modalities which will govern the relationship of humans with the most vital objects in their environment. That is, the objects are not presented simply as objects, but

---

42. To understand what is presented in Gen 2–3 regarding man's involvement in cultivation, and the differences in the pre- and post-Fall condition, it is helpful to consider a number of things. First, the term עבד, which is used in both verse 5 and verse 15, means "to work" or "to serve," and only due to the context is it often translated "to cultivate." That is not to say that this translation is incorrect, but rather to point out that the connotation which one places on the term "cultivate" can influence the understanding of these verses. The entire situation is enlightened by noting the object of the work described in these two verses. In verse 5 man is presented as serving the ground (האדמה), whereas in verse 15 he is presented as serving the garden (גן; cf. Hendel, *The Text of Genesis 1–11*, 44 for discussion of the 3fs suffix). Based upon verse 9, the garden is best understood as an orchard since it is specifically described as consisting of trees, with no mention of herbs, etc. This concept is reinforced by considering the disjunctive nature of verses 5 and 6. Those verses seem to present a background of the narrative introduced in verse 4 and then elaborated upon beginning in verse 7. (Note the explanatory כי followed by two reasons joined by the conjunctive ו.) In this disjunctive section, it appears that the narrator asserts that no plants were in, or growing out of, the ground because there was no rain and because there was no man to "work" the ground. Since there were no plants growing out of the ground, and since the garden was actually an orchard, the "work" of man presented in verse 15 involved taking care of the trees, rather than working the soil, and thus is not presented as arduous in any sense. (Note the infinitive construct indicating the purpose for man being placed in the garden. The purpose, namely, to take care of the garden, must coincide with the nature of that garden, i.e., orchardry.) It is not until Gen 3:23 that man is mentioned as working the soil, which, of course, is post–Fall. Part of the curse following the Fall was that man would eat, as the result of hard labor, from the ground (3:17–19) rather than from the trees which provided his food previously. Therefore, it appears that from the perspective of his labor, when man was originally placed in the garden his function was to take care of the trees which God had planted, but in the post–Fall state, having been cursed and cast out of Eden, he was destined to arduous work with the soil. This perspective is supported by the narrator's use of terminology, forming an inclusio with the expression (שיח השדה, 2:5; 3:18) used in reference to the lack which began the story and the resolution of that deficiency signaling the narrative's conclusion.

43. According to White, this characterization provides the interpretive framework for the following narrative (*Narration and Discourse*, 117).

rather in relation to humans and their potential response to them. In addition, that response is given in internal terms (i.e., attraction).

The trees also introduce concepts which will play a major role in the story, namely, life in contrast to death and the knowledge of good and evil.[44] Although, as previously discussed, Gen 1 includes the theme of life; there is no hint of death in that account.[45] However, the introduction of a tree of life in the Eden narrative in and of itself implies the possibility of death since, if eating provides continued existence, there must be the potential for death.[46] Although the introduction of the knowledge of good and evil is not as easily characterized, it seems to present the man's dependence upon God in matters of discernment. Thus the man is initially characterized by implication as having neither independent life nor the knowledge of good and evil.[47] These "deficiencies" are compensated for by the sovereign provision of God in the paradise of Eden, the former by the tree of life and the latter, presumably, by God.

The second major feature of the garden is the availability of water, and it also must be understood within the context of the story. The beginning of this narrative presented a lack in the earth in terms of irrigation; however, the garden is just the opposite.[48] Not only is there abundant water

---

44. Some scholars refer to the tree of the knowledge of good and evil as the tree of death. Cf. Bonhoeffer, *Schöpfung und Fall*, 84; Landy, *Paradoxes of Paradise*, 211; Tsevat, "שני העצים אשר בתוך הגן," 40; and van Wolde, *Words Become Worlds*, 35.

45. This phenomenon is probably directly related to the fact that the creation account is presented in terms of God's work and purposes. From the perspective of divine purpose, death is not an option.

46. So also van Wolde, *A Semiotic Analysis of Genesis 2–3*, 190. This view is further supported by understanding that the term חיים is probably functioning in this context as a genitive of product in that the tree produces or sustains life. Although the details are not entirely clear, the context of Gen 3:22 indicates that in some sense the tree of life would have provided sustenance for Adam and Eve so that they could, in spite of the Fall, continue to live. This perspective is affirmed by Fretheim who argues that the significance of the tree of life must be understood based on 3:22. It has two basic thrusts: (1) to be in its presence and eating of it represents communion with God; (2) to be separated from it represents the broken nature of that relationship and hence the impossibility of continued life. The tree of life is a means of continuing life. See Fretheim, *Creation, Fall, and Flood*, 73; idem, *The Pentateuch*, 75; and contra Barr, *The Garden of Eden and the Hope of Immortality*, 4, 13–14.

47. White, *Narration and Discourse*, 118.

48. Understood within the context of the story, as well as the order in which it is presented, the lack introduced in the first part of the narrative is probably best understood as setting up the paradisaical nature of the garden rather than foreshadowing the fate of man. Man does, in fact, end up in the place of hardship, but it is by virtue of losing the

coming into the garden to water it, but the abundance is so great that it flows out again, benefitting the rest of the world.[49] However, of even further significance is the change in the connotation of water. Whereas the creation narrative had presented the waters of the sea in terms of that which was unsuitable for life, flowing water now is characterized as the source of life.[50]

A final characteristic of the garden, albeit implied through figural representation rather than explicit characterization, is its connection with the divine presence. Wenham argues that the Eden narrative should be understood as an archetypal sanctuary. In support of his idea he refers to (1) the verb הלך in the *hithpael* (see 3:8, cf. Lev 26:12; Deut 23:15; 2 Sam 7:6–7); (2) the guarding by the *cherubim*; (3) the tree of life; (4) man's charge to serve and keep it (cf. Num 3:7–8; 8:26; 18:5–6); (5) the connection with a river (cf. Ps 46:5; Ezek 47); (6) gold, as in the tabernacle and temple; (7) the tree of knowledge of good and evil (cf. Ps 19:8–9, and the law being kept in the holy of holies, and the Decalogue in the ark [Exod 25:16; Deut 31:26]); and (8) the parallels often noted between the end of the creation account and the tabernacle building of Exodus 25–40.[51] This figural representation of Eden as sanctuary, hence indicative of the divine presence, is further

---

privilege of inhabiting the garden.

49. The rivers present the garden as the source of fertility to the outside world. One river flows from Eden to water the garden, and then becomes four rivers, bringing prosperity to other regions. This presentation is probably another instance of connoting the multiplication of life, especially since in the context water is presented as a source of growth. The first river, the least known in terms of either the river itself or the region which it watered, is elaborately described as a rich land. The next two rivers are known in terms of the renown of lands, significant and prosperous, to which they flowed. (Cush probably refers to the Mesopotamian region as evidenced by its use within the Primeval History. Cf. Gen 10:6–8. See also Speiser, *Genesis*, 20.) Nothing additional need be said about the final river other than its name since the prosperity of its region was well known. Thus, the blessing of fertility is the reason for this extensive digression, presenting Eden as the source of that which gives the world its abundant life. So also Westermann, *Genesis 1–11*, 215–17.

50. This dichotomy of the figural representation of water continues throughout Scripture. Water in terms of the seas retains a negative connotation, whereas flowing fresh water is continually characterized as the source of life.

51. As will be discussed in chapter 6, identification of the implied readership of Gen 1–11 is difficult. However, the correspondence with Exodus 25–40 would probably have been evident to all. So Wenham, "Sanctuary Symbolism in the Garden of Eden Story," 19–26. Cf. Alexander, *From Paradise to the Promised Land*, 21; Beale, "Eden, the Temple, and the Church's Mission in the New Creation," 8, 15; Dumbrell, "Genesis 2:1–17: A Foreshadowing of the New Creation," 59; and Hart, "Genesis 1:1–2:3 as a Prologue to the Book of Genesis," 333.

Creation in the Hands of Humanity

supported by Ezekiel's presentation of Eden as the mountain of God (Ezek 28:12–16).

Therefore, Eden is not simply a paradise, but is so in terms of the contrasts between (1) sustenance without labor versus food from laborious toil, and (2) water as the source of life versus that which is unsuitable for life. Additionally, the presence of the Lord may be figured in this presentation of paradise.

Contingency

Following the detailed description of the garden, the main line of the narrative resumes with the presentation of man's life in this wonderful paradise.[52] The placement of man in the garden is reiterated, accompanied by a statement of his function; however, an important contingency is now introduced, once again through the vehicle of speech, thus slowing the narrative and signaling something of importance. Having been placed in the garden and given the task of caring for it, the man is now faced with a commandment.[53] This commandment is worded in a way which alludes to both the man's blessed situation (freedom to eat) and the fact that it is not necessarily permanent (death from disobedience).[54] Thus, the narrative

---

52. Verses 15–16 should probably be taken together in that they follow the parenthetical digression and together develop the placement of v. 8 by stating the general situation of that placement (i.e., purpose/ function, and blessing/restriction).

53. Westermann asserts that the prohibition is simply a statement of the necessary accompaniment of freedom. It is a warning that, given the two different planes of man and God, the gift of freedom to man naturally includes limitations (Westermann, *Genesis 1–11*, 224–25). However, Stordalen argues that the term צוה indicates that God is not issuing a warning, but rather a command. He asserts that צוה על denotes a provisional instruction from a superior. Therefore, motivation for the decree seems linked to divine command rather than rationale. See Stordalen, *Echoes of Eden*, 226–27.

54. The first part of God's speech focuses on the privilege of eating freely of all the trees of the garden, thus presenting both freedom of action and freedom of choice. Freedom of action is inferred by the infinitive absolute followed by a finite form of the same verb. Regarding freedom of choice, Fishbane suggests that the blessing of man implies that he has a will, while the prohibition against eating of the tree is to be understood in light of chapter 1 which presents the clear hierarchy of God's rule over man. This combined characterization has the effect of creating a tension between divine and human will. See Fishbane, *Biblical Text and Texture*, 18. White argues similarly, seeing the central conflict of the narrative as one of desire, initially implied in this section but then fully developed in the temptation itself. Thus, the potential conflict is not with the serpent, but rather the potential inner conflict of desire versus obedience. See White, *Narration and*

reaffirms the man's blessed situation while simultaneously creating tension by characterizing it as contingent.

Unexpected Problem

The next section of the set-up presents the development of an unexpected problem. Now the narrator, in what appears to be a completely unrelated digression and, once again, by the important means of speech, introduces something quite unforeseen: "It is not good that man is alone."

Although much can be and is said about this section, its function in the story is a critical matter in that it intensifies the plot and highlights an important theme. First, it begins to focus attention on the significance of the unity of humanity which was introduced in Day 6 of creation. In spite of his life in paradise, the man's situation is not complete in the eyes of God; he needs a companion. In response to that need, God creates animals. However, the failure of animals to resolve the crisis creates tension and anticipation. This facet of the narrative serves to highlight the formation of the woman in a way otherwise not possible.[55] Just as in the presentation of a story the failure of an apparent resolution of a problem creates tension and heightens expectation, the same is the case in biblical narrative.[56]

This unexpected development of man's aloneness also introduces additional characters into the story in a potentially competitive relationship

---

Discourse, 119-22.

55. Animals are introduced in Gen 1 apart from any function or purpose—the only thing presented in this way. They are presented as earth creatures on the sixth day, and appear to function as a foil for humanity, serving to emphasize the latter's uniqueness. This presentation in Gen 2 seems to function similarly in that animals function as a foil for humanity, serving to emphasize the unity of male and female humans. This contrast between humankind and land animals is further signaled by several other features. First, in Day 6 of creation animals were introduced as נפש חיה (Gen 1:24). The fact that the man is presented in the same manner in the Eden narrative immediately implies a comparison. However, since it is obvious from both accounts that there are some major differences as well, not the least of which is that humanity has dominion over the animals, attention is drawn to a comparison/contrast. Second, in the sixth day of creation humankind was given עשב and עץ for food while animals were only given עשב, again creating comparison and contrast. This particular feature is later developed even further when the man and woman are expelled from the garden to eat עשב.

56. So also Hauser, who notes the elongated discussion of the search for a companion among the animals, echoed by "and he brought her to the man," and the further strengthening of the image by the addition of the term הפעם which he translates "finally." See Hauser, "Intimacy & Alienation," 386-87. Cf. also Collins, *Genesis 1-4*, 139.

Creation in the Hands of Humanity

with the man, thus setting up the subsequent temptation. The contrast of the woman with the animals, in the context of suitable companionship for the man, heightens the tension created when, later in the story, the woman is approached by the most crafty of those whom the man found unsuitable to be his companion.

Resolution

With the creation of the woman, the unexpected problem of the man's aloneness is resolved. However, this resolution is presented in a way which further highlights a major theme by repeatedly drawing attention to the marvelous character of the unity of man and woman. Rather than simply stating that the man now has an appropriate companion, the narrator reiterates the point in a number of ways. First, he utilizes the important vehicle of speech as the man eloquently presents his own analysis in two separate statements. Not only is the woman suitable, but she is "bone of my bone, flesh of my flesh."[57] Then, the man names her in such a way as to demonstrate the closeness of the relationship with himself (אשה from איש). Second, the narrator adds his own comment that, because of this unity, man will leave father and mother to be joined to his wife, and they will become one.[58] Thus the narrative presentation of the close relationship of the man and woman, by both a character and the narrator, formulates an obvious focus on the theme introduced in Day 6 of creation, namely, unity in plurality of humanity. This emphasis placed on the perfect suitability of the woman for the man and their complete oneness is important in that it sets up the seriousness of the effects of their sin.[59]

---

57. Biblical statements referring to being of the same bone and flesh seem to indicate close personal relationships, particularly in connection with associated responsibilities and loyalties, rather than simply sexual union (cf. Gen 29:14; 37:27; Judg 9:2–3; 2 Sam 5:1; 19:12–14; 1 Chron 11:1).

58. The "becoming one flesh" demonstrates further relationship with Gen 1 in that the unity of the plurality of humanity once again alludes to both community and the generation of life. So also Bonhoeffer, *Schöpfung und Fall*, 94; and Fretheim, *The Pentateuch*, 76.

59. Another possible effect of the formulation of the narrative is suggested by White who sees the use of an animal to present the temptation as indicating that the focus is not on the external action of an enemy, but on the conflict within (White, *Narration and Discourse*, 129).

Transition

The ending of the chapter introduces what Walsh labels the "strangely obtrusive theme" of nakedness, and, in so doing, provides a summarizing exemplification of the theme of unity in plurality.[60] Shame results from one's perception of individuality, the awareness of self as distinct and separate from others.[61] Therefore nakedness apart from shame epitomizes the concept of total unity with others and lack of concern for self.

The mention of nakedness also sets up a transition into the next phase of the story. The wordplay created by "nakedness" (ערומים) with "craftiness" (ערום) in Gen 3:1 joins the two sections while simultaneously signaling a potential problem.

Summary of the Set-up

The set-up section of the Eden narrative is extensive and complex, but clear nonetheless. It picks up the issues of Day 6 of the creation account and presents them in such a way as to emphasize and develop the same key themes, namely, (1) the vitality of earth, especially in relationship to humanity, and (2) the unity in plurality of humankind. As will be seen, the development of these themes sets the stage for the disastrous calamity and results of humanity's sin.

Climax and Resolution[62]

Transition

The way in which this next section of the story is introduced is disruptive in that there is an abrupt shift in scene and subject matter. It is further

---

60. Walsh, *Style and Structure in Biblical Hebrew Narrative*, 163.

61. See pages 81–85 of this book.

62. This section, comprising the next two scenes, is the most difficult of the entire story to approach from the perspective of literary analysis. So much attention has been placed on the details of this section that it is virtually impossible to "read it for the first time," getting a sense of the "big picture" and the overall plot apart from the bias of "preconditioning." In the following analysis, every attempt will be made to limit discussion to the main plot of the narrative, which will require avoiding a number of issues on which considerations of this story generally focus. Their avoidance here is not intended to diminish the importance of these issues. Rather, this approach is consciously taken with the view that important issues which surface in the details of a narrative are best

complicated by the focus on two subordinate characters (the serpent and the woman), rather than the two principal ones (Yahweh Elohim and the man). Unfortunately, because of our familiarity with the story, we do not sense this disruption, and hence its impact is generally lost.

Although the section begins with the introduction of a new character, the serpent, he is not introduced as a new entity, but rather as the most crafty member of a group which has already played a role in the story. Given this type of introduction, it is best to view the serpent from that perspective. That is, he is the most crafty of those among whom the man had not found any suited to be his helper. It is this *rejected* character who is presented as approaching the woman, the one who has just been praised as an excellent companion. When viewed in this respect, a significant tension is created. Two secondary characters, who have been presented in a potentially competitive situation in their relationship to the protagonist, now interact. And, to make matters worse, the instigator is presented as extremely crafty.[63]

Man's Failure to Rule

In spite of the presentation of the Fall in terms of an interaction between secondary characters, the emphasis is clearly on the man.[64] God does not initiate a conversation with either the woman or the serpent. His initial question is directed to the man, "And the Lord-God called to the man, 'Where are you?'" The apparent reason the woman and the serpent are

---

considered when the main plot and the overall theological framework of the story as a whole is understood.

63. Based on some studies of the perception of serpents in the ancient Near East, the fact that this particular animal approached the woman may well have added tension. Benjamin notes that serpent characters in ancient Near Eastern material are both helpers and adversaries. If this were a recognizable feature, then his appearance would raise the question of which trait he would exhibit. See Benjamin, "Stories of Adam and Eve," 50. From a different perspective, Joines compares the serpent's role in the account to its usual ancient Near Eastern symbolism. She concludes that it represents the embodiment of a strange combination of life, wisdom, and chaos. Its underlying purpose in the garden is to deceive and destroy humankind and, thus, basically symbolizes chaos in that respect. See Joines, "The Serpent in Gen 3," 1–11. Regardless of which view is correct, a serpent probably was freighted with connotation to the ancient reader, adding characterization.

64. So also Collins, *Genesis 1–4*, 152 fn. 9.

addressed is because of the man's obvious attempt to divert blame away from himself.[65]

Not only is the man the prime concern, but it is his action rather than his motivation which is the principal issue. The character of the man's action is couched in terms of the interaction between the serpent and the woman. The conduct of subordinate characters generally does not determine the outcome of the story for a protagonist, except in terms of either its impact on him or his reaction to the situation. In this case it is not the impact which is significant, since the interaction between the serpent and the woman is not presented in terms of some momentous event which has cataclysmic effects on the man. Rather, the events are recounted in a manner totally unrelated to the man other than the simple statement, "and he ate." This feature locates the significance in his reaction, namely, his choice to participate; however, in view of this conclusion, the absence of any indication of the basis for the man's reaction provides an additional clue to the story's emphasis. With the man being the main character, the conspicuous absence of any motivating factor places the focus on the fact of his sin and its effect, rather than the cause.

Even though the main concern is action and its effect rather than motivation, the narrative does imply the character of the man's sin by the manner in which the story is framed.[66] In the presentation of the Fall, he is seen as passive.[67] The setup of the story has been about the man—his unexpected paradisaical placement, his interaction with God, and the gift of a perfect companion. With that as the background, his strictly passive role in the climactic event is unexpected. This surprising development serves to highlight the nature of the event. In a story which is essentially about him, the man passively allows his fortune and that of the earth to be reversed through interaction between one over whom he had dominion and his suitable helper. This presentation of passivity is in direct contradiction to his prior characterization and highlights his failure to fulfill the role divinely assigned to him in creation.

---

65. The attempted diversion is evident not only in the content of the man's accusation, but also in his emphasis placed on the woman by means of the redundant pronoun: "The woman you gave me, *she* . . . ."

66. Here, as will be seen again in the story of Cain, features which are significant but not main line are presented by characterization and innuendo.

67. So also Eslinger, "A Contextual Identification of the bene ha'elohim and benoth ha'adam in Genesis 6:1–4," 67.

The man and his sin as the central focus of the story is further highlighted by the Lord's response to his attempt to divert blame towards his wife. At first it appears that his strategy works since the Lord turns and confronts the woman. The woman uses a similar strategy and diverts the blame to the serpent. Again, evasion seems to work as the Lord immediately, and without asking any question, condemns the serpent. At this point the reader must wonder if the couple has successfully averted disaster. However, the Lord proceeds to turn back to the woman, pass judgment on her, and then return back to the starting point, namely, confrontation of the protagonist. This effect would not have been created had the Lord not followed the diversion. If he had proceeded by dealing entirely with one character and moving to the next, no particular focus would have been created. However, in confronting only the man, being diverted away to other matters, dealing with those matters, and then coming back to the man to finish what he had started, the man and his conduct remain the focus of attention.

The sin of the man as the central issue, and specifically in terms of his passivity, is further highlighted by the manner in which God condemns him. First of all, the basis of his judgment is explicitly stated; however, the reason for the serpent's punishment was the vague, "because you have done this," while no basis at all is given when meting out judgment on the woman. These omissions highlight the explicit presentation of the basis for the man's judgment: not simply his eating, but rather his eating as the direct result of his obeying his wife.[68] Whereas the man's only responsibility thus far in the narrative was to obey God, he not only listened to his wife, but did so even though it required disobedience of God. However, his action is not here featured so much as disobedience of God as much as the failure to assume the responsibilities for which he was created.

Finally, the judgments issued also demonstrate that the story is about the man and his failure. Regardless of the theological implications which may be drawn from the text, the punishment of the serpent is presented in

68. Although the man's actions are the focus, his motivation is woven in as a secondary element. God's characterization of the man's actions as "listening to his wife" is informative when compared with the narrative presentation of his sin. Verse 6 states that she gave to her husband and he ate. That is, there is absolutely no mention of the interaction between the two, nor the motivation of the man for taking. However, God's statement that he listened to his wife implies communication, communication which was not presented before. This allusion to communication may well be a subtle connection of the man with the explicitly stated motivation of the woman. Since the focus of the story is his action and its effect, he is judged for that. However, that judgment is couched in such a way that he is associated with the motivations of his wife.

terms of future interaction between him and the woman and their respective offspring. The punishment of the woman is presented in terms of her increased pain and her interaction with the man. However, the judgment on the man affects creation itself, rather than simply interaction with other beings. The significance of this fact for the story is evidenced by the way the climactic event is set up. First, the entire section is entitled, "This is what happened to the earth and the heavens." Second, the story is introduced in terms of the relationship between man and the ground, specifically the lack of a cultivator, but leaves that issue hanging. However, the judgment of the Lord provides closure for the reader who, realizing from experience that burdensome labor is required to produce food and having seen the man introduced in terms of that function, was surprised to see him placed in paradise. Third, the story was set up with man having free access to the source of life, living in a garden in Eden. It is only in terms of the punishment of the man, not the serpent or the woman, that this paradisaical situation is affected. The story specifically states that it is because "the man" (not the couple) gained the knowledge of good and evil that the banishment occurred.[69] Even the banishment itself is presented in terms of "the man" rather than the couple.

Summary

Primary Theme

The analysis of the literary features of the garden story reveals that it develops matters introduced in Day 6 of the preceding creation account. Specifically, the primary issue concerns the failure of the man to properly fulfill his divinely appointed role in creation. This failure results in a negative impact on all of his sphere of influence and is presented specifically in terms of loss of unity with his wife (corresponding to unity in plurality and the image of God), his relationship with the earth (corresponding to subduing) and the loss of a peace with at least part of the animal world (corresponding to dominion).

---

69. Along these lines Boomershine asserts that a comparison between the judgment rendered upon the man and that upon the woman "conveys an implicit invitation to recognize that the man was the one who was finally responsible for the transgression." See Boomershine, "The Structure of Narrative Rhetoric in Genesis 2–3," 119.

Creation in the Hands of Humanity

Secondary Themes

The presentation of man's failure and its impact on creation is presented along with secondary matters, which relate to subjective issues of man's inner being as opposed to simply his actions.

Loss of God's Blessings

One secondary theme involves the ironic effect of humanity's self-serving seizure of autonomy. That is, the result of mankind taking upon himself the responsibility to decide his own welfare is a loss of his own well-being in terms of the blessings which he had received in creation. This loss is presented in terms of separation from God, estrangement from fellow human beings, pain in fulfilling divinely assigned roles, and even death itself.

Understandably, in most discussions of the effects of the Fall the subject of death seems to take precedence. Not only does it represent the ultimate expression of loss experienced by humanity in relation to existence on the earth, but the fact that the couple did not physically die on the very day in which they ate is a matter of particular concern. However, it may be helpful to view the subject from the perspective that death seems to be portrayed as the loss of God's blessings, rather than the cessation of physical life. That is, possibly death should be understood in terms of the loss of vitality, or, in medical terminology, as morbidity as opposed to mortality. This perspective is supported by the creation account in which the emphasis on life is not presented in the opposite polarities of "alive" versus "dead." Rather, it is characterized in progressively higher forms of life, with greater blessings and freedom, and even culminates in life which reflects that of God himself. Accordingly, consistency of characterization would argue that the sentence of death in the Eden narrative is best understood from the same perspective. This suggestion is supported by the fact that the loss of humanity's welfare in Gen 3 directly correlates to the presentation of humanity in the creation account. Whereas in the creation account humanity is introduced in terms of unity in plurality, this oneness is lost in the estrangement of the couple. In Gen 1 humanity is blessed with productivity, but, in Gen 3, their sin results in that productivity being accompanied by pain and labor in childbearing. At creation, humanity is blessed with food apart from any indication of the need for labor, but now they are not only removed from the garden—the source of food apart from labor—but they are condemned to eke out sustenance from an uncooperative ground. Finally, they are banned from the source of ongoing life, the tree of life, with the result that they eventually return to the dust from which they came. Thus, the warning by God that they would surely die in the day they ate the forbidden fruit can be understood as completely fulfilled if death is viewed from the perspective of a loss of original blessings bestowed by God, rather than simply the cessation of physical existence. Of course, the culmination of death as the loss of blessing is the forfeiture of physical life and is so featured in the genealogy of Gen 5.

This concept is argued by others as well, and in a way which corresponds well to the entire discussion of the Eden narrative in this book. For example, Trible understands death to be "living death" as opposed to "fulfilled life," with the inclusio of "in the sweat of your face you will eat bread" and "in pain you shall eat of it" presenting a living death. She sees this "existential death" as merging with mortality at the restriction from the tree of life.[70] According to Bonhoeffer, death is man having to live in a destroyed world until he returns to the dust; it is having to live before God without drawing life from God and living only out of its own resources, that is, by its own acquired knowledge of good and evil.[71] Although one may argue that this approach is importing concepts from outside the text, this is not the case. For example, Collins rightly argues from the perspective of presentation of the story that, since God is a "reliable" character and the serpent is not, what happens determines the meaning. He concludes that the man does, in fact, die immediately, but that death involves more than loss of physical life.[72] Rather, the loss experienced by humanity as a result of the Fall includes multiple blessings originally bestowed by his creator, with physical death being the ultimate expression and inevitable result of that loss.

Faith and Obedience

The Eden narrative also introduces the secondary themes of faith and obedience.[73] By comparing the wording of the serpent to that used by God,

70. Trible, *God and the Rhetoric of Sexuality*, 123, 132, 136.
71. Bonhoeffer, *Schöpfung und Fall*, 85–86, 124, 132.
72. Collins, "What Happened to Adam and Eve?" 12–44.
73. Their secondary nature is evident in the fact that they are presented in discussion of the secondary characters, namely, the serpent and the woman. However, they

Creation in the Hands of Humanity

one observes a two-pronged attack utilized by the serpent, namely, creating doubt as to God's loving faithfulness and undermining the certainty of God's judgment. These features, which are also evident in the speech of the woman, correspond to matters of faith and obedience.

The serpent begins his interaction with the woman by questioning what God had said; however, his intention becomes evident when one notes the manner in which he speaks to the woman. God, in his original interaction with the man to which the serpent refers, states מכל עץ הגן אכל תאכל ("from every tree of the garden you may freely eat"). This wording emphasizes a positive perspective in several ways. First, מכל is preposed, likely providing emphasis ("from *every* tree"). Second, the speech begins with the presentation of what is bountifully provided rather than what is restricted. The serpent, on the other hand, although using the same words, portrays God's speech in a negative light. First, he takes the positive provision of food and rephrases it as a prohibition, "you shall *not* eat from every tree of the garden" (לא תאכלו מכל עץ הגן). This change in wording has the effect of causing "all" (כל) to be associated with what is prohibited rather than what is provided. Additionally, by moving מכל from the preposed emphatic position where it appears in God's original statement to a more common placement he further detracts from God's bountiful blessing. The omission of the infinitive absolute (תאכלו vs. אכל תאכל) reinforces this characterization even more. Thus, the serpent's minor rephrasing of God's speech has the subtle effect of placing the emphasis upon denial rather than provision.

This characterization of God's speech is apparently intended to undermine the woman's perception of God as a creator who seeks the best interests of the man and the woman. This ultimate purpose, implied in the initial question, is clarified and further developed by the serpent's comments following the woman's response. First, the phrase "God knows" (ידע אלהים) immediately suggests that God is holding something back from them.[74] Then, the explicit statement regarding *what* God knows ("you will be as God/gods") asserts that God is holding something back for himself. This assertion by the serpent has the effect of raising doubts about humans being able to trust him while simultaneously implying that the serpent, as opposed to God, is really looking out for their best interests. Therefore, by creating alienation between humankind and God, the serpent leads the woman into distrust of God. It is this context in which the direct disobedi-

---

are nonetheless portrayed as important concerns in that they appear in reported speech.

74. Fretheim, *The Pentateuch*, 78.

ence occurs. Thus, although the act is disobedience, the narrative portrays it as originating from lack of faith.[75]

In addition to undermining the woman's faith in God, the serpent, both directly and indirectly, indicates that the judgment of God is not as inevitable as one might think. In an indirect subversion, the serpent refers to what God said as "speaking" (אמר), whereas what God did was command (צוה). Next, he directly contradicts God's statement of the consequences of eating לא מות תמתון ("You will not surely die" or "Surely you will not die"). Thus, not only does he initiate distrust of God, but he also denies that God will follow through in judgment.

The response of the woman to the serpent's comments further develops these same themes, thus indicating an intentional presentation of the story which emphasizes matters of faith and obedience. First, the woman's response exhibits a perspective of God which is inclined toward the serpent's characterization of him. In response to the initial question she exaggerates God's prohibition in a manner which can be inferred as indicating some degree of displeasure with God's restriction ("you shall not touch it").[76] That is, she makes God's command more restrictive, thus implicating God by responding in kind to the serpent's own characterization of the original command. In addition, the woman's response limits God's bountiful blessing by omitting the infinitive absolute (i.e., "you may eat" rather than "you may freely eat") and by omitting כל ("all"). Thus the woman's response to the serpent's initial question continues to focus on the restrictive aspect of God's speech rather than upon his bountiful provision for them.[77]

---

75. Cf. Emmrich, "The Temptation Narrative of Genesis 3:1–6," 13; Fretheim, *The Pentateuch*, 78; Hauser, "Intimacy & Alienation," 390.

76. Cf. Alter, *Genesis: Translation and Commentary*, 11; White, *Narration and Discourse*, 131. In an interesting aside, Emmlich suggests that the original audience would have understood the woman's added prohibition as relating to Moses' warning about adding to the commandments of the Lord (Deut 4:2). See Emmrich, "The Temptation Narrative," 14.

77. The woman gives the tree of the knowledge of good and evil a location which is not presented in the original presentation of chapter 2. She refers to it as the tree in the midst of the garden. First, by using the modifier "in the midst of the garden" rather than "knowledge of good and evil" she gives it a central location, thus very likely providing focus. Second, the original narrative does not refer to this tree as in the midst of the garden, at least not directly. Rather, it is the tree of life which is said to be in the midst (2:9). Although the syntax of the following clause allows for one to understand the tree of knowledge to be in the same location, the priority and focus remains on the tree of life. The woman's response refers only to one tree in the midst of the garden, and that is the prohibited tree. Thus, her focus continues to be on restriction rather than provision.

Creation in the Hands of Humanity

Just as the woman's response seems to indicate an inclination toward seeing God in the same negative light as that portrayed by the serpent, her answer also demonstrates a correspondence with the serpent's belittling the certainty of God's judgment. She follows the wording of the serpent by referring to God's prohibition as something said (אמר), rather than a command (צוה). Additionally, she seems to treat death as a consequence (פן) rather than judgment.[78]

These matters of faith and obedience are not simply presented in the context of a discussion between secondary characters; they are also associated with the primary character in that the man listened to (i.e., obeyed) his wife. Thus, humankind's self-serving grasp of autonomy is couched in terms of failing to trust that the God who gave them life and placed them in paradise can be trusted to look out for their best interests.[79]

Continued Tensions

The creation account is presented in a way that focuses on God's work in terms of life but simultaneously raises questions regarding the continuation of that vitality as creation is placed into the hands of humanity. The Eden narrative reveals the legitimacy of these concerns by explaining the impact of human failure on the vitality of creation; however, even though the feared effect is actually presented, it is done so in a manner which does not allow the tension to dissipate. In Gen 1 the positive characterization of life was left under a shadow, but here the negative presentation of death features a ray of light in hope for future life as the man names his wife.[80] Conspicuously separated from the "naming" scene prior to the Fall, the man's naming of his wife immediately following the pronouncement of

---

78. Although there is some debate over the matter, the original statement by God seems to characterize it as a judgment rather than a consequence, as evidenced by usage of צוה. First, the term צוה would argue that God is not issuing a warning, but rather a command. On this subject Stordalen notes that צוה על denotes a provisional instruction from a superior which should be faithfully observed (Stordalen, *Echoes of Eden*, 226–27). As further support for the idea that God's speech is not simply a warning against, for instance, a poisonous tree, Alter argues that the infinitive absolute followed by the conjugated form of the same verb adds emphasis, and, in the case of the verb "to die," is the pattern used in the Bible for the issuing of death sentences (Alter, *Genesis*, 8).

79. Cf. Fretheim, *The Pentateuch*, 78; Stordalen, *Echoes of Eden*, 237; and Walsh, "Genesis 2:4b–3:24," 173.

80. So also Fretheim, *Creation, Fall, and Flood*, 91; Gage, *The Gospel of Genesis*, 45; and Turner, *Genesis*, 33.

death directly associates it with that condemnation. Even though he had just been told that he would return to the dust from whence he came, he introduces hope by naming the woman "the mother of all living," focusing attention on life in terms of future generations.[81] This focus upon life in future generations, particularly in the face of evident death, reflects a hope which will be interwoven throughout the Primeval History.[82] Thus, as the creation account presents a tension by emphasizing vitality of life under a shadow, the Eden narrative continues this tension from the opposite perspective, namely, death accompanied by a hope for future life.

The Self-Destructive Effect of Humanity's Failure to Rule: The Theology of Gen 4

As discussed above, Gen 4 is the second part of the larger narrative of chapters 2–4, containing many parallels to the first section. Not only are the overall structures of each story similar, but the content is as well. Together with a transition which clearly connects the two stories, these features make it apparent that the story of Cain is to be understood in terms of its connection with the Eden narrative. That relationship seems to be one in which the latter narrative develops the secondary issues introduced in the former. Specifically, while the garden story focuses on the actions of creation's vice-regent and the effect of those actions, the story of Cain deals with the subjective issues of man's inner being which were introduced as a secondary theme.

---

81. So also Fretheim, *The Pentateuch*, 79; Galambush, "'*adām* from '*adāmâ*, '*iššâ* from '*îš*," 45; Mann, *The Book of the Torah: The Narrative Integrity of the Pentateuch*, 21; Sasson, "The 'Tower of Babel' as a Clue to the Redactional Structuring of the Primeval History," 215; and, similarly, Hess, *Studies in the Personal Names of Genesis 1–11*, 111; Ramsey, "Is Name-Giving an Act of Domination in Genesis 2:23 and Elsewhere?" 24–35; and Williams, "The Relationship of Genesis 3:20 to the Serpent," 372–73.

82. Although considering a separate topic, Robinson observes the sense of future life through posterity. Regarding the notion of Israel's sense of corporate responsibility, Robinson states the following: "The whole group, including its past, present, and future members, might function as a single individual through any one of those members conceived as representative of it. Because it was not confined to the living, but included the dead and the unborn, the group could be conceived as living forever." See Robinson, *Corporate Personality in Ancient Israel*, 25–26.

Preliminary Issues

As with the Eden narrative, familiarity with the story of Cain and Abel tends to prevent today's reader from focusing on important clues presented in the literary formulation. One distracting issue, which is almost always encountered, is the debate regarding Cain's sacrifice. Therefore, just as in the case of the knowledge of good and evil in the Eden narrative, it is advisable to deal with this issue prior to considering the story itself.

Cain's Offering

A logical question which invariably arises in the mind of the reader of this story is why God accepted Abel's sacrifice while rejecting Cain's. Although much ink has been spilled delving into this matter, two impressions surface when considering this question from the perspective of the literary presentation. First, the characterization of Cain's sacrifice is rather clear, and second, this issue is not the focus of the story.

The characterization of Cain's sacrifice is presented by the narrator in a negative light and in a way which evokes a comparison. First, the syntax of the Hebrew text invites a comparison by presenting both Abel's and Cain's offerings in a contrastive manner ("Cain brought [ויבא קין] ... but Abel brought [והבל הביא]" followed by "The Lord looked upon Abel and his offering" [וישע יהוה אל הבל ואל מנחתו] "but upon Cain and his offering he did not look" [ואל קין ואל מנחתו לא שעה]; note the pre-positioning of a *waw* plus a non-verb in a *wayyiqtol* narrative sequence). In addition to this invitation to compare, the mention of Cain's sacrifice as "fruit of the ground" characterizes it in negative terms. Throughout the previous sections fruit was primarily associated with trees (1:11, 29; 3:2, 3, 6), and the only time it was connected with the ground was in conjunction with the term ארץ ("earth"). Therefore, this novel association of fruit with האדמה ("the ground") evokes the previous negative characterization of the ground. Since the garden story was explicitly presented within the context of "the ground," and, specifically its connection with the sin of the man, this expression in this context must not be understood apart from its association with the curse.[83] Thus, the characterization of Cain's offering is negative.

The term מבכרות further supports the idea that this is a negative presentation. The fact that "firstfruits" from the ground are possible (Exod

---

83. See Herion, "Why God Rejected Cain's Offering," 52–55.

23:19; Lev 2:14) but not offered by Cain, while the presentation of Abel's offering is portrayed in these terms, seems to draw attention to a difference in the quality of the respective offerings. Additionally, God's rejection, reinforced by his subsequent conversation with Cain ("If you do what is right ..."), implies the existence of some type of shortcoming.

Even though it is rather evident that Cain's sacrifice is couched in a negative manner, the avoidance of any direct evaluation is telling. Not only is the sacrifice itself presented apart from any explicit critique by the narrator, but God's conversation with Cain continues to avoid any reference to an evaluation of the offering. This characterization through implication and allusion makes it clear that although something is wrong, the nature of the wrong is not the issue. It is simply part of the setting in which "the issue" takes place.[84]

Brotherly Conflict

The foregoing review of the literary presentation of the narrative reveals that, although it plays into the setup of the crisis, Cain's offering is not the primary focus of the account. Rather, the main issue is his response; however, it is not *simply* his response, but rather that response in relationship to his brother.

In addition to being signaled by the setup, this primary issue is further highlighted in that the development of the story concentrates on Cain's attitude. To a first-time reader, this is a surprising twist since the innuendo in the presentation of the preceding narrative is that the nature of the offering would be addressed. That is, as the brothers are introduced in potentially competing occupations, and the sacrifice of one is accepted by the Lord while the other is rejected, the reader would anticipate some development of that matter; however, interest is piqued when the nature of the respective sacrifices is completely ignored. Rather, the story develops with a concentration on Cain's attitude: he was enraged. This direction continues with God's first interaction with Cain, which again does not address the sacrifice but rather his attitude, and specifically his motivation ("Why are you angry ... ?). Then God counsels him in a way that continues this emphasis on what was transpiring in his heart and mind rather than his outward

---

84. Cf. Borgman, *Genesis*, 31; Hauser, "Linguistic and Thematic Links," 300; Mathews, *Genesis 1–11:26*, 272.

Creation in the Hands of Humanity

behavior, again featuring his motivation ("If you do well,[85] will not your countenance be lifted up?").[86]

This development of the story's conflict in terms of the inner being, particularly featuring motivation, presents a strong contrast to the prior narrative and thus draws attention to the relationship between the two stories. In the garden story, the focus was the failure of the man in his responsibility to exercise dominion on behalf of God. Secondary to this focus were matters of the portrayal of unity in plurality and personal motivation. The story of Cain picks up those secondary issues and develops them by featuring Cain's self-serving ambition in relationship to (lack of) oneness with his brother.[87]

The concern of the story of Cain with the unity of humanity is evidenced by the emphasis on the relationship between the two characters. As will be discussed below, Cain is introduced into the story with much fanfare. By comparison, however, Abel appears only as "his (Cain's) brother."[88] The

---

85. Although the Lord mentions Cain's action ("doing well") which may allude to the presentation of an acceptable sacrifice, the question itself addresses his response (i.e., his countenance) more than his action.

86. The construction of this speech is very elliptical, and the subject of considerable debate. However, the infinitive construct שאת ("lifting up") is best understood in direct connection with ויפלו פניו ("his face fell") and continuing the focus on Cain's attitude rather than his acceptance along with his sacrifice (cf. *NIV, RSV*, "will you not be accepted"). Additionally, although the expression ויפלו פניו appears only in this passage, the parallelism of Num 6:26 referring to the Lord's lifting up his countenance and giving peace associates that "lifting up" of the face with peace and prosperity. This supports the natural inclination to assume that the "falling" of the face is associated with the anger of Cain and is probably reflective of inner turmoil (opposite of inward peace). Further, the aspect of the imperfect form תמשל seems to support the focus on Cain's attitude. Conceivably, that aspect could arguably be any of the following: (1) possibility, (2) injunction, or (3) obligation. However, the injunctive imperfect does not seem to fit the counseling tenor of God's comments. Although the obligatory imperfect is probably the best choice, both an imperfect of obligation, denoting responsibility, and an imperfect of possibility, referencing ability and thus, in this context, implying choice, focus on Cain's inner motivation. Contra Gruber, "The Tragedy of Cain and Abel," 95–97.

87. Additionally, the concern with responsibility continues to play a role. Cain's rhetorical response to God's inquiry sheds light on this matter by the utilization of the term "keeper." A form of the term שמר ("keeper") is used twice in the prior episode (Gen 2:15; 3:24). In the first case, it refers to one of the man's two responsibilities in the garden, while in the second, it is used of the angel, guarding the way to the tree of life. Thus, in both cases it is directly associated with responsibility. These prior nuances are probably continued in this instance in that Cain directly refers to his own responsibility, denying that it involves caring for his brother.

88. As Fishbane and Miller state, Abel is only an agent in the account. See Fishbane,

presentation of Cain's sin and God's response continues to emphasize that relationship. Although the statement that Cain killed Abel is very succinct, it contains two references to the relationship. The narrator does not simply present the facts by saying that "Cain spoke to Abel and then killed him in the field," nor does he focus on the name Abel by saying "Cain spoke to Abel and then killed Abel in the field." Rather, Cain is presented as speaking to Abel, *his brother*, and then killing Abel, *his brother*.[89] The emphasis here, as throughout the entire story, is on the relationship. Throughout the account, the name Abel is used five times, three of which are accompanied by an explicit reference to the relationship. In the immediate context of Cain's action, Abel is referred to twice, in immediate succession, as "his brother," thus drawing attention, not simply to the crime, but also to its heinousness because of the relationship. Next, the Lord confronts Cain and asks him concerning the whereabouts of "Abel, *your brother*." The immediate response is not, "Am I his keeper?" but, "Am I *my brother's* keeper?" which, through obvious repetition, again draws attention to the relationship. This repetition is continued with the Lord's response to Cain repeatedly referring to Abel, not with his name or with a pronoun, but with the expression "your brother." This exceedingly redundant utilization of an expression, in both speech and narrative comments, clearly demonstrates that the brotherly relationship of Abel to Cain is a critical concern of this presentation.[90]

Biblical Text and Texture, 25; and Miller, *Genesis 1–11: Studies in Structure and Theme*, 40.

89. The omission of Cain's speech is conspicuous by its absence, raising the question of what he actually said. Although there is considerable support for the accidental omission of Cain's speech due to homoioteleuton or parablepsis (cf. Samaritan Pentateuch, Old Greek, Vulgate, Syriac, and Hendel, *The Text of Genesis 1–11*, 46–48), the rhetorical effect of an intended omission is such that the MT may be correct, especially when noting a similar omission in reference to Ham in chapter 9. That is, this omission may well serve as an indicator that the subsequent events are the issue rather than content. Just as the nature of the sacrifices was not the focus, neither is Cain's speech. So also Rendsburg, *The Redaction of Genesis*, 15. Further support of the MT is offered by van Wolde who makes an additional suggestion regarding the rhetoric and its furtherance of the story, seeing this omission as representing Cain's lack of respect toward Abel. See van Wolde, "The Story of Cain and Abel," 34–35.

90. Van Wolde sees additional support for this idea by proposing that the usage of איש in Gen 4 should be understood specifically within its context, namely, Eve gives birth to a man and his brother, presenting the theme for the story—a man and his brother (van Wolde, "The Story of Cain and Abel," 27).

Creation in the Hands of Humanity

Hope

An additional connection with the previous story is the continued rhetorical emphasis on the hope for life in the midst of morbidity. As will be discussed, the narrative opens and closes with the focus upon hope for future life, while the story itself presents further deterioration of the vitality introduced in the creation account.

Summary

In summary, the literary presentation of the story of Cain focuses on secondary elements introduced in the Eden narrative. Specifically, it concentrates the readers' attention on the self-serving motivations of humanity.

The Story

Introduction

The manner in which this story is introduced immediately begins to set up the situation which is to follow. First, even though this episode is not about them, the man and woman from the garden are used to introduce the main characters. This type of presentation establishes a direct connection with the previous narrative and indicates that this episode is to be understood in light of the former story.[91] Second, the man continues to be referred to as האדם ("the man"), while the woman is referred to by a name given but by which she had never before been mentioned. The utilization of her name generates an immediate connection with the prior account, invoking the implications of the events surrounding her naming. As discussed above, her name is presented in such a way and at such a point in the narrative that it places the emphasis on hope for humankind.

Further allusions to the Eden narrative in a manner which evokes hope are seen in the woman's initial statement. She had acquired an איש, a man. In view of the fact that the only other character so named was the one condemned to return to the dust, it appears from her statement that she is presenting a replacement for this איש, and, hence, continued life.[92] Thus,

---

91. So also Mathews, *Genesis 1–11:26*, 263.
92. So also Westermann who states, "She sees in the child she has borne the (future) man" (Westermann, *Genesis 1–11*, 290).

the introduction of this section constructs a setting which not only follows, but is related to the account of the Fall, and which implies the human hope for continued life through children, even in the face of impending death.[93]

The introduction also establishes the main character of the story. With the hope for continued life placed in future generations, that hope is presented as embodied in Cain, thus focusing attention on him. He is introduced by name and with an explanation of the rationale behind that name. In contrast, Abel appears only as Cain's brother. Abel's appearance, along with the meaning of his name ("fleeting"), mentioned apart from any etiology, characterizes his participation in the narrative and reveals that he is only a secondary character.[94] Thus, at the very outset the human characters are introduced, and the primary one is identified. Additionally, that identification is presented in such a way as to create anticipation and hope for continued life.

In addition to signaling the subject of hope, the introduction also foreshadows the conflict which will develop.[95] First, Cain is a farmer while Abel is a shepherd, and each offers the fruit of his own particular labor. Second, even though Cain is initially presented in terms of positive potential, his occupation and offering immediately connect him with his father and the associated curse, creating a distinction between him and his brother.[96]

---

93. This hope is presented as that of the woman rather than of the narrator or God as evidenced in its expression primarily in terms of human speech.

94. Hess states: "The roles of the name bearers in the narrative concur with the explicit or implied etymologies of names themselves in suggesting the degree of activity and significance assigned to the name bearer. In these ways the West Semitic etymologies and wordplay available to each of the names provide a suggestion of their role and importance in the text. The etymology and related wordplay integrate the name, the name bearer, and the narratives of which they are a part." See Hess, *Personal Names of Genesis 1–11*, 123. Accordingly he sees Abel's name carrying the thought of that which is ephemeral and transitory, corresponding to his role in the narrative. Wenham comments that the meaning is too obvious to warrant comment, and means "breath" or "vanity," and alludes, unwittingly, to the shortness of his life. See Wenham, *Genesis 1–15*, 102. Additionally, Rudman argues that although there are some attempts to link the name "Abel" with Assyrian *ablu*, "son" or Jabal and Jubal, the consensus remains that the name is intended to portray transitoriness and mortality. See Rudman, "A Little Knowledge is a Dangerous Thing," 463.

95. So also Brodie, *Genesis as Dialogue*, 152.

96. This presentation in terms of implied association rather than explicit narrative comment serves to continue the literary characterization while avoiding the mistake of making that issue the point of the narrative. It also forebodes ill with reference to the hope that is associated with Cain.

Creation in the Hands of Humanity

Then, God's rejection of Cain and his sacrifice, while accepting Abel and his offering, brings the potential conflict to a head.

Climax and Resolution

As discussed above, the climax of the story is presented in a manner which focuses attention on Cain's self-serving motivations. It paints a picture of dependence upon his own assessment for matters related to his welfare as he refuses to accept divine counsel and kills his brother.[97] Even his response to God's judgment reaffirms the focus on self-serving motivations. In contrast to the prior episode in which there is absolutely no response from those receiving punishment, Cain complains, seeking relief. Even Cain's fear is related to self-serving human motivation, namely, concern for his life at the hands of those who would seek revenge.

The story of Cain also continues the development of the effects of the sin of humanity upon itself. The loss of personal welfare which was portrayed in Gen 3 is continued in the presentation of Cain's judgment. The loss of unity with fellow human beings is further exacerbated as Cain is banished from the companionship and security of his family, cursed to be a fugitive and wanderer.[98]

---

97. In this section there is a major syntactical problem related to God's counsel to Cain prior to the murder. A review of various discussions of the matter reveals that conclusions reached, although possibly significant to the exegesis of the text, do not impact the overall emphasis of the story as proposed above. It may be significant to note, however, that the only discussion of this text found which does not require an emendation of the text asserts that the overall concern of the episode is with Cain's attitude toward his brother. In an extended discussion on the entire verse, van Wolde takes רבץ as a substantival participle meaning "lying in wait for." She argues that the grammatical and semantic problems of the verse can be resolved without altering the text by taking the two terms חטאת and רבץ as both functioning as subjects: at the door is sin, the sin of lying in wait. Thus she sees parallelism between 7a and 7b with the ms suffix in 7c referring back to רבץ. She proposes that Yahweh is urging Cain to lift up his head and look at his brother, with "looking" meaning "favorably disposed towards." See van Wolde, "The Story of Cain and Abel," 31–32. However, as Chisholm has pointed out in personal communication, there is a problem establishing that the root רבץ means "lying in wait."

98. So also Robinson, "Literary Functions of the Genealogies of Genesis," 602; and White, *Narration and Discourse*, 165. Additionally, the participle נע, "quiver, wave, waver, tremble," and the participle נד, "move to and from, wander," comprise a hendiadys meaning "wandering fugitive" (cf. Isa 6:4 where they are used in synonymous parallelism). Scholars commonly note that there is no precedent for this expression indicating a Bedouin lifestyle. Given the context of separation from land, this specific terminology, along with cursed "from the ground," should probably be understood to connote expulsion

Genesis 1–11

Epilogue

The story ends with an epilogue which continues the presentation of the issues featured throughout the story, namely, the progressive development of death in terms of humanity's self-serving motivations, albeit with hope for future life.

Deterioration

Although the account begins with the characters expressing hope for future life centered in a new man, this new man simply contributes to the downward path. Instead of providing hope by carrying on life, he contributes to and hastens death by killing his brother. With the recounting of additional generations, this downward spiral is presented as rapidly continuing, culminating in the even more heinous self-serving crime of Lamech.[99] Displaying

---

from family, and the land of security and sustenance, that is, from the place of blessing (cf. 2 Kgs 21:8).

The expression Cain uses, מעל פני האדמה ("from upon the face of the ground"), occurs thirty-three times in the Old Testament and is commonly translated as "the face of the earth," usually understood as indicating presence on the surface of the entire earth. However, in some passages the expression is modified with a relative clause, thereby limiting the scope, usually to a *specific region* (e.g., 1 Kgs 8:40; 9:7; 2 6:31; Jer 35:7). In the case of Cain, the ground from which he was cursed is undesignated in verse 14, but modified by a relative clause in verse 11. Clearly the referent is the same in both verses since in verse 14 Cain is directly referring to the curse pronounced in verse 11. Therefore Cain was probably cursed from the specific location where he previously lived and the region where he killed his brother. The construction in verse 11 supports this interpretation since, in the vast majority of cases, the collocation of מן + the article + a noun + אשר, occurring eighty-seven times, has the relative pronoun limiting, rather than simply describing, the noun.

The fact of Cain building a city affirms this idea in that it probably represents an attempt to provide security for himself in the face of his punishment. So also Bush, *Notes on Genesis*, 105; Hamilton, *Genesis 1–17*, 238; Gonzales, *Where Sin Abounds*, 66; and Wittenberg, "Alienation and 'Emancipation,'" 111. Contra Sarna, *Genesis*, 36.

99. Even the genealogy itself is presented in negative terms. So also Dumbrell, *The Faith of Israel*, 24; Hamilton, *Genesis 1–17*, 239–40; Kikawada and Quinn, *Before Abraham Was: The Unity of Genesis 1–11*, 56; and Wilson, *Genealogy and History in the Biblical World*, 148, 55. Further, Rudman suggests that technological progress is a development of humankind's ability to think independently (Rudman, "Knowledge is a Dangerous Thing," 463). If that is true, even the theme of autonomy is continued. Dumbrell sees it as introducing human aggression, which, if valid, would continue to develop the idea of conflict with fellow human beings (Dumbrell, *The Faith of Israel*, 24). Further, Gonzales proposes that, in his invocation of a curse, Lamech takes upon himself the prerogatives

the character of his forefather, Lamech, like Cain, kills his fellow human being; however, consistent with its placement at the end of the downward progression, his act is characterized in even more ominous and blatant terms. First, instead of killing one who is most naturally understood as his peer, as did Cain, he kills a mere boy.[100] Then, he arrogantly declares his own welfare by referring to God's protection of Cain and invoking even greater divine protection for himself, all in apparent oblivion to the ethical nature of his actions. Thus, the focus on self, in contrast to that of fellow humans (i.e., loss of unity in plurality), is presented as continuing and worsening.

Hope

In spite of the presentation of degradation, the idea of hope in continuation of life through future generations is once again presented at the end of this episode. This hope, introduced from the man and woman's perspective and originally concentrated in Cain, is renewed; however, it is now associated with a new son and is presented in a way that shifts the attention away from human efforts to the work of the Lord.

Cain's introduction was highlighted by the implications of the name Eve and Eve's statement at his birth which was formulated in such a way that she was the subject ("I have acquired"). In the introduction of Seth, God is the subject ("God has appointed"), there is no association with the name "Eve" and its connotations, and Seth is presented in connection with people beginning to call on the name of the Lord. Thus, the episode ends not only by continuing the idea of hope, but with that concept associated with a renewed looking to the Lord as opposed to self.

In this regard, the name Enosh may be significant. Although the argument is not very strong, the etiology of the name may associate it with weakness, and, occurring as a name for man, it is sometimes thought to connote humankind in weakness, rather than strength.[101] If valid, this

---

of God (Gonzales, *Where Sin Abounds*, 69).

100. Wittenberg notes that by placing איש and ילד in parallelism, attention is focused on the youthfulness of Lamech's victim and portrays the act as aggression against the weakest of society. See Wittenberg, "Alienation and 'Emancipation,'" 113; so also Alter, *Genesis: Translation and Commentary*, 20. Gevirtz, too, sees the victim as a boy, but a young upstart, a would-be hero-warrior rather than the weakest of society. See Gevirtz, "Lamech's Song to His Wives (Genesis 4:23–24)," 405–15.

101. See Harris, Archer, and Waltke, eds., *Theological Wordbook of the Old Testament*, 345–348.

could be seen as an additional literary feature which provides the innuendo of man in recognized weakness calling on the Lord. This idea would be supported by an emphasis on the change in perspective presented by the episode beginning with אדם and ending with אנוש.

In a similar vein, Hess proposes that in 4:25 the uses of אדם as a personal name indicates that something new is about to happen. It signals the movement from a generic representative of humanity to a specific person participating in the *toledot* of Genesis. This idea is supported by the semantic parallel of Enosh with Adam which causes one to expect Enosh to fulfill a parallel role, serving as a new beginning to the human race. He also alludes to the role of the two names in relation to each other elsewhere in Scripture as possibly pointing to the role of Enosh as a second Adam.[102]

In view of the movement from negative to positive connotations at the end of the Cain story and the possible validity of the foregoing discussion of the name Enosh, a major shift is signaled. This shift will be further developed in Gen 5–11.

Summary

The story of Cain develops the Eden narrative. The tension between death and hope for future life is continued with the presentation of the worsening condition of humanity, albeit followed by a ray of hope through the intervention of the Lord. The self-serving motivation of humanity is developed by featuring direct aggression against fellow human beings for the purpose of benefitting self and with the ironic effect of such self-centered activity progressing in the exacerbation of the loss of blessing.

---

102. See Hess, *Personal Names of Genesis 1–11*, 132.

5

Judgment, Deliverance, and Salvation
The Theology of Gen 5:1—11:27

GENESIS 5:1–11:27 IS A large section including a variety of material. Some of that material (e.g., the flood) has been the subject of much detailed study and debate; however, since the concern of this present study is to ascertain the overall theological message of the entire section, particularly as it relates to the development of the concepts introduced in the previous chapters, many frequently discussed issues and other significant matters will be passed over in view of surveying the entire section.

Although the legitimacy of taking this entire section as one whole has been partially addressed in chapter 2 of this book, it will be further developed here through a consideration of the structure of Gen 5:1–11:27 and the implications of that structure upon the understanding of the authorial intent. Following the discussion of structure, there will be a consideration of the content itself along with its theological implications as a development of Gen 1–4.

Structure

The overall structure of Gen 5–11 is rarely discussed. Perhaps this is because there is little disagreement regarding the identification of most subunits while even the relationship between them is frequently agreed upon (e.g., the significance of the sons of God episode prior to the flood, and why

Babel follows the Table of Nations). However, seldom is there any attempt to address the structure of the entire section, especially in a manner that explains the logical relationship of the various parts and their contribution to the understanding of the whole. This lack must be met, especially in view of the goal of this work to ascertain the theological message of the Primeval History.[1]

Genealogy with Narrative Inserts

The first indicator of the structure of this section is the title: "This is the book of the *toledot* of Adam." Although Gen 5 is generally referred to as the *toledot* of Seth, according to the text it is really that of Adam. It is "what happened," "what developed," from Adam, not Seth.[2] The next important, and generally misunderstood, feature of this section is the reference to "image" (5:3). The common approach taken, although with little rationale, is to understand Adam's bearing a son in his image as indicating a continuation of the divine image.[3] This approach, however, does not properly reflect

---

1. Questions regarding the unity of the flood account have been the subject of much discussion. One of the more recent important works in this regards is that of Emerton who, addressing the work of Cassuto and Wenham, argues that the two primary discrepancies in the flood narrative are the chronology and the number of animals taken into the ark. See Emerton, "An Examination of Some Attempts to Defend the Unity of the Flood Narrative in Genesis: Part 1," 401–20; idem, "An Examination of Some Attempts to Defend the Unity of the Flood Narrative in Genesis: Part 2," 1–21; Cassuto, *Genesis: From Noah to Abraham*, 32–47; and Wenham, "The Coherence of the Flood Narrative," 336–48. However, whether or not there were sources, and whether or not the account contains contradictions, the final canonical form still must be dealt with as an intended unity. Even a number of source critics support this proposition when they acknowledge the existence of a purposeful and creative redactive unity. E.g., Blenkinsopp, *The Pentateuch*, 77; and Mann, *The Book of the Torah*, 22. Anderson accurately characterizes the situation when he argues for taking up the flood story as a unity and within its greater context, regardless of potential sources, in order to understand the whole theologically. See Anderson, *From Creation to New Creation*, 73.

2. The usage of the term ספר ("book") is an indication that this particular *toledot* is of special significance, probably because of its all-inclusive character. Although it is common to propose source explanations for the appearance of the term, this would mean that its use here while with no other *toledot* most likely is the result of sloppy redactive work which the creative literary structure of the section argues against. Rather, the significance of the term is highlighted by the fact that the next time this type of expression is used with a genealogy is with that of Jesus in Matt 1. Therefore, the only two occurrences are in connection with the genealogies of federal heads (cf. Rom 5; 1 Cor 15:22, 45).

3. Cf. Alter, *Genesis*, 23; Hess, *Studies in the Personal Names of Genesis 1–11*, 137;

Judgment, Deliverance, and Salvation

what is being said. The text presents Seth being born in *Adam's* image and likeness, not God's. Although Mathews connects this reference to the passing down of the divine image, he notes that it is reasonable to take the text as indicating that Adam passed down his own image.[4] However, since the closest direct reference to God is in verse two, it is not simply reasonable that the 3ms suffix refers to Adam, but clearly indicated by the following: (1) a contextual break between verses two and three, (2) the beginning of verse three with a genealogical form, and (3) the beginning of verse three with ויהי. Therefore, this section begins with the text stating that the following is the "book of what developed from Adam," who bore children in his own image.[5]

Although Adam's genealogy begins in chapter 5, there is some disagreement regarding its end. The traditional perspective has been that it ends with the introduction of Noah. However, in recent years a number of scholars have noted that 9:28–29 appears to be the ending of the biographical entry of Noah which begins in 5:32.[6] This means that the flood narrative is actually a narrative insert into the presentation of Noah and thus an expansion of the Adamic genealogy itself.[7]

The validity of the proposition that the Adamic genealogy continues at least through 9:28–29 is evidenced in the structural pattern of this section. In chapter 5 the following pattern is used:

> PN1 lived x years and begat PN2.
> PN1 lived after he begat PN2 y years
> and begat sons and daughters.
> All the days of PN1 were z years;
> and he died.

The entry for Noah is as follows:

> Noah was five hundred years old and begat Shem, Ham and Japheth (5:32)
> (flood narrative, introducing the *toledot* of Noah).

Waltke and Fredricks, *Genesis*, 110, 112; and Westermann, *Genesis 1–11*, 356.

4. Mathews, *Genesis 1–11:26*, 308, 310.

5. So also Gonzales, *Where Sin Abounds*, 72.

6. Hamilton, *Genesis 1—17*, 260; Mathews, *Genesis 1–11:26*, 296; Turner, *Genesis*, 42; Waltke and Fredricks, *Genesis*, 113; Wenham, *Genesis 1–15*, 129; and Wilson, *Genealogy and History in the Biblical World*, 161.

7. So also Anderson, *Creation to New Creation*, 67; and Waltke and Fredricks, *Genesis*, 124, 151. Cf. Wilson, *Genealogy and History in the Biblical World*, 161.

> Noah lived after the flood 350 years (9:28).
> All the days of Noah were 950 years (9:29);
> and he died (9:29).

It is evident that, although there are some differences (which will be discussed below), the entry for Noah follows the same basic form of the genealogy of Adam, albeit including the flood narrative.

The idea of a narrative insert is not foreign to the Adamic genealogy;[8] the biographical entries of both Enoch and Lamech clearly set a precedent for narrative presentations within this particular genealogical structure. Although the flood story might be considered too extensive to be considered such an insertion, the fact that the formulaic entry for Noah begins prior to the flood and is completed after the deluge account argues for an intentional structuring in order to clarify that the genealogy is to be understood in this way.

If the structurally based perception that the Adamic genealogy continues through 9:28-29 is legitimate, then it follows that the genealogy of Shem in Gen 11 is likewise an extension of that of Adam. This relationship is evidenced in the fact that the same basic form of Adam's genealogy resumes once again in Gen 11:10. The form, representing the exact pattern in chapter 5, less the death statements, is as follows:

> PN1 lived x years and begat PN2.
> PN1 lived after he begat PN2 y years
> and begat sons and daughters.

The form of the Shem genealogy is even closer to that of Adam than the Noahic entry. Therefore, if it is valid to understand 9:28-29 as a continuation of the Adamic genealogy, as do many scholars, then it would seem to be even more appropriate to extend that perception to the genealogy of Shem.[9] Therefore, the section Gen 5:1-11:27 appears to be one unit, comprising a single genealogy with narrative inserts.[10]

---

8. It also appears in extrabiblical literature, such as the Sumerian King List. See Pritchard, *Ancient Near Eastern Texts Relating to the Old Testament*, 265-66.

9. The significance of the differences between the genealogies of Adam and Shem are important, providing clues to the understanding of the entire section. This matter will be developed later.

10. This approach is similar to that of Westermann who, although taking this position, does not develop its significance for understanding the theological message of the section. He sees the genealogies as stretching from creation to Abraham with a series of "happenings" set into those genealogies. They are "an essential constitutive part of

Significance of Genealogies as Genre

If Gen 5:1–11:27 is a genealogy with narrative inserts, then the first matter that must be addressed is the significance of such a form. Studies of ancient Near Eastern genealogies, particularly the research of Robert Wilson, provide some help along these lines.[11] Following his study of modern oral genealogies, ancient Near Eastern king lists, and biblical genealogies, Wilson concludes that there are significant similarities in both form and function between the genealogies of the ancient Near East and those of Israel, with both sharing some of the characteristics of modern oral genealogies. Specifically, segmented genealogies (those listing multiple lines from an individual) apply to the relationship of groups within a social context, while linear genealogies (those listing single descendants) relate a person or persons to someone or some group in the past; however, when genealogical

---

the primeval story and form the framework of everything that is narrated in Gen 1–11 ... They give continuity to all that happens which makes the biblical account of the origins unique in its kind in the history of religions. A coherent and summary history is prefaced, by means of the genealogies, to the salvation history which begins in Gen 12" (Westermann, *Genesis 1–11*, 3, 6).

The approach that understands Gen 5:1–11:27 as a genealogy with narrative inserts may resolve the confusion which has existed regarding the combination of genre types in this section. Although the significance of the genealogies has been observed, suggestions regarding their exact function along with the narrative have been myriad. For example, Renaud sees the genealogies working together with the *toledots* to express the theology of the section. See Renaud, "Les généalogies et la structure de l'histoire sacerdotal dans le livre de la Genèse," 5–30. Clines states that there are clues within the narrative section of Gen 1–11 which indicate that the genealogies were intended to express some theological purpose. See Clines, *The Theme of the Pentateuch*, 66. Similarly, Bailey sees the genealogies of chapters 5 and 11 as crucial episodes even though they lack any plot structure. See Bailey, "Some Literary and Grammatical Aspects of Genealogies in Genesis," 267–82. Some scholars understand the genealogies as functioning simply as links between the narrative segments. For Fishbane the Genesis genealogies link the narratives and determine the basic movement of the cycle. See Fishbane, *Biblical Text and Texture*, 28; and similarly, Huey Jr., "Are the 'Sons of God' in Genesis 6 Angels? Yes," 11–12. Kikawada sees the genealogies as interludes between stories, giving substance to the blessing/command of 1:28 "be fruitful and multiply." See Kikawada and Quinn, *Before Abraham Was*, 68.

11. For a full discussion of ancient Near Eastern genealogies, and their relationship to biblical material, refer to the following: Aufrecht, "Genealogy and History in Ancient Israel"; Chavalas, "Genealogical History as 'Charter'"; Hess, "The Genealogies of Genesis 1–11 and Comparative Literature"; Johnson, *The Purpose of the Biblical Genealogies with Special Reference to the Setting of the Genealogies of Jesus*; Malamat, "King Lists of the Old Babylonian Period and Biblical Genealogies"; Robinson, "Literary Functions of the Genealogies of Genesis"; Wilson, "The Old Testament Genealogies in Recent Research"; and idem, "Between 'Azel' and 'Azel.'"

Genesis 1–11

variants do occur, they should be considered from the perspective of variance in function rather than from an attempt to harmonize errors. In fact, one of the principal conclusions of his study is that form and function are inextricably linked. He states: "Future study of the biblical genealogies must be guided by the principle that genealogical structure and function are interrelated. One genealogical feature cannot be studied in isolation from the other."[12] He further comments: "An analysis of genealogical function is thus crucial for an accurate understanding of any given genealogy, for often the function of a genealogy is intimately related to its form."[13] Therefore, genealogies should be studied and understood from the perspective of function, with changes in form presenting clues as to that function. Applied to the present discussion, the changes in form of the Adamic genealogy, e.g., narrative inserts, give clues as to its function in the Primeval History.

Insert of the Flood Account

In accordance with the conclusions of Wilson's research, a narrative insertion into a genealogy presents material of importance.[14] This is demonstrated by the minor insertions into the genealogy of chapter 5, namely narrative comments regarding Enoch and Lamech. The significance of these additions is signaled by a comparison of the Adamic genealogy with that of Cain and reveals significant parallels since both lines include entries for an Enoch and a Lamech. Both cases of Enoch include a presentation related to the effects of a given way of life.[15] The son of Cain receives some temporary security on the earth while the son of Jared escapes death and receives permanent life in the presence of God. In the case of the two Lamechs,

---

12. Wilson, "Interpreting Biblical Genealogies," 21.
13. Wilson, "Old Testament Genealogies," 182.
14. So also Alter, *Genesis*, 23.
15. The association of Enoch with life is further evidenced in the slight adjustment in the formulation of the genealogy. Instead of the expected "and [father] lived after he begat [son] . . . ," the Enoch entry states "and Enoch walked with God after he begot Methuselah . . . " That is, in place of "living" the narrative substitutes "walking with God," thus alluding back to the prior narratives in which communion with God was a feature of *shalom* before the Fall. Additionally, although it is sometimes questioned, God "taking" Enoch is a reference to his leaving the earth apart from death. This is indicated in two ways. First, the statement that God took him parallels and replaces the standard entry in the genealogical form that he died. Second, the fact that the term לקח is repeatedly used in 2 Kgs 2 with reference to Elijah being taken into heaven apart from death supports the concept that it has the same reference here.

Judgment, Deliverance, and Salvation

both are presented along with reported speech. The first justifies himself, asserting that his sin should go unpunished, while the second expresses hope for deliverance from the consequences of sin in general.[16] Thus, the parallels between the narrative insertions into both of these genealogies indicate that they are not random, but rather intentionally structured, and therefore represent important material.[17]

The significance of the large narrative insertion of the flood account is also evident and signaled both rhetorically and structurally. First, as discussed above, the genealogical structure begun in chapter 5 continues in chapter 11, albeit with a significant change.[18] The emphasis on death in the former, indicated by redundant statements, is omitted from the latter.[19] The

---

16. Similarly, Hess observes that Cain's Enoch is attached to a city, but Seth's moves beyond human culture into the realm of the divine. Cain's Lamech utters a cry for vengeance while Seth's expresses hope for a better life for his descendants. Hess, *Personal Names of Genesis 1-11*, 141-42. Mathews notes that both Lamechs are presented as transitional figures and their genealogies include segmentation (Mathews, *Genesis 1-11:26*, 280-82).

17. As will be discussed below, the comparison serves to imply a basis for hope in a genealogy which is focused on death.

18. This phenomenon is a prime example of Wilson's point that changes in form are functional.

19. The phrases "all the days of PN1 were x years" and "and he died" are unnecessary in that the prior lines of the form already provide that information.

It is interesting to note that scholars commonly see genealogies themselves as connoting hope for life. Blenkinsopp understands the birth of the son as the pivotal position of the overall chronological system in chapter 5, thus focusing on life (Blenkinsopp, *The Pentateuch*, 72). Mathews asserts that genealogies "indicate that hope prevails through Adam's successors." (See Mathews, *Genesis 1-11:26*, 309.) Mann also sees the theme of hope in the concept of life through future generations. See Mann, *The Book of the Torah*, 21; cf. Dempster, "Geography and Genealogy, Dominion and Dynasty," 70, 77. Contrary to this proposition, many scholars see the genealogy of Gen 5 as actually *focusing* on the continuation of life, rather than on death with a subliminal implication of hope. The basis for this position is the understanding of the genealogy as that of the elect son, Seth, and as focusing on the image of God and the blessing of 1:26-28. Cf. Clines, "Theme in Genesis 1-11," 294; Hamilton, *Genesis 1-17*, 255-56; Johnson, *Purpose of Biblical Genealogies*, xv; Robinson, "Genealogies of Genesis," 599; Waltke and Fredricks, *Genesis*, 112; and Wilson, *Genealogy and History in the Biblical World*, 164. However, in spite of this widespread perception that the genealogy of Gen 5 is related to the continuation of life in the image of God, if the proposal made above that the genealogy is Adam's rather than Seth's, and that the image presented in 5:3 is Adam's rather than God's image, this common association loses much of its basis. In fact, the understanding of this genealogy as that of Adam, and the image in 5:3 being Adam's rather than God's image, meshes extremely well with the proposal that the emphasis of this line of descent is on death. Whereas humankind in God's image was characterized by life, as a result of Adam's sin

question this raises in the mind of an alert reader is, What happened to cause such a shift? Thus, the rhetorical effect of this change is to focus the reader's attention on the narrative insert of the flood account.

Lest the effect of the change in form be overlooked, attention is focused on the flood narrative by means of overall structure as well. As is often noted in studies of these chapters, preceding and following the flood account are genealogical presentations comprising ten generations each. Additionally, each group of ten generations is a linear genealogy ending in a segmented entry which includes three sons. The fact that these similarities are not coincidental is evident in that the favored son of the first group of ten generations is the initial entry of the second group. Thus, an extensive narrative insert between two presentations of ten generations in segments of a genealogy which are related to each other also focuses attention on that narrative.

Thus, these rhetorical and structural features of Gen 5–11 serve to pique the interest of the readers by focusing attention on the flood account for the purpose of answering the specific question, "Why the loss of emphasis on death?"

The Flood Account

Literary and structural features are not only helpful in understanding the overall perspective and purpose of Gen 5–11, but they also assist in the study of the flood account itself. Accordingly, the following discussion will first consider these features as indicators of the authorial intent. Then, the themes which have been introduced in Gen 1–4 and continued in chapters 5–11 will be identified, and the nature of their development reviewed.

Literary Features and Their Significance

The flood account is sometimes considered as beginning with the presentation of the account of the sons of God in 6:1 and sometimes with the *toledot* of Noah in 6:9. The insertion of a *toledot* in the midst of what appears to be a logically continuous presentation is at first troubling, but, upon further consideration, is helpful in understanding the significance of the story of

---

the passing on of his own image to his children resulted in death to all. This seems to be the perspective of Paul, who states that "in Adam all die" (1 Cor 15:22).

Judgment, Deliverance, and Salvation

the flood. Additionally, the account of the flood itself, beginning in Gen 7:1, is presented with a literary crescendo and decrescendo, providing an intentional focal point. This focal point is also signaled by the logical flow of the story. By placing the reader's attention on this point the author provides an answer to the question raised by the overall structure of these chapters: "Why the loss of emphasis on death?" Thus, the literary features and structure of the story of the flood provide significant help in ascertaining the emphases of the account.

Toledot of Noah

Although the *toledot* of Noah structurally indicates a major break in the narrative, the nature of this juncture is seldom discussed. Perhaps a clue to its significance can be seen in noticing the movement from the matter of the corruption of humanity and the imposition of judgment to God's deliverance through judgment.

Genesis 5:1–6:8 presents the spread of Adam's sin and its consequences throughout humankind, resulting in God's decision to destroy all flesh. However, prior to the presentation of that destruction, the theme of deliverance is introduced. It is foreshadowed by both Lamech's longing for deliverance from the curse of the ground and by the statement that Noah found favor in the eyes of the Lord. The latter statement ends the section as indicated by the *toledot*, a marker indicating the beginning of another section. The next section, "what happened with Noah," presents God's deliverance of Noah through the destruction which he has decided to bring upon the earth. That is, the story following the *toledot* statement of 6:9a represents a significant break in the narrative because the matter to be taken up is the deliverance of Noah through the judgment which God had just promised at the end of the immediately preceding pericope. Therefore, the story of Noah is not simply a continuation of the preceding narrative, expounding upon the promised judgment. Rather, it is actually about deliverance through that judgment.

This change in focus introduces for the first time in Gen 1–11 the idea of deliverance; up to this point it has never been directly portrayed. Although God has provided mitigation in judgment (e.g., the mark on Cain), judgment pronounced was judgment experienced.[20] However, now God's

---

20. Enoch probably represents a foreshadowing of the idea of deliverance in that he is presented as taken out of the earth apart from death.

chosen one and those who follow him will experience *deliverance* from the judgment which God is bringing upon all others, and then entrance into salvation (i.e., a "new" creation).[21]

The introduction of the concept of deliverance leading to salvation is accompanied by the introduction of another concept, namely, mediation.[22] Prior to the flood narrative, each character, as well as humanity in general, has been presented apart from any idea of another human being functioning as his representative; however, with Lamech's statement that Noah would deliver "us," the idea of one person effecting change for others is first encountered.[23] Although Lamech looks to Noah as the one who will deliver humanity by providing comfort from the curse on the ground, it turns out that Noah himself must experience deliverance—deliverance from God's judgment upon all flesh. However, he does function in a mediatorial role as he leads his family in faith and obedience to the Lord and gathers animals into the ark. The narrator does not present any communication between Noah's family or the animals and God, but rather God's plans for them are communicated through Noah, and Noah leads them in obedience, which in turn results in their deliverance from judgment.[24]

---

21. Fretheim correctly notes the difference between deliverance (i.e., redemption) and salvation. He states that "the objective of God's work in *redemption* is to free people to be what they were *created* to be, the effect of which is named salvation." See Fretheim, *God and World in the Old Testament*, 10, with original emphasis. That is, redemption is deliverance while salvation is entrance into blessing.

22. The term "mediation" is used here in a very broad sense. It is meant to convey the idea of one person functioning as a "go-between" between God and others. It will later take on various functions such as leader, intercessor, prophet, priest, etc. In the flood narrative, Noah functions as a mediator (1) as he receives God's word which applies to his entire family, (2) as he leads his family in obedience to God's command, and (3) as he protects the animals. Following the flood, this concept of mediation is developed somewhat with judgment of humanity placed in the hands of humanity ("by man shall his blood be shed") as well as by Noah's pronouncement of both a blessing and a curse—activities previously seen only as actions of God.

23. One might point out that Adam's sin affected all humanity; this is not the concept of mediation; rather, it is cause and effect. The actions of human beings affect others as well as themselves; however, in the case of Lamech, he is looking for Noah to accomplish something for "us" which they were not able to accomplish for themselves. Hence, a type of mediation is presented.

24. This introduction of human leadership will turn out to be important as it includes the essential characteristics required in Israel's king.

Judgment, Deliverance, and Salvation

Crescendo–Decrescendo

Other structural features of the flood account give clues as to its significance in the larger narrative. The following breakdown reviews the content of each successive pericope, demonstrating a crescendo–decrescendo effect.

> *7:1–5* This section includes God's command to bring animals into the ark, since God will bring rain in order to destroy life. It concludes with the terse statement that Noah did what God said.

> *7:6–10* This section begins with the brief statement that the flood of waters was on the earth, followed by a description of people and animals entering the ark. The section concludes with a brief statement that the waters of the flood were on the earth. This presentation employs recapitulation, and by doing so creates a crescendoing effect. Verses 7:1–5 present the command to bring the animals into the ark, followed by the statement that Noah did it; however, verses 6–10 do not carry the story forward from the ending of the previous section (Noah having brought the animals into the ark), but rather pick up the story and carry it forward from a point already presented in verses 1–5. Simultaneous with this recapitulation, the presentation of the flood intensifies. Whereas in the first pericope the impending event is presented as only rain, in this section it is characterized as a flood of waters—a significant intensification.

> *7:11–16* This section states that the fountains of the deep and the windows of heaven were opened, and it rained 40 days. The entry into the ark is once again given, this time with a fuller description of both the people and the animals. Thus, the crescendoing effect by means of recapitulation is continued. The intensification of the description also continues. Whereas in the first section the flood is presented simply as rain and, in the second pericope, as a flood of waters, now it is characterized in the cosmic terminology of the opening of the windows of heavens and the fountains of the deep.

> *7:17–24* This last section contains the fullest, most repetitive, and most intense characterization of the destructive event. The flood was on the earth, the waters increased, the waters prevailed and increased greatly, the mountains were covered, all flesh died, and the waters prevailed 150 days.

Thus, these four sections provide descriptions of the flood using recapitulation, that is, each section picking up the narrative at a point in time in the midst of the prior section, but carrying the narrative further forward.

Additionally, with each section the description of the devastation of the flood intensifies, culminating in unimaginable destruction.

Just as the onset of the deluge is presented with a crescendoing effect, the abatement of the waters is characterized by decrescendo. This effect is created as follows:

> 8:2 This verse states that the fountains of the deep and the windows of heaven closed, and the rain stopped, thus characterizing the end of the flood in the similar cosmic terms presented in the final stages of its onset.
>
> 8:3–4 The next section presents the waters as slowly abating for 150 days and the ark resting on Ararat. Unlike the previous verse, which portrays the cessation of cosmic catastrophic phenomena, this portion softens the presentation by describing a more common, natural process which occurs over an extended period of time.
>
> 8:5–12 This section seems to slow the pace of the description of the flood's abatement even more by first presenting a continued retraction of the waters and an extended presentation of the drawn-out process of birds gradually leaving.
>
> 8:13–14 Finally, the waters are presented as completely dissipated and the ground surface as dry, culminating in the concluding statement that the earth is dry.

Thus, the reversal of the flood is presented in cosmic terms of the fountains of the deep and windows of heaven closing, then as the waters abating to the point of the ark resting on Ararat, then to the point at which the tops of mountains were visible, then to where the raven would not return, then to where the dove would not return, then to the point at which the surface of the ground is dry, and finally to the point where the earth is dry.

This crescendo–decrescendo structure of 7:1–24 and 8:2–14 respectively provides a literary focus and simultaneously mimics the actual experience of the flood. That is, as the deluge worsens, there is a sense of steadily increasing calamity until it reaches a peak and then begins to wane. At the center of this process is the climax, the turning point when the calamity's intensification ceases, and conditions begin to improve. This climax is the statement that God remembered the inhabitants of the ark (8:1).[25] That

---

25. This same focus of the presentation of the flood itself is noted by a number of scholars who argue for a chiastic structure which centers on 8:1. E.g., Anderson, "From Analysis to Synthesis," 433; Anderson, *Creation to New Creation*, 72; Dorsey, *The Literary*

is, the crescendo–decrescendo structure focuses attention on the point at which things change, with that point being an independent, subjective activity of God, presented without any apparent basis but that God, in his sovereignty, had compassion on the inhabitants of the ark.[26]

Logical Flow of the Story

With the structural focal point of the Primeval History being the flood narrative and the pivotal event of the flood narrative being God's remembrance of his creatures, it appears that the key theological point of the Primeval History is the change in stance taken by God from one of judgment to one of redemption.[27] However, not only is this point communicated through the section's structure, it is also made by the logical flow of the story in that the flood narrative facilitates God's transition from a decision to de-

---

Structure of the Old Testament, 52; Longacre, "The Discourse of the Flood Narrative," 89–133; Maier, "The Flood Story: Four Literary Approaches," 107; Ross, *Creation and Blessing*, 191; Waltke and Fredricks, *Genesis*, 125; and Wenham, "The Coherence of the Flood Narrative," 337–42. However, Bailey criticizes the popularity of this idea, presenting a solid argument. He notes, among other things, the fact that most chiastic proposals leave out parts of the text, and then identify sections which range in size from part of a verse to several verses. See Bailey, *Noah: The Person and the Story in History and Tradition*, 156–58. See also Emerton, "Unity of the Flood Part 1," 401–20; idem, "Unity of the Flood Part 2," 1–21; and van Wolde, "A Text-Semantic Study," 24.

26. Similarly, Fretheim notes that God here *chooses* to be a savior and to be active in that salvific activity. See Fretheim, *The Pentateuch*, 47.

Related to this matter there is a debate regarding whether the Lord made a covenant with Noah prior to entering the ark (see, for example, Dumbrell, *Covenant and Creation*, 11–43). Does the statement of 6:18 refer to the covenant of chapter 9, a separate covenant involving deliverance from the flood, or an implied creation covenant? If the reference is to deliverance from the flood, then 8:1 could be taken as God remembering that covenant, thus contradicting the above statement that there is no apparent basis other than God's sovereign will. However, if 8:1 does, in fact, allude to a covenant established in 6:18, then that covenant itself is presented in terms of God's will and apart from any explanation of motivation (Noah finding favor being separated from the statement of his righteousness by the major division indicator of a *toledot*. If 6:18 alludes to an implied creation covenant, then once again the portrayal refers to God's sovereign choice. Therefore, regardless of this debate, the remembrance of the inhabitants of the ark is the result of an unexplained choice on the part of God. Along these lines Campbell and O'Brien comment that this section grapples with one of the deepest theological issues, namely, that how a far-from-holy humankind can remain in relationship with an all-holy God is presented as a mystery in the text. That is, as stated above, the basis of God's action remains a mystery. See Campbell and O'Brien, *Rethinking the Pentateuch*, 28.

27. So also Anderson, *Creation to New Creation*, 141–42.

stroy (6:1–8) to his commitment never again to lay waste the earth by flood (8:21–9:17).[28]

The logical flow of the flood account is indicated by a consideration of the references to the hearts of the Lord and of humankind (see 6:5–6, 8:21). In the passage which provides the background and basis for God's destruction, the narrator states that the Lord's heart was grieved (ויתעצב אל לבו) when he observed that the thoughts of man's heart were only evil continually (וכל יצר מחשבת לבו רק רע כל היום). But then, following the flood, the Lord says in his heart (ויאמר יהוה אל לבו) that the thoughts of man's heart are evil from his youth (יצר לב האדם רע מנעריו). The connection between these two passages is unmistakable as indicated by both their content and terminology. That is, the content includes the same basic observation by the Lord about the heart of man, and, in both cases, it is made with a reference to his own heart. These obvious clues concerning a connection between these two statements are not just aesthetic. Rather, they ensure that the point being made is not missed by the reader.

That profound point is further signaled by the curious fact that the reason given for the Lord's destruction of humanity and the earth is the very same reason given for his commitment not to bring such devastation again. These observations raise the same basic question as that implied by the structural focus: "Why the change?" That is, why is the evil of man's heart the basis for destroying the earth, and then, soon after, the basis for not destroying the earth? It appears that the narrator purposefully gives no clear motivation for this opposite response on the part of God, presenting it simply as his sovereign decision. The result of this literary presentation repeatedly focusing on the same issue while presenting no explicit answer serves two purposes. First, the presentation of the story itself characterizes deliverance as something found in the obscurity of the purposes of the transcendent creator. Second, it serves to heighten the anticipation of the reader, causing him to look for possible answers as the narrative continues to develop in subsequent episodes.

---

28. Although the presentation of covenant issues throughout these chapters justifiably receives much attention, this is material which, once again, must be passed over in the interest of ascertaining the overall message of the story as indicated by its literary construction.

Judgment, Deliverance, and Salvation

A New, Different Beginning

The presentation of the flood account in terms of God's change in response is supported by the often noted feature of its presentation in terms of de-creation and re-creation and the characterization of Noah as a new Adam, both of which contribute to the portrayal of a new and different beginning.

DE-CREATION, RE-CREATION AND A NEW ADAM

An often observed feature of the flood account is that it is presented in terms of a reversal of the original creation of Gen 1. In the creation account, the waters above were separated from the waters below, and then the waters below were restricted, allowing the dry land to appear. Living creatures were then created in the order of birds, animals, creeping things, and man. The destruction of the flood is presented as a reversal of this process. First, in the statement of the Lord's intention to destroy all flesh, the order is given as man, beasts, creeping things, and birds (see 6:7). This is a direct reversal of the order in which they appeared in the creation account (see 1:20–27).[29] Then, in the account of the flood itself, waters are released, the dry land disappears, and the waters above and the waters below are again combined into one. However, the allusions to creation do not end there; God uses a wind to begin the post-flood re-creative process (ויעבר אלהים רוח על הארץ) just as the רוח אלהים signaled the beginning of the creation account (cf. 1:2 and 8:1). The waters above and waters below are seen as separating once again in that both the windows of heaven and the fountains of the deep close. Then, the reappearance of the earth is described using יבש, the verbal form of the noun used for the dry land in chapter 1 (יבשה, cf. 1:10 and 8:14). If there is any question of the post-flood account presented in terms of re-creation, it is certainly removed in the observation that it, too, concludes with a blessing upon humankind to be fruitful, multiply, and fill the earth.[30]

---

29. Chisholm has observed that the order of creation is reversed when God is the subject of the destructive action, as he was of the creative action. This pattern obviously omits sea creatures which were not affected by the flood. In 7:21, 23, which present the actual account of the destruction, the presentation follows the creation order. Chisholm Jr., "The Genesis Flood Account: Some Observations and a Question."

30. Waltke structures the parallels as follows:
Phase 1: Precreation–the Spirit moving over the waters (earth, deep, spirit/wind, waters, deep)

Not only is the revival of the earth presented as a re-creation, but Noah is characterized as a new Adam. Some of the similarities are as follows: (1) both Adam and Noah are uniquely associated with the image of God (Gen 1:26–28; 5:3; 9:6), (2) both interact with animals (Adam names, Noah preserves), (3) both receive the same commission to be fruitful, multiply, rule the earth,[31] (4) both work the ground (3:17–19; 9:20), (5) both ingest the product of the earth, one by eating and one by drinking, (6) both face problems involving nakedness as a result of ingesting the product of the earth, (7) both experience the discernment of their nakedness and are clothed by another, (8) the failures of both result in curses (Adam's on the earth, Noah's on Canaan), (9) both have three named sons, (10) the consequence of each one's actions falls on others (Adam on humankind, and Noah on Canaan), and (11) both have sons who experience judgment, hope, and division into the blessed and the cursed.[32]

This very clear and repeated allusion to creation in the flood account is not simply aesthetic. Just as the literary characterization of God's heart in response to man's heart serves to focus on a change, so does the characterization of a re-creation of the earth. Further, the change signaled by these creation allusions is the very same one brought forward by the overall structure of genealogy with inserts of Gen 5:1–11:27, namely, the shift in focus from death to life.[33] In the events immediately following the creation

---

First Day–there is no need for recreation of light
Phase 2: Second Day–restraint of the waters, establishing borders between sky and earth (1:6–8; 8:2b)
Phase 3: Third Day–establishment of dry land (1:9, 8:3–5)
Fourth Day–there is no need to renew vegetation
Phase 4: Fifth Day–winged creatures in the skies (1:20–23; 8:6–12)
Phase 5: Sixth Day–living creatures of sky and land populate the earth
Phase 6: Appearance of the nuclear family who bear God's image
Phase 7: blessing on humanity (1:28; 9:1–2)
See Waltke and Fredricks, *Genesis*, 128–29.

31. The Noahic blessing omits "subdue the earth." It is interesting to observe that the conditions in the re-creation recognize the Fall and do not restore things to their original pristine condition. Whereas previously there was no hostility presented between humanity and animals, that now occurs (corresponding to "have dominion" of Gen 1). Similarly, whereas humanity was to subdue the earth, with an implied authority, the curse on the ground in Eden apparently undermined the effectiveness of that authority to some extent (corresponding to "subdue"). These matters are areas for further study.

32. Adapted from Gage, *The Gospel of Genesis*, 9–15; and Waltke and Fredricks, *Genesis*, 127–28.

33. Similarly, Sarna notes that the air of pessimism about the seemingly incorrigible

account, the curse and its effects are prominent, with blessing only implied as a possible hope; however, in the events following the re-creation, even though the condition of humankind does not change, the implication of a future hope becomes far more prominent.[34]

A Different Beginning

Although original creation and post-diluvial creation are presented similarly, the subsequent events of the latter contain an increased focus upon life, representing a new beginning. Adam's history is presented as corruption, resulting in the eventual death of all as graphically presented in the genealogy of Adam. The only positive feature is seen in humanity's hope and its looking to God; however, in the post-flood situation associated with Noah, there is a significant move from implied hope to one made overtly possible through an explicit promise by God. Whereas the full fruition of antediluvian humanity resulted in God's relenting of having made humankind, following the flood he covenants never again to destroy all flesh in this manner. Rather than destroy humankind, he begins his salvific work—another theme commonly associated with creation throughout Scripture—to restore humanity to its intended position of blessing and representation.

---

nature of man presented in the previous narratives is now relieved by an emphasis on life, new birth, and the potential for a fresh start for humanity. See Sarna, *Genesis*, The JPS Torah Commentary, 85.

34. There is another very significant shift signaled by the narrator between the pre- and post-flood narratives. Prior to the flood the focus has been humankind in general but following the deluge it is on the nations. Previously, the subject matter has been of existential concerns, things true of all humankind, but then it shifts to things corresponding to the realities of the author's own times. The pre-flood geographical references are vague and, for the most part, do not seem to correspond to the world of the original audience (e.g., prominent but apparently unknown rivers, unknown configuration of rivers, and, of course, Eden). However, in the post-flood account the extensive references to peoples and places are well-known and still existing. Prior to the flood there is no reference to Israel, but the accounts of the cursing of Ham and the Table of Nations seem to present everything from Israel's perspective. Thus, while presenting a shift from a focus upon death to hope for life, the narrator simultaneously moves from "pre-historical" existential questions to the realities of the current world. This change moves the reader from consideration of the fundamental bases of existence to dealing with the implications of those issues on present life. Cf. Fretheim, *Creation, Fall, and Flood*, 57.

Summary

The overall presentation of Gen 5–11 exposes the account of the deluge as the point at which the emphasis of the section transitions from death to life and from despair to hope. A consideration of the introduction of the *toledot* of Noah in the midst of a logically flowing story signals a change in momentum of the larger narrative. It signals a transition from emphasis on judgment to presentation of deliverance and the introduction of human mediation. The internal structure of the flood narrative itself presents its own central issue. The presentation of the flood as a crescendo and decrescendo features God's remembrance of the inhabitants of the ark as the pivotal point. The fortunes of humanity and the earth change as God, in his sovereignty, chooses to respond in deliverance.

The logical flow of the narrative, signaled by clear literary indicators as discussed above, reinforces the centrality of this action by God. The narrator clearly presents God's evaluation of humanity before and after the flood as having remained unchanged. Nevertheless, that evaluation serves as the basis for both the flood and the covenant to never again impose such a judgment. Although the basis for judgment and grace being the same raises obvious questions in the mind of the reader, no clear answer is provided. The resolution lies, as in the structural presentation, in the obscurity of the will of the sovereign creator.

Thus, the creative presentation of the flood narrative, utilizing both structure and the flow of the story, the latter indicated by clear literary markers, places the emphasis on God and his decision to respond to humanity with salvation rather than destruction.[35]

Development of Human Corruption

A consideration of the presentation of the various components of the flood narrative reveals that, while presenting a major shift from death to life, from despair to hope, with both shifts centered in the action of a sovereign God, it does so in a manner which reinforces the depraved characterization of humanity in the Eden and Cain narratives.

---

35. This change in God's dealings from judgment to deliverance is a focal point in other biblical passages, such as the Song of Moses and Isa 40–48.

Judgment, Deliverance, and Salvation

Introduction to the Flood

TRANSITIONAL FUNCTION

The first part of chapter 6 serves as a bridge between the multiplication of humankind over the earth and the subsequent flood narrative. The connection with the previous narrative is accomplished by a variety of means. The temporal reference to the multiplication of humanity on the earth clearly alludes back to the genealogy of chapter 5 which, by its very nature, involves the spread of humanity. The direct reference in Gen 6 to the birth of daughters of men immediately following the close of chapter 5 provides an obvious allusion to those births. These features ensure that the reader understands this section to be in association with the preceding material.

CHARACTERIZATION OF HUMANITY

Further references are made to the previous narrative by way of both content and terminology. Humankind[36] is presented as "seeing" (ראה) and "taking" (לקח) what they had chosen, alluding to the Fall of the Eden narrative through both terminology and concept (cf. 3:6).[37] By characterizing the spread of humanity throughout the earth in terms of the same self-gratifying autonomy initiated in Eden, the entire world is presented as filled by humankind, as God intended, but with self-serving creatures rather than his faithful representatives.[38] Thus, this section which introduces the flood

---

36. Once again a subject is encountered which is too complex to address within this present study. The position taken here is that the "sons of god" in reference to human beings better fits the overall context of judgment upon humanity than does a reference to angelic beings. The reason for the usage of such terminology is understood to be a rhetorical allusion to the humanity of Gen 3.

37. The addition of the phrase מכל אשר בחרו ("from all which they chose") may well portray uninhibited exercise of autonomy in choosing what is beneficial to one's self, thus strengthening the allusion to chapter 3.

38. The theological point of these verses is a matter of much discussion. Some of the more popular suggestions propose that the section deals with polygamy, sin and violence, and a breach of the divine-human boundary. With regard to polygamy, it is suggested that monogamy is first broken by Lamech, and now totally destroyed. Further, it is sometimes observed that Jesus associates the flood with some type of looseness with regards to marriage (Matt 24:37-39; Luke 17:26-27). The suggestion of violence and corruption is seen as evidenced in the usage of שחת and the usage of בשר to denote the temporal, corruptible side of human nature. The breach of the divine-human boundary is understood in terms of the "sons of God" as a reference to divine beings who then

does so in a manner which characterizes the corruption of humanity as the development of the sin in Eden.

In addition to ראה and לקח, the narrator uses other terminology and rhetoric to reinforce this negative portrayal of the character of humanity in the days immediately preceding the flood. Humankind is referred to as "sons of God," a rhetorical device which satirically associates him with his grasp of autonomy, that is, his attempt to become like God, who knows good and evil. This depiction is continued in verse four which presents a parenthetical addendum and which continues the characterization of humanity as prideful.[39] That is, a picture of humankind is painted using a number of expressions which evoke the image of man "in all his glory" by means of the expressions נפילים ("giants"), גברים ("mighty men, heroes"), and אנשי השם ("men of renown").[40]

Not only does this section characterize humankind in general in terms reminiscent of the pride of the fallen man and woman, it also presents God's response with a literary creativity which draws attention to the contrast between the self-centered evaluation of humankind and an

---

produce semi-divine offspring. Cf. Breukelman, "The Story of the Sons of God Who Took the Daughters of Humans as Wives," 83–94; Cassuto, "The Episode of the Sons of God and the Daughters of Man (Genesis vi 1–4)," 17–28; Gilboa, "Who 'Fell Down' to Our Earth?," 66–75; Hendel, "Of Demigods and the Deluge," 13–26; Kio, "Revisiting the 'Sons of God' in Genesis 6.1–4," 234–396; VanGemeren, "The Sons of God in Genesis 6:1–4," 320–48.

39. This verse is disjunctive. The *Qatal* form of the verb in 6:4a, and the reversal of subject-verb order indicates that it does not continue the temporal line from the prior verse. The resumptive statement of 4aa–ab comprises expressions of vv. 1–2 and, by doing so, connects the two parts of the story. The first section focuses on the relationship between the sons of God and daughters of men and especially Yahweh's response. See Vervenne, "All They Need is Love," 36.

40. Although the perspective taken above seems to be unique, a number of scholars recognize the rhetorical features which are behind this approach. The use of the definite article on *nephilim* in 6:4 is generally understood to indicate a specific or well-known group or class. Along with the usage of the term in Numbers, the connotation seems to be semi-divine heroic figures (cf. Alter, *Genesis*, 27; Hamilton, *Genesis 1–17*, 270; and Mathews, *Genesis 1–11:26*, 338). The idea that this expression is rhetorical rather than ontological is supported by the position taken by Mathews regarding "*gibborim*" and "men of the name." He argues for "name" referring to the motif of prideful autonomy, and the rhetorical contrast between the human perception of *gibborim* as men of renown and God's perception as corrupt (Mathews, *Genesis 1–11:26*, 339–40). Thus, others have noticed the strong rhetorical features included in this terminology, although apparently not considering the possibility that *all* of the expressions used of humankind in this section are rhetorical.

accurate assessment by God. The passage presents God as "seeing" (ראה) and does so in direct contrast to the prideful observation (ראה) of man;[41] however, in that the only prior occurrences of God "seeing" are found in Gen 1, these verses probably simultaneously allude to the creation account as well. In Gen 1, God saw (ראה) his creation under the dominion of humankind and evaluated it as "very good." Now, however, he once again sees creation in the hands of humankind, but this time sees only "evil" (רעה) rather than good (טוב).[42] The narrator further strengthens this allusion to and contrast with creation by the subsequent use of the verbs ברא ("create") and עשה ("make").[43] Because of this new evaluation, God repented that he had made man and decided to destroy what he had created. Thus, both the terminology and content of these verses form a link and a contrast to God's original creation, all because of the faithless and autonomous activity of his representatives.[44]

Therefore, using heavily nuanced terminology along with satire, the narrator introduces the devastating judgment of the flood in terms of the previously presented corruption of humanity. As Blenkinsopp states, these verses decode the preceding genealogy, presenting the negative moral character which leads up to the recounting of the judgment of the deluge.[45]

Post-Flood Epilogue

The narrator uses the presentation which follows the account of the flood to portray a new filling of the earth with the corruption of humanity, rather than with God's faithful representatives.

The overall topic of repopulation of the earth is signaled by the reintroduction of Noah's sons as those from whom the earth was populated.[46]

---

41. The correspondence between man's character and God's response is highlighted by the rhetorical use of לב ("heart") in reference to both man and God. So also Alter, *Genesis*, 28.

42. Note the further allusion to the sin of the garden, utilizing the same terms used to express the knowledge of good and evil.

43. Cf. Sailhamer, *The Pentateuch as Narrative*, 88.

44. There may also be another link with Gen 3 with the usage of the term עצב. If this is true, the Lord as well as the woman is presented as suffering pain because of the condition of humankind. This concept is further portrayed in the ironic use of man's heart (6:5) and the Lord's heart (6:6).

45. Blenkinsopp, *The Pentateuch*, 74.

46. The section beginning with 9:18–19 is presented in such a way as to clearly

Genesis 1–11

The character of this extensive section as a presentation of the repopulation of the earth is also evidenced in the parallels between Gen 5 and the Table of Nations in that both utilize a genealogical form which describes humanity spreading over the earth.[47]

---

designate change in direction of the narrative and the end of the flood account. First, the opening statement takes the reader back to the exit from the ark, that is, prior to the last change in direction of the narrative. Second, the sons of Noah are reintroduced as the ones from whom the earth was repopulated.

47. Although there are various nuances to the way in which the Table of Nations is understood, there is widespread agreement that it functions to portray the dispersal of the nations throughout the earth. Hamilton asserts that this genealogy is a fulfillment of the divine blessing regarding multiplying and filling the earth (Hamilton, *Genesis 1–17*, 330). Both Cassuto and Wenham note the lack of comprehensiveness of the list, seeing it as no attempt to provide an exhaustive list but rather simply to demonstrate the dispersal of humankind (Cassuto, *Genesis: From Noah to Abraham*, 180; Wenham, *Genesis 1–15*, 214). Along the same lines, Sarna comments on the structural features of the genealogy, noting three major groupings, each with its own caption, and a "generalizing closing recapitulation" which characterizes the human race in territorial, linguistic, familial and national divisions (Sarna, *Genesis*, 67). Thus, regardless of the particular nuance, this list is commonly understood as a presentation of the population of the earth.

Another fundamental function of the genealogy is understood as the presentation of the relative kinship of humanity. Hess, in agreement with Johnson and Westermann, states that, whatever else it may do, the Table of Nations emphasizes the common humanity of all peoples who share in the failures and hopes of a common ancestry and ultimately in a common creation in the image of God. See Fretheim, *Creation, Fall, and Flood*, 122; Hess, "The Genealogies of Genesis 1–11 and Comparative Literature," 68; Johnson, *Purpose of Biblical Genealogies*, 77; and Westermann, *Genesis 1–11*, 704–06. Hamilton also argues for this approach, understanding the presence of perplexing associations of names (e.g., Nimrod from Cush, or a Hamitic Canaan rather than a Shemitic Canaan) as testifying to the function of this list as an expression of the ecumenic nature of civilization (Hamilton, *Genesis 1–17*, 332).

Related to this idea of common kinship, the genealogy is also frequently understood as presenting Israel, although part of all humanity, emerging as the line of blessing (e.g., Waltke and Fredricks, *Genesis*, 106). Hamilton notes that the term גוי ("nation") is consistently used in this chapter while עם ("people") never is. He asserts that the latter term denotes close family connections, whereas the former refers to large conglomerates held together externally rather than internally. This phenomenon is consistent with the character of the chapter in that, theologically, the chapter affirms Israel as part of one world governed by God, but also as the nation chosen to carry the knowledge of him throughout that world. Thus, Israel is presented both as part of humanity, and also as God's chosen vessel (Hamilton, *Genesis 1–17*, 334, 346).

Cassuto seems to combine all of these approaches, proposing a threefold aim: (1) to demonstrate that divine providence is evidenced in the distribution of nations as in other concerns; (2) to show the relationship between Israel and the nations; and (3) to teach the unity of postdiluvian humanity. He understands the lack of detail to be intentional, with the purpose of the author being to simply provide vague allusions. See Cassuto, *Genesis:*

Judgment, Deliverance, and Salvation

Nevertheless, this extensive narrative does not simply present the repopulation of the earth, but does so in a manner which demonstrates that the corruption of humanity has not changed. Following the parallel sections portraying the population of the earth (Gen 5 and the Table of Nations), the corrupt moral character of that filling is presented (i.e., Gen 6:1–8 and the Babel story). Arguing for this perspective, Kline adds the following observations: (1) the mystery of iniquity developed in this age toward a climactic episode of defiance, beginning with 9:20ff; (2) the account of Nimrod corresponds to 6:4, in that both use *gibborim* and the spirit of the two ages is the same, with the kingdom builders of Shinar, like the ancient *gibborim*, bent on a name (11:4; cf. 6:4); and (3) each episode leads directly to the divine reckoning and intervention.[48]

Further, an intended association between the character of the two populations of the earth is signaled by a number of features. Both immediately follow someone's sin, which impacts subsequent generations (Adam's affecting humanity and Ham's impacting Canaan and his posterity).[49] Additionally, the content of the post-flood spread of humanity seems to make allusions to the sinful conditions which led up to the judgment of the flood in that the twofold mention of the mighty Nimrod as a גבור (10:8, 9) is reminiscent of the pre-flood characterization of prideful men as גברים (6:4). This presentation of humankind in his sinful greatness is reinforced by references to the aspirations of humanity at Babel (cf. self-preservation concerns of Cain with reference to his city, 4:17) and the beginning of *his* (Nimrod's) kingdom (10:10).

If there was any question about this negative characterization of the repopulation of the earth by humanity, it is dispelled by the Babel story.

From Noah to Abraham, 187.

48. Kline, "Divine Kingship and Genesis 6:1–4," 200–2.

49. Additionally, the sin of Ham reiterates previously introduced themes. Although there is much debate regarding this passage, the focus of the narrative is most probably the contrasted responses of Ham and his brothers. One drew attention to Noah's nakedness while the other two hid it. The usage of nakedness and everything entailed by that term implies that Ham exacerbated the loss of unity in plurality of humanity (i.e., exposing the shame of individuality), while his brothers functioned as "their brother's keeper." The subsequent spread of nations and repopulation of the earth, especially in view of the curse and blessing, seems to signal how this lost sense of unity, whether corporate or personal, will characterize interaction among people in the world at large. Similarly Tomasino, "History Repeats Itself," 128–30.

For additional parallels between pre- and post-flood presentations, see Steinmetz, "Vineyard, Farm, and Garden," 193.

Genesis 1–11

Although there is sometimes a debate over the presence of a chiastic structure in this account,[50] its rhetoric and irony are unmistakable and widely recognized. Ironically, although humanity attempts to prevent its being scattered over the face of the earth, the actions of the people directly precipitate their dissipation. Presented by means of a wordplay, humankind seeks to make there (שם) a name (שם), but God visits them there (שם) and scatters them prior to the re-introduction of the line of Shem (שם).[51] Additionally, the people's actions are initiated by "Come! Let us ... " as is the response of God. All of these features serve to focus attention on the characterization of humanity as self-seeking and disobedient, just as in Eden.[52] This occurrence of this presentation within a section which features humanity filling the earth repeats the characterization of humanity prior to the flood.[53] As asserted by Blenkinsopp, the entire section of 10:1–11:9

---

50. For example, Kikawada and Quinn, Fishbane, Dorsey, and Walsh propose some type of chiastic structure while van Wolde provides serious criticism of this type of approach. See Kikawada and Quinn, *Before Abraham Was*, 30–31; Fishbane, *Biblical Text and Texture*, 36; Dorsey, *The Literary Structure of the Old Testament*, 53; Walsh, *Style and Structure in Biblical Hebrew Narrative*, 94; and van Wolde, *Words Become Worlds*, 94.

51. The wordplay on שם probably functions additionally as a connection between the Babel story and the pre-flood condition (cf. אנשי השם, "men of the name").

52. It is interesting to note that, in contrast to disobedience which characterized original sin, the account of Noah seems to focus on obedience. First, God informs Noah of what he is about to do and directs him, in great detail, to prepare (vv. 13–21). This segment ends with an emphatic statement that Noah obeyed. (The statement ויעש נח ככל אשר צוה אתו אלהים כן עשה, translated literally, "And Noah did according to all which God commanded him, thus he did," is emphatic via redundancy.) Then, once again God speaks, commanding Noah to enter the ark (7:1–4). Once again, this speech is concluded with a narrative statement regarding Noah's obedience. The section 7:6–8:14 moves from the pattern of divine communication followed by obedience, to a narrative account of the flood event itself. Then, once again following the account of the flood, the text resumes the pattern of divine speech to Noah (command to exit the ark) followed by a narrative statement of obedience. Therefore, the flood story is characterized by a pattern, namely, divine speech followed by human obedience, with an account of the flood event inserted. This feature may signal that God's salvific intervention may be related to a proper expression of dependence and submission on the part of humanity.

53. For the Table of Nations and the Babel story as a unit, see Waltke. He argues that these sections are a unit with two acts, with the second act, Babel, explaining the first act. He supports this idea with the mention of keywords and foreshadowing: (1) ארץ, indicating territories/earth (10:5, 20, 31–32; 11:1, 8–9); (2) לשון, tongue/language (10:5, 20, 31) and שפה (11:1, 6–7, 9); (3) Nimrod foreshadowing the tower, associated with "build" (בנה), cities (עיר) in Babylon, Shinar; and (4) foreshadowing division with Peleg. See Waltke and Fredricks, *Genesis*, 161–63.

Judgment, Deliverance, and Salvation

demonstrates that the drive for power and status exercises its corrupting influence here as it did previously.[54]

The narrative following the flood performs another important function as well. While completing the portrayal of a second filling of the earth by corrupt humanity, this section also serves to move the narrative from primal history into the world known and recognized by the original audience. This adjustment in perspective signals the apparent transition from matters fundamental and foundational to humanity as a whole to the consideration of how these concerns are played out in history (i.e., transition from primeval history to salvation history).[55]

Summary

The analysis of both the structure of Gen 5:1–11:29 and the presentation of the flood, including both its introduction and epilogue, reveal the same overall scope and purpose of these chapters. It conveys that nothing has changed, yet everything has changed. Nothing has changed in that humanity remains the same self-centered creature it was prior to the destruction of the flood. However, everything has changed in that God has chosen to respond to that corruption differently: whereas before he reacted by reversing creation, he now commits to do so never again; whereas the emphasis in the genealogy prior to the flood was on death, albeit containing a ray of hope, the genealogy following the flood no longer emphasizes death, thus bringing hope to the forefront.[56]

---

54. Blenkinsopp, *The Pentateuch*, 88.

55. Similarly, Alter, *Genesis*, 40; Fretheim, *The Pentateuch*, 69, 71, 83; Sarna, "The Anticipatory Use of Information as a Literary Feature of the Genesis Narratives," 78; and Steinmetz, "Vineyard, Farm, and Garden," 194–95.

56. That hope, of course, unfolds itself immediately following in the account of the call of Abram.

6

Summary and Implications

Introduction

THE THESIS OF THIS book is that Gen 1–11 presents a coherent theological message which is identifiable by means of a literary-theological exegesis of the text. Succinctly stated, that message is that humankind must, in unity, demonstrate faith and obedience toward God while functioning as God's representative and expectantly awaiting his full blessing, which will be realized when God restores to its full intended vitality the creation corrupted through humanity's failure. This chapter will review the foregoing theological exegesis for the purpose of demonstrating that the Primeval History contains a theological coherency and that the coherency can be expressed by the suggested message statement. This chapter will also briefly consider the function of the message of Gen 1–11 within its context and its significance to the implied readers. It will then conclude with a consideration of potential implications of this study.

Coherent Theological Message

The theological exegesis reviewed in the prior chapters of this book reveals several features which argue for the presence of a coherent theological message in Gen 1–11, namely, (1) theological themes are developed in each section, (2) a consistent tension is maintained throughout the entire Primeval History, and (3) a hierarchical relationship between theological ideas and tensions is suggested by the manner in which the narrative is formulated.

Summary and Implications

Theological Themes

The preceding theological exegesis has argued that God's work of creation is presented in Gen 1:1–2:3 in terms of fullness and vitality of life. The account is presented entirely from God's perspective in that the purposes, action, and evaluations are his alone; however, in a somewhat surprising manner, given the overall focus on divine activity, God chooses to have humanity represent him by creating them in his image and giving them dominion.

Whereas the creation account focuses on the work of God, the Eden narrative emphasizes the work of humanity as they function as God's representative in creation. This emphasis is achieved by focusing on secondary themes featured in the creation account, which themes are further developed in the Eden account, namely, humankind's role as God's representative and its failure in fulfilling that responsibility. The primary issue of humanity's failure does not regard the subjective matters of sin (e.g., seizure of autonomy, lack of faith, and disobedience), but rather the failure's actual occurrence which has impacted the sphere of humanity's representation. This failure of humanity is presented specifically in terms corresponding to the original characterization of his creation. That is, humanity's sin affects (1) the relational unity in humanity (related to creation in the image of God) resulting in disharmony between the man and the woman and a blight upon humanity's reflection of God, (2) his relationship with the earth (related to the command to subdue) resulting in obstacles between the man's labor and earth's productivity, and (3) his relationship with the animal world (related to dominion) resulting in conflict. In addition to developing the secondary themes relating to humanity that were implied in the creation account, the Eden narrative introduces more subjective issues relating to matters of the inner man and his own well-being. Specifically, the Fall is presented in terms of humanity's self-serving seizure of autonomy through distrust and disobedience of God. Ironically, humankind's taking upon themselves the privilege to decide their own welfare results in a loss of that welfare because of God's judgment and is presented in terms of death, the latter including separation from God, estrangement from fellow human beings, pain in fulfilling divinely assigned roles, and physical death. Thus, the story of the garden not only develops issues related to humanity's representative role in God's work—his corruption of God's creation when he should have been ruling and subduing—but also introduces matters related to his own well-being.

Just as the Eden narrative takes up secondary themes of the creation account, so the Cain story develops the secondary, subjective concerns introduced in the garden. The self-serving motivation of humanity is developed in the direct aggression of human being against fellow human being (Cain against Abel, Lamech against a boy) for the purpose of benefitting self. The ironic effect of such self-centered activity is additional divine judgment and further exacerbation of the loss of personal welfare resulting from taking upon oneself the right of determining and acquiring that welfare in independence of God. This further corruption of humanity is then presented as continuing to spread to future generations and worsening as humankind persists in his own efforts to improve the quality of his existence while attempting to evade the natural and divinely imposed consequences of his seizure of autonomy (cf. Lamech).

Following the same literary pattern found in the interrelationships of the prior sections, Gen 5–11 once again takes up the secondary themes of the prior section and develops them. Whereas the Cain story focuses upon humankind's exercise of self-centered autonomy in terms of conflict with his fellow human being, the secondary theme of the spread of the sinful condition throughout humanity is fully developed in this next section. These chapters emphasize the spread of mankind's sinful condition which fills the world with corruption; however, the structure of these chapters indicates that the primary point of Gen 5–11 is the way that God deals with this corruption. Although the righteous response of God is initially judgment, as one would expect from his previous responses in the Eden narrative and the story of Cain, this time, because of humanity's hopeless condition, God chooses to initiate deliverance and salvation. The structure of the pre- and post-flood genealogies provides a change of emphasis from death to hope for life while simultaneously focusing on the flood account as the pivotal event. The internal structure, storyline, and rhetoric of the flood narrative itself focus attention on God's sovereign decision to provide deliverance. Thus, even though the earth is once again repopulated with corrupt humanity (cf. the curse of Canaan, the Table of the Nations, and the Babel story), the initiation of God's salvific activity ends the Primeval History with hope in spite of humanity's intractable corruption (cf. the absence of emphasis on death in the Shem genealogy).

Summary and Implications

Tension

The finale to the Primeval History, as discussed above, is not simply an unexpected open-ended conclusion to a story, but is a feature which has been creatively developed throughout the narrative. The creation account introduced a tension into the story; even though nothing of the experience or perspective of humanity is mentioned, thus ensuring that the creation account remains focused on the purposes and activity of God, there appears to be an implication that all may not proceed smoothly. By using the term "subdue," the creation account subtly implies that, in spite of the overall presentation of completeness and perfection, there remains something which requires further intervention on the part of humanity. This idea is furthered by the rhetorical effect of the characterization of creation in utopic terms—a condition obviously unknown to the implied reader and which thus foreshadows the subsequent occurrence of disaster. However, in spite of these negative implications, the seventh day is nevertheless presented in a way which features ultimate perfection. Thus, the account is structured in a manner which implies the development of problems but simultaneously portrays a perfect outcome, thereby creating a tension between the final success of God's work and the implied disruptions on the way to its completion.

The negative implications of the creation account are realized in the subsequent presentations of the Eden narrative, the Cain story, and the flood account while always accompanied by allusions to a positive future. Though the man and woman in Eden are condemned to death, the man anticipates future life even in the face of death as he gives to his wife the name Eve, "the mother of all the living." Although the story of Cain presents the spread and worsening of humanity's self-serving corruption, the account ends with humankind calling upon the Lord (cf. Enosh). Even the catastrophic judgment of the flood is followed by God's commitment never again to respond to humanity's intractable evil in such a manner.

In addition to this tension between hope in God's deliverance and despair over humanity's corruption being continually developed throughout the Primeval History, it is presented from a full array of perspectives: (1) knowing the end from the beginning, as seen in the creation account; (2) humanity's hope for future life even in the face of certain death, as presented in the Eden narrative; (3) hope for a change in heart in humanity even though there seems to be intractable corruption, as seen in the story of

Cain and its epilogue; and (4) hope in God's provision of deliverance without regard to any change in humanity, as presented in the flood narrative.

Hierarchical Structure

Not only are the foregoing theological themes and tension introduced and developed in Gen 1–11, but the structure of the section gives clues as to how these issues are to be understood. Each section is presented with clear indications of primary themes accompanied by subordinate concerns; however, the presentation of each successive section is made in terms of the secondary issues presented in the prior narrative. This structure implies a hierarchical relationship between the theological issues in which the concerns of any given segment should be understood in terms of those of the previous narrative. Following this hierarchical structure, everything ultimately must be understood in terms of God's work. Subordinate to that fact is God's choice to accomplish his work through humanity. The fact of humanity's representative role then leads to the problems caused by humanity's failure, which in turn are to be understood in terms of egocentrically motivated independence of God expressed in disobedience and lack of faith. Finally, these characteristics thoroughly permeate all of humanity, and, as a result, the creation over which it has influence. It is this complex of theological ideas, in this hierarchical priority, in which God acts in either judgment or salvation.

Suggested Message Statement

The literary-theological exegesis presented in the body of this work has resulted in the identification of a complex of theological ideas and their interrelationships as summarized above. They can be further compacted into a single suggested message statement.

Even though the theological presentation of Gen 1–11 subsumes all points under the presentation of all things as the work of God, its existence in the form of human communication requires that it be understood as a message to humanity. Thus, the suggested message statement must reflect a charge to humanity which reflects his *raison d' être*: representation of God.

The hierarchical structure reflected in the Primeval History requires that all responsibilities placed upon humanity, as well as the consequences of success or failure, are understood as subordinate to what God is working

Summary and Implications

in creation. Therefore, the suggested message statement should portray the supremacy of God's work while simultaneously focusing on the responsibility of humanity.

The message statement should also attempt to reflect the specific priorities regarding human responsibility which are featured in the theological presentation of Gen 1–11. In that the failure of humanity is presented primarily as disobedience, the primary responsibility of humankind is best understood as obedience; however, since the underlying basis for disobedience is portrayed as lack of trust in God, faith must be a necessary component of that obedience.

Finally, the suggested message statement must reflect the tensions present in the Primeval History. First is the tension between present difficulty and future perfection, evident in humanity's hope for deliverance from death and restoration to the full blessings intended by God. Second is the tension between the responsibility of humanity and the sure accomplishment by God of his purposes, seen in the focus on human responsibility while subordinating outcomes to God's salvation.

Therefore, reflecting these essential features and the interconnection of themes contained in the theological presentation of Gen 1–11, the suggested message statement of the Primeval History is thus stated: Humankind must, in unity, demonstrate faith and obedience toward God while functioning as God's representative and expectantly awaiting his full blessing, which will be realized when God restores to its full intended vitality the creation which was corrupted through humanity's failure.

Contextual Function and Significance to Readers

Since this book has argued for the existence of a coherent message in Gen 1–11, it is appropriate to consider the function of that suggested message within its literary context as well as its significance for the implied readers. If there is a coherent message, one would anticipate that it has a recognizable function within the literary context in which it appears. Additionally, the existence of a message would also imply that it has some significance for the implied readers. These matters will be considered by reviewing the identity and situation of the implied readers and the function of the Primeval History within the Pentateuch.

Genesis 1–11

Implied Readers

The broader context of the Primeval History is the Pentateuch, and, in spite of the impact of critical approaches, there has been little to no debate regarding unity in its final form. Regardless of whether its perceived discontinuities are considered to be indicators of compilation and/or redaction, or, alternatively, functional creativity,[1] it is recognized that the Pentateuch presents itself as one whole.[2]

If the self-presentation of the Pentateuch is that it is a unity, who then are its implied readers? From a traditional and canonical perspective, the Pentateuch is widely understood as written by Moses. In this case, the implied readers would be Israel on the plains of Moab, poised to enter Canaan. From the perspective of critical scholarship there are many and varied views regarding the formulation of the Pentateuch; however, regardless of the exact manner in which one sees it as taking its final form, in this case the implied readership would be a later generation of Israel. In view of these widely varying perspectives, it is problematic to suggest a more specific identification of the implied readership than simply the nation of Israel; however, it *was* the nation of Israel, whether on the plains of Moab or at some later point in their history, for whom the message of the Primeval History and also the Pentateuch was initially intended.

The Message of the Pentateuch

Just as is the case with Gen 1–11, in spite of all that has been written on the Pentateuch, there is a remarkable paucity of works which address an overall message. Since it is beyond the scope of this study to validate the presence of a coherent message of the Pentateuch and to suggest a message statement, the pioneering work in this area done by well-known scholars will be referenced for the purposes of discussing the message of the Primeval History within its larger context.

---

1. See, for example, Valiquette, "Exodus–Deuteronomy as Discourse," 47–70.
2. For a discussion of the recognition of the Pentateuch as a unit see Blenkinsopp, *The Pentateuch*, 1–3.

Summary and Implications

Significance of Deuteronomy within the Pentateuch

The character of Deuteronomy provides particular help in understanding its overall message. In suggesting an approach to reading the Pentateuch, Fretheim points out that the way a story ends is important for the interpretation of the whole.[3] Accordingly, he argues that the ending of the Pentateuch should be considered both in terms of the last chapters of Deuteronomy and Deuteronomy as a whole. This type of an approach highlights Deuteronomy's use of hortatory language and its open-ended conclusion.

Homiletic Character of Deuteronomy

Fretheim describes Deuteronomy as hortatory, written in concert with the rest of the Pentateuch, using a rhetorical strategy designed to impress upon the reader, Israel, all that has preceded, intensely and urgently appealing for a present response in her present circumstance.[4] That is, the lengthy homiletic presentation that concludes the Pentateuch represents a conscious design intended to communicate the message of the whole and to achieve desired results.

If the parenesis of Deuteronomy is intentionally combined with the historical narrative of the Pentateuch for the purpose of generating a response, the essence of the message of the whole may well be found in the specific exhortations contained in the closing homilies. The specific exhortations in Deuteronomy are as follows:[5]

> Deut 4:1: "And now, Israel, pay attention to and adhere to the statutes and ordinances I am about to teach you, in order that you might live and go in and possess the land that the LORD, the God of your fathers, is giving you."

---

3. Fretheim, *The Pentateuch*, 24.
4. Ibid., 53–54.
5. Deuteronomy 5 begins the actual presentation of the statutes and commandments ("Hear, O Israel, the statutes and commandments which I am telling you this day . . . ") which in turn ends with Deut 26:16–19 ("This day the Lord your God has commanded you to keep these statutes and ordinances . . ."), followed by the presentation of blessings and curses. Thus the specific exhortations are included in the introduction to the ordinances and at their conclusion. Thus, from a homiletical perspective, Deuteronomy is constructed as one might expect: (1) example (history of disobedience, Deut 1–3), (2) exhortation to obey (Deut 4), (3) presentation of requirements and consequences (Deut 5–29), (4) restatement of the exhortation and consequences (Deut 30).

Deut 4:5–6: "See, I have taught you statutes and ordinances, just as the Lord my God commanded me, that you may do so in the land into which you enter to possess it. And you must keep and do them; for that will be your wisdom and your understanding before the peoples that will hear all these statutes, and say, 'Indeed this great nation is a wise and understanding people.'"

Deut 4:9: "Be very careful that you do not forget the things which you have seen, or disregard them all your life. Rather, you must teach them to your children and grandchildren."

Deut 4:23: "Be careful lest you forget the covenant of the Lord your God which he made with you and make yourselves an image of any kind as the Lord your God has forbidden you."

Deut 4:40: "Keep his statutes and his commandments which I command you this day in order that it might go well with you and your children after you, and that you might live long in the land which the Lord your God is giving to you forever."

Deut 30:15–30: In this section Moses calls upon them to love the Lord, walk in his ways, and keep his commandments. He places before them life and good, death and evil (v. 15), and again, life and death, blessing and cursing (v. 19).[6]

The one prominently recurring challenge evident in these verses is obedience. This repeated command to obey the Lord is frequently associated with consequences, namely, life and blessing in the land as a result of obedience, and cursing and death as the effect of disobedience. Thus, the message which is presented to both Israel the listener (on the plains of Moab) and Israel the reader (the implied reader) is a call to the people to obey the Lord, knowing that obedience results in blessing and life while disobedience leads to cursing and death.

---

6. Loving the Lord is associated with keeping his commandments, cf. 5:10; 7:9; 10:12; 11:1, 13, 22; 19. The people are called upon to love the Lord their God. The word for "love" (אהב) is a term that was commonly used in ancient Near East Treaties, suggesting that a vassal's attitude toward his suzerain should be one of reverential fear, loyalty, and obedience. Thus the concept of loving one's master may be understood as an essential component of the notion of obedience. For a full discussion of this topic see Moran, "The Ancient Near Eastern Background of the Love of God in Deuteronomy."

Summary and Implications

Open-ended Conclusion

Another key feature of Deuteronomy is the fact that the ending leaves things open-ended. Fretheim summarizes the situation as follows:

> The ending defers the fulfillment of the promise; it gives to the Pentateuch the character of an unfinished symphony. The promise is left suspended and the people are dispirited and fearful (31:6). The future is not simply filled with delights; it is fraught with danger. And the danger comes, not just from Canaanites, but from the inner recesses of their own hearts (31:20–29).
>
> The considerable body of law in the Pentateuch, even the ending of Deuteronomy (30:11–14), implies that obedience is possible; a community of life and well-being can be created in the land of promise. Human responsibility with respect to life in community is recognized as basic to the shape that the promised future takes. But the same ending also subverts that confidence with repeated drumbeats speaking of Israel's inclination to infidelity and warning of consequent disaster (28:15–68; 29:17–28; 30:17–19; 31:16–29; 32:15–35).[7]

This type of open-ended conclusion has the rhetorical effect of causing the reader to fill in the ending for himself. In order to bring the story to a conclusion the reader must think through options while considering the relative probabilities in view of the presentation of the story up to that point. Such contemplation tends to draw the reader into the story, placing himself in the situation in order to consider how he would act in those circumstances. Israel, then, reading this narrative, would relive the decisions and action of her forefathers and be challenged to consider the necessity of obedience in her present situation. Thus, the rhetorical effect of the open-ended conclusion to the story complements the hortatory character of the ending of the Pentateuch by personally engaging the reader.

Correspondence of Ending and Beginning

If the key to understanding the Pentateuch is the ending (Deuteronomy), then the significance and function of Primeval History, i.e., the beginning, is probably found in its relationship with that ending.[8] Does it simply

---

7. Fretheim, *The Pentateuch*, 54.

8. Once again, in his rare narrative approach to the Pentateuch as a whole, Fretheim argues that the Primeval History, functioning as the beginning of the Pentateuch,

provide a background, or does it have a more significant function? Two factors indicate that it functions as more than mere background material: (1) the essence of its message is the same as that of Deuteronomy, and (2) just as does Deuteronomy, it fails to provide resolution but leaves things open-ended.

The perspective of the essence of the Pentateuch's message discussed above corresponds well with the message of Gen 1–11, which is extensively developed in this book. In addition to other parallels, there seems to be a special and direct correspondence to the Eden narrative. In Eden the man was placed in a paradisaical environment and warned that disobedience to God's command would result in death. This situation is similar to that of Israel on the plains of Moab as they receive the exhortations of Moses. In view of the promise of a paradisaical land "flowing with milk and honey," they are commanded to obey God and are warned that disobedience would result in cursing and death. Thus, it appears that the essence of the message to Israel in Deuteronomy is the same as that exemplified in regards to humanity in general in the Primeval History, namely, obedience leads to the enjoyment of blessing and life while disobedience results in cursing and death.[9]

In addition to containing the same basic message, there are other correspondences between Deuteronomy and Gen 1–11. Just as the charge to humanity in Eden is presented within the broader context of humanity's existence as representative of God, the exhortations to Israel are portrayed as serving God's purpose that she function as his representative among the nations. Not only is Israel's formation introduced in Exodus as having the purpose of her being God's mediator to the nations,[10] this characterization is evident in a number of important texts in Deuteronomy.[11] As Fretheim

---

corresponds to Deuteronomy, the ending, and intensifies the themes for the implied audience. See ibid., 56–58.

9. Alexander notes that the choice between life and death, blessing and cursing, all tied to obedience as presented in Deut 30, is frequently referenced in summary descriptions of Deuteronomy. See Alexander, *From Paradise to the Promised Land*, 162.

10. Cf. Exod 19:5–6. According to Dumbrell and Merrill, this text can be considered the central purpose statement regarding God's election of Israel. See Dumbrell, *Covenant and Creation*, 80–81; and Merrill, "A Theology of the Pentateuch," 12.

11. For example, the famous credo of Deut 26:5b–9, possibly an expression of a fully developed and widespread confession of Israel, fails to include any reference to Sinai. Although this omission is surprising considering the covenant nature of Deuteronomy, it seems to be more than simply coincidence since the identical phenomenon also occurs in 6:20–24 with another presentation of the same credo. Once again, in Josh 24:2–13

Summary and Implications

states, "The deliverance of Israel is ultimately for the sake of the entire creation. The issue for God finally is not that God's name be made known in Israel; the scope of the divine purpose is creation-wide, for all the earth is God's. God's purpose is to so lift up the divine name that it will come to the attention of all the peoples of the earth."[12] Therefore, just as humanity was to function as the image of God in creation, Israel was to serve as his representative to all peoples.

Another connection between Deuteronomy and Gen 1–11 is the emphasis on land as a place of blessing. Deuteronomy makes allusions to humanity's initial placement primarily in the portrayal of entrance into Canaan as a return to Eden.[13] Additionally, existence in the land is portrayed in terms of life and prosperity (e.g., "that you may live," "that it may go well with you," and "that you may live long in the land," cf. Deut 4:26, 40; 5:16,

---

the same omission of Sinai occurs in what appears to be another presentation, although embellished, of this original statement of belief. Without any reference to Sinai the content of this credo focuses on God's provision of deliverance rather than on covenantal matters and may indicate that the covenant and the attendant responsibilities should be understood within the broader perspective of God's election and deliverance of Israel and its associated function as God's representative to the nations.

This proposition is supported by the form critical proposal that Deuteronomy is reflective of a suzerain-vassal treaty. The very nature of this type of treaty presupposes a salvation history (historical prologue) with a promise of future blessing for continued faithfulness. Sinai is presented as the "ceremony" at which this agreement was formulated and initially ratified. Deuteronomy presents the renewal of this covenant upon the entrance into the land—the actual receipt of the "future blessing." Therefore, the significant issues here are the salvation history and the fulfillment of the promises for future blessing. That is, the underlying confession of the people represents what the suzerain has done for them and the initiation of the covenant as well as its renewal is because of their blessings. Therefore the primary issue is not the act of initiation of the covenant, but rather the salvation that is the basis for that covenant.

Additionally, the theology of the Song of Moses presents God's universal perspective and representational purposes for Israel. Yahweh is seen as the one who intervenes in judgment upon the faithlessness and disobedience of his representative, but eventually intervenes in deliverance for his own sake. Thus the witness to Israel places her responsibility as God's servant within the broader perspective of what God is accomplishing through his own work and in view of his overall universal purposes.

12. Fretheim, *God and World in the Old Testament*, 119.

13. Cf. Deut 6:10–11; 7:13–15; 8:7–10; 11:8–17; 14:29; 15:4, 6; 16:15; 28:3–6, 11–12; 29:5–6; 33:24 Along these lines Dumbrell states, "Primarily, Deuteronomy offers Israel life in the Promised Land, with such a life depicted as a return to Eden" (Dumbrell, *The Faith of Israel*, 67).

Genesis 1–11

29, 33; 6:2–3, 18; 8:16; 11:9; 12:25, 28; 17:20; 22:7; 25:15; 28:63; 30:5, 18, 20; 32:47).[14]

Still another significant correspondence between the exhortation to Israel at the end of the Pentateuch and Gen 1–11 is the overall perspective with which one is left at the end of each respective section. The Primeval History ends with hope for the future dependence upon God's provision but with the acute awareness that disobedience results in loss of blessing. This is the same manner in which Deuteronomy, and hence the Pentateuch as a whole, ends.[15] Israel is presented with hope for God's future blessing while being made very aware of her responsibility to obey and of the consequences of disobedience.[16]

Function of the Correspondence of Beginning and Ending

It is one thing to observe the rhetorical strategy of the Pentateuch with both its beginning and ending emphasizing the same themes. It is a different

---

14. Fretheim observes a number of parallels between the beginning and ending of the Pentateuch which, he asserts, function as an intensification for the implied readers of the themes presented: (1) the first human beings in Eden and the newly redeemed people of God on the verge of entry into the land are representatives of God and partners in the furtherance of his divine purposes; (2) each is commanded to obey and is presented with consequences of life and death; (3) in both cases God engages the human, the image of God, as co-creator; (4) the inclination of each is toward failure (see Gen 6:5; 8:21; Deut 31:21, 27); (5) God's engagement of humanity as co-creator continues in both cases in spite of humanity's failure; (6) in both cases there is a promise of movement from judgment to blessing (see Gen 9 and Deut 29–32). See Fretheim, *The Pentateuch*, 56–57. These themes correspond closely with those identified in the theological exegesis of this book.

15. Fretheim sees Deut 29–34 as the ending of both Deuteronomy and the Pentateuch and which leaves "loose ends." He proposes that this character is particularly applicable to the implied readers who are "leaning into the future, but wondering what that future might hold." Some of the ideas which he cites as included in this uncertainty are as follows: (1) the future is filled with delights but fraught with dangers, both from outside and from within their own hearts; (2) obedience is possible, along with a community of life and well-being, but there is an inclination to infidelity; (3) there is basis for hope with a genuine sense of expectancy, but found not in their own potential for obedience, but rather in God's faithfulness. See ibid., 54–55. See also Postell, *Adam as Israel*, for an excellent treatment of the relationship between Genesis 1—3 and the Torah with its forward-pointing hope in a future work of God.

16. Just as Gen 1–11 combines the requirement for obedience with the underlying necessity for faith, the Pentateuch as a whole includes a strategy which emphasizes faith. See Schmitt, "Redaktion des Pentateuch im Geiste der Prophetie."

Summary and Implications

matter altogether to understand specifically how that beginning is to function with respect to the ending. That is, does it simply function as one part of an inclusio, introducing exactly the same concepts which are reiterated at the end? Westermann seems to think that it is far more than that when he describes the Pentateuch as two concentric circles placed around the account of Israel's deliverance from Egypt. The outer circle includes the story of the primeval events, which has the effect of extending Israel's experiences to world events in the broadest sense of the word.[17] He sees this presentation as critical for exegesis in that it gives the narrative of Israel and her history a universal perspective.[18] In his discussion of the theology of Gen 1–11, he suggests that, because of the Primeval History, Israel's sin as part of the history of the people of God is deliberately set in the broader context of sin, guilt, and punishment outside the history of Israel. That is, the history of God's dealings with his people shows the following:

> Punishment and forgiveness cannot be restricted to Israel alone, but must extend in some way beyond these limits to the broader horizon of sin and revolt as part of the human condition. The effect of the disorder which the sin and revolt of humanity has brought into creation is such that Gen 12 is not the beginning of a course of salvation history which is played out and runs to its goal within the enclosed framework of a community chosen by God; rather, God's saving action is concerned with humanity and the world and must be bound up in some way with the sin and revolt of humankind. So sin as part of the human condition—and the primeval story is dealing with this—is linked with history: God's dealing with his people and his concern with human sin are brought into relationship.[19]

In short, Westermann proposes that the Primeval History functions for Israel as an orientation of her history within the broader history of humanity, thus giving it a universal context. This perspective is echoed by Fretheim who, speaking about Gen 1–11, comments, "It seems clear that this material is not laid out simply to give the reader some basic information about the world or the beginnings of things. Rather, the strategy is to catch the reader up into *a universal frame of reference.*"[20]

17. Westermann, *Genesis 1–11*, 2.
18. Ibid., 4.
19. Ibid., 67.
20. Fretheim, *The Pentateuch*, 44. Cf. Blenkinsopp, *The Pentateuch*, 54, 86; Campbell and O'Brien, *Rethinking the Pentateuch*, 26; and Whybray, *Introduction to the Pentateuch*, 35.

Westermann's discussion is helpful for considering the particular function of the similarities in the message of Gen 1–11 and that of the Pentateuch as a whole. That is, those parallels serve to portray the concerns for Israel on the Plains of Moab as characteristic of those of all humankind. The necessity to obey is not something imposed solely on Israel because of her relationship with Yahweh, but rather something which is required of all humanity because of its relationship with the Creator. What is required of Israel is simply that which is incumbent upon all humanity.[21] But it is far more than that. As Fretheim asserts:

> It makes clear the intentions of God's redemptive work. The opening chapters demonstrate that God's purposes in redemption are not finally centered on Israel; they are universal in scope.... Israel comes on the scene only within the context of all the nations/families of the earth (Gen 10–11); Israel's election and reception of the divine promises are specifically tied back into this world family in Gen 12:1–3, "in you all the families of the earth shall be blessed." All these families are the ultimate concern of God; they are the ones who stand in need of the blessing (especially in view of sin and its effects). The ancestral narrative is punctuated with this divine mission in and through Israel (18:18; 22:18; 26:4; 28:14), and this is concretely shown in the various interactions between Israel's progenitors and virtually every people in Israel's environs.[22]

Therefore, Gen 1–11 can be understood as not only reinforcing the exhortation of Deuteronomy by reflecting the same essential message, but also as demonstrating that the message to Israel is reflective rather than determinative of God's message to all humankind.

Significance of the Message for the Implied Reader

In view of the foregoing discussion one can understand that the significance of the message for the reader, Israel, is that she is representative of God's interaction with humanity. That is, although she is to function as God's mediator to the nations, God's blessings do not originate with her

---

21. In a discussion which has similar implications, Emmrich discusses the themes of the temptation narrative played out in the Pentateuch. He argues for the writing of the creation accounts after the Pentateuch for the purpose of literarily laying the groundwork for the theology of the Pentateuch. See Emmrich, "The Temptation Narrative of Genesis 3:1–6."

22. Fretheim, *The Pentateuch*, 45.

and flow through her to the world. Rather, she is simply representative of God's interaction with all of humanity. As God's people she is special, but only in that God has chosen her as the vehicle, not the source, of blessing. Therefore, Israel must understand her existence to be an example and communication of God's message with the final object of blessing being all of humanity, rather than her being that final object herself.

Potential Implications

If Gen 1–11 is a unity with a coherent message, and that message corresponds to the message of the Pentateuch, which, in so doing, serves to place the exhortations to Israel within a universal context, then biblical theology, which tends to consider Gen 1–11 as simply background information, may do well to consider whether this introductory section of the canon serves a greater function than has been commonly thought.

As discussed in chapter 1 of this book, late twentieth century theological works on biblical theology generally treat Gen 1–11 simply as prolegomena, having little particular significance other than providing background material from which to pick up concepts or themes. That is, there has been a significant lack of consideration of the early chapters of Genesis as a unit with a coherent message and as having a function other than supplying background information. However, if, as argued in this study, the Primeval History is intentionally constructed for the purpose of conveying a theological message, and that message has a specific function within the overall context of the Pentateuch, which, in turn, provides significant foundational material from which the remainder of the Hebrew Scriptures draws, then the possibility is raised that the Primeval History has a greater significance for biblical theology than has generally been thought. That is, if it is a coherent section which provides a message and serves a function within a foundational section of Scripture, the Pentateuch, its significance and function may well extend beyond that section. The fact that imagery and themes introduced in these early chapters of Genesis are found also in the closing chapters of Revelation seems to support this possibility. This is a perspective which requires a great deal of additional work but, if pursued, may serve to further biblical theological studies.

Bibliography

Abela, Anthony. "Is Genesis the Introduction of the Primary History." In *Studies in the Book of Genesis: Literature, Redaction and History*, ed. A. Wénin. BETL, vol. 155, 397–406. Leuven: Leuven University Press, 2001.

Alexander, T. Desmond. *From Paradise to the Promised Land: An Introduction to the Main Themes of the Pentateuch*. Grand Rapids: Baker, 1995.

Alter, Robert. *The Art of Biblical Narrative*. New York: Basic Books, 1981.

———. *Genesis: Translation and Commentary*. New York: W. W. Norton & Company, 1996.

Amit, Yairah. *Hidden Polemics in Biblical Narrative*. Biblical Interpretation Series, ed. R. Alan Culpepper and Rolf Rendtorff, vol. 25. Leiden: Brill, 2000.

———. *Reading Biblical Narratives: Literary Criticism and the Hebrew Bible*. Minneapolis, MN: Fortress, 2001.

Andersen, Francis I. *The Sentence in Biblical Hebrew*. The Hague: Mouton, 1974.

Anderson, Bernhard W. "From Analysis to Synthesis: The Interpretation of Genesis 1–11." In *I Studied Inscriptions from before the Flood: Ancient Near Eastern, Literary, and Linguistic Approaches to Genesis 1–11*, ed. Richard S. Hess and David Toshio Tsumura. Sources for Biblical and Theological Studies, ed. David W. Baker, 416–35. Winona Lake, IN: Eisenbrauns, 1994.

———. *From Creation to New Creation*. Old Testament Perspectives, ed. Walter Brueggemann. Minneapolis, MN: Fortress, 1994.

Ansell, Nicholas John. "The Call of Wisdom/The Voice of the Serpent: A Canonical Approach to the Tree of Knowledge." *CSR* 31 (2001): 31–57.

Aufrecht, Walter E. "Genealogy and History in Ancient Israel." In *Ascribe to the Lord: Biblical and Other Studies in Memory of Peter C. Craigie*, ed. Lyle Eslinger and Glen Taylor. JSOTSup, ed. David J. A. Clines and Philip R. Davies, vol. 67, 205–25. Sheffield: Sheffield Academic Press, 1988.

Bailey, Lloyd R. *Noah: The Person and the Story in History and Tradition*. Studies on Personalities of the Old Testament, ed. James L. Crenshaw. Columbia, SC: University of South Carolina Press, 1989.

Bailey, Nicholas Andrew. "Some Literary and Grammatical Aspects of Genealogies in Genesis." In *Biblical Hebrew and Discourse Linguistics*, ed. Robert D. Bergen, 267–82. Dallas, TX: Summer Institute of Linguistics, 1994.

Bar-Efrat, Shimon. *Narrative Art in the Bible*. New York: T. & T. Clark, 2004.

Barr, James. *The Garden of Eden and the Hope of Immortality*. Minneapolis, MN: Fortress, 1993.

Bibliography

Barth, Karl. *The Doctrine of Creation.* Translated by J. W. Edwards, O. Bussey, and Harold Knight, *Church Dogmatics*, Vol. III.1. Edinburgh: T. & T. Clark, 1958.

Beale, Gregory K. "Eden, the Temple, and the Church's Mission in the New Creation." *JETS* 48 (2005): 5–32.

Benjamin, Don C. "Stories of Adam and Eve." In *Problems in Biblical Theology: Essays in Honor of Rolf Knierim*, ed. Henry T. C. Sun and Keith L. Eades, 38–58. Grand Rapids: Eerdmans, 1997.

Bird, Phyllis A. "'Male and Female He Created Them': Genesis 1:27b in the Context of the Priestly Account of Creation." In *I Studied Inscriptions from before the Flood: Ancient Near Eastern, Literary, and Linguistic Approaches to Genesis 1–11*, ed. Richard S. Hess and David Toshio Tsumura. Sources for Biblical and Theological Studies, ed. David W. Baker, 329–61. Winona Lake, IN: Eisenbrauns, 1994.

Blenkinsopp, Joseph. *The Pentateuch: An Introduction to the First Five Books of the Bible.* Anchor Bible Reference Library, ed. David Noel Freedman. New York: Doubleday, 1992.

Bonhoeffer, Dietrich. *Schöpfung und Fall.* Dietrich Bonhoeffer Werke, ed. Martin Rüter and Ilse Tödt, vol. 3. München: Chr. Kaiser, 1989.

Boomershine, Thomas E. "The Structure of Narrative Rhetoric in Genesis 2–3." *Semeia* 18 (1980): 113–29.

Borgman, Paul. *Genesis: The Story We Haven't Heard.* Downers Grove, IL: InterVarsity, 2001.

Botterweck, G. Johannes, and Helmer Ringgren, eds. *TDOT*. 11 vols. Grand Rapids: Eerdmans, 1975.

Bratcher, Margaret Dee. "The Pattern of Sin and Judgment in Genesis 1–11." PhD diss., Southern Baptist Theological Seminary, 1984.

Breytenbach, A. P. B. "The Connection between the Concepts of Darkness and Drought as well as Light and Vegetation." In *De fructuoris sui: Essays in Honour of Adrianus van Selms*, ed. I. H. Eybers, et al. Pretoria Oriental Series, ed. A. van Selms, vol. 9, 1–5. Leiden: Brill, 1971.

Brodie, Thomas L. *Genesis as Dialogue: A Literary, Historical, and Theological Commentary.* New York: Oxford University Press, 2001.

Brown, Francis, et al. BDB. Boston: Houghton, Mifflin and Company, 1906. Reprint, Peabody, MA: Hendrickson, 1999.

Brown, William P. "Divine Act and the Art of Persuasion in Genesis 1." In *History and Interpretation: Essays in Honour of John H. Hayes*, ed. M. Patrick Graham, et al. JSOTSup, ed. David J. A. Clines and Philip R. Davies, vol. 173, 19–32. Sheffield: JSOT Press, 1993.

Brueggemann, Walter. "The Kerygma of the Priestly Writers." *ZAW* 84 (1972): 397–414.

———. *The Land: Place as Gift, Promise, and Challenge in Biblical Faith.* 2d ed. Overtures to Biblical Theology. Minneapolis, MN: Fortress, 2002.

Bush, George. *Notes on Genesis.* Vol. 1. New York: Ivison, Phinney & Co., 1860. Reprint, Minneapolis: James & Klock, 1976.

Campbell, Antony F., and Mark A. O'Brien. *Rethinking the Pentateuch: Prolegomena to the Theology of Ancient Israel.* Louisville, KY: Westminster John Knox, 2005.

Cassuto, U. *A Commentary on the Book of Genesis: From Adam to Noah.* Translated by Israel Abrahams. Jerusalem: Magnes, 1964.

Chavalas, Mark. "Genealogical History as 'Charter': A Study of Old Babylonian Period Historiography and the Old Testament." In *Faith, Tradition, and History: Old*

Bibliography

Testament Historiography in Its Near Eastern Context, ed. A. R. Millard, et al., 103-28. Winona Lake, IN: Eisenbrauns, 1994.

Childs, Brevard S. *Introduction to the Old Testament as Scripture.* 1st American ed. Philadelphia: Fortress, 1979.

———. *Myth and Reality in the Old Testament.* Studies in Biblical Theology, ed. H. H. Rowley, et al., vol. 27. Naperville, IL: Alec R. Allenson, 1960.

Chisholm, Robert B. Jr. *From Exegesis to Exposition: A Practical Guide to Using Biblical Hebrew.* Grand Rapids: Baker, 1998.

———. "The Genesis Flood Account: Some Observations and a Question." Unpublished paper presented in the Creation Symposium, Dallas Theological Seminary, 2004.

Clark, W. Malcolm. "A Legal Background to the Yahwist's Use of 'Good and Evil' in Genesis 2-3." *JBL* 88 (1969): 266-78.

Clements, R. E. *Old Testament Theology: A Fresh Approach.* Atlanta: John Knox Press, 1979.

Clifford, Richard J. "The Hebrew Scriptures and the Theology of Creation." *TS* 46 (1985): 507-23.

———. "Theme in Genesis 1-11." *CBQ* 38 (1976): 483-507.

Clines, David J. A. "The Image of God in Man." *TynBul* 16 (1967): 53-103.

———. *The Theme of the Pentateuch.* JSOTSup, ed. David J. A. Clines, et al, vol. 10. Sheffield: University of Sheffield, 1978.

Cohn, Robert L. "Narrative Structure and Canonical Perspective in Genesis." *JSOT* 25 (1983): 3-16.

Collins, C. John. "What Happened to Adam and Eve? A Literary-Theological Approach to Genesis 3." *Presb* 27 (2001): 12-44.

Collins, John J. *Genesis 1-4: A Linguistic, Literary, and Theological Commentary.* Phillipsburg, NJ: P&R Publishing, 2006.

Combs, Eugene. "Has YHWH Cursed the Ground? Perplexity of Interpretation in Genesis 1-5." In *Ascribe to the Lord: Biblical and Other Studies in Memory of Peter C. Craigie*, ed. Lyle Eslinger and Glen Taylor. JSOTSup, ed. David J. A. Clines and Philip R. Davies, vol. 67, 265-87. Sheffield: Sheffield Academic Press, 1988.

Culley, Robert C. "Action Sequences in Genesis 2-3." *Semeia* 18 (1980): 25-33.

Delitzsch, Franz. *A New Commentary on Genesis.* Clark's Foreign Theological Library, vol. 1. Edinburgh: T. & T. Clark, 1899.

Dempster, Stephen G. "Geography and Genealogy, Dominion and Dynasty: A Theology of the Hebrew Bible." In *Biblical Theology: Retrospect and Prospect*, ed. Scott J. Hafemann, 66-82. Downers Grove, IL: InterVarsity, 2002.

DeRoche, Michael. "The *rûaḥĕlōhîm* in Gen 1:2c: Creation or Chaos." In *Ascribe to the Lord: Biblical and Other Studies in Memory of Peter C. Craigie*, ed. Lyle Eslinger and Glen Taylor. JSOTSup, ed. David J. A. Clines and Philip R. Davies, vol. 67, 303-18. Sheffield: Sheffield Academic Press, 1988.

Descamps, A. L., André de Halleux, and BédaRigaux, eds. *Mélanges bibliques: en hommage au R. P. BédaRigaux.* Gembloux: Duculot, 1970.

Dorsey, David A. *The Literary Structure of the Old Testament: A Commentary on Genesis-Malachi.* Grand Rapids: Baker, 1999.

Dumbrell, William J. *Covenant and Creation: A Theology of the Old Testament Covenants.* Carlisle, CA: Paternoster, 1984.

———. *Creation, Fall, and Flood: Studies in Genesis 1-11.* Minneapolis, MN: Augsburg, 1969.

Bibliography

———. *The End of the Beginning: Revelation 21–22 and the Old Testament.* Eugene, OR: Wipf and Stock, 1985.

———. *The Faith of Israel: A Theological Survey of the Old Testament.* 2d ed. Grand Rapids: Baker, 2002.

———. "Genesis 2:1–3: Biblical Theology of the Creation Covenant." *ERT* 25 (2001): 219–30.

———. "Genesis 2:1–17: A Foreshadowing of the New Creation." In *Biblical Theology: Retrospect and Prospect,* ed. Scott J. Hafemann, 53–65. Downers Grove, IL: InterVarsity, 2002.

———. *God and World in the Old Testament: A Relational Theology of Creation.* Nashville, TN: Abingdon, 2005.

———. *The Pentateuch.* Interpreting Biblical Texts, ed. Gene M. Tucker. Nashville: Abingdon, 1996.

Emerton, J. A. "An Examination of Some Attempts to Defend the Unity of the Flood Narrative in Genesis: Part 1." *VT* 37 (1987): 401–20.

———. "An Examination of Some Attempts to Defend the Unity of the Flood Narrative in Genesis: Part 2." *VT* 38 (1987): 1–21.

Emmrich, Martin. "The Temptation Narrative of Genesis 3:1–6: A Prelude to the Pentateuch and the History of Israel." *EvQ* 73 (2001): 3–20.

Eslinger, Lyle. "A Contextual Identification of the *bene ha'elohim* and *benoth ha'adam* in Genesis 6:1–4." *JSOT* 13 (1979): 65–73.

Fields, Weston W. *Unformed and Unfilled.* Phillipsburg, NJ: P&R Publishing, 1976.

Fishbane, Michael. *Biblical Text and Texture: A Literary Reading of Selected Texts.* New York: Schocken Books, 1979. Reprint, Oxford: Oneworld Publications, 1998.

Fokkelman, J. P. *Narrative Art in Genesis: Specimens of Stylistic and Structural Analysis.* Amsterdam: Van Gorcum, 1975.

Forrest, Robert W. E. "Paradise Lost Again: Violence and Obedience in the Flood Narrative." *JSOT* 62 (1994): 3–18.

Freedman, Tuvia. "רוח אלהים—and a Wind from God." *JBQ* 24 (1996): 9–13.

Fretheim, Terence E. *Creation, Fall, and Flood: Studies in Genesis 1–11.* Minneapolis, MN: Augsburg, 1969.

———. *God and World in the Old Testament: A Relational Theology of Creation.* Nashville, TN: Abingdon, 2005.

———. *The Pentateuch.* Interpreting Biblical Texts, ed. Gene M. Tucker. Nashville: Abingdon, 1996.

Froebe, Dieter. *Der Sonderfall des Menschen und der Sündenfall der Theologie: Einliterarische Auslegung der Vorgeschichte Israels (Gen. 2,4b–11,32) im Zusammenhang der hebräischen Bibel.* Theologie, vol. 56.Münster: Lit, 2004.

Futato, Mark D. "Because It Had Not Rained: A Study of Gen 2:5–7 With Implications for Gen 2:4–25 and Gen 1:1–2:3." *WTJ* 60 (1998): 1–21.

Gage, Warren Austin. *The Gospel of Genesis: Studies in Protology and Eschatology.* Winona Lake, IN: Carpenter Books, 1984.

Galambush, Julie. "*'adām* from *'adāmâ*, *'iššâ* from *'îš*: Derivation and Subordination in Genesis 2.4b–3.24." In *History and Interpretation: Essays in Honour of John H. Hayes,* ed. M. Patrick Graham, et al. JSOTSup, ed. David J. A. Clines and Philip R. Davies, vol. 173, 33–46. Sheffield: JSOT Press, 1993

García Martínez, Florentino, ed. *The Dead Sea Scrolls Translated: The Qumran Texts in English.* Translated by Wilfred G. E. Watson, 2d ed. Leiden: Brill, 1996.

Bibliography

Garrett, Duane A. *Rethinking Genesis: The Sources and Authorship of the First Book of the Bible.* Ross-shire, Great Britain: Christian Focus Publications, 2000.

Gevirtz, S. "Lamech's Song to His Wives (Genesis 4:23–24)." In *I Studied Inscriptions from before the Flood: Ancient Near Eastern, Literary, and Linguistic Approaches to Genesis 1–11*, ed. Richard S. Hess and David Toshio Tsumura. Sources for Biblical and Theological Studies, ed. David W. Baker, 405–15. Winona Lake, IN: Eisenbrauns, 1994.

Goldingay, John E. *Old Testament Theology.* Vol. 1, *Israel's Gospel.* Downers Grove, IL: InterVarsity, 2003.

Gonzales, Robert R. Jr. *Where Sin Abounds: The Spread of Sin and the Curse in the Book of Genesis with Special Focus on the Patriarchal Narratives.* Eugene, OR: Wipf& Stock, 2009.

Gowan, Donald E. *From Eden to Babel: A Commentary on the Book of Genesis 1–11.* ITC, ed. Frederick Carlson Holmgren and George A. F. Knight. Grand Rapids: Eerdmans, 1988.

Gruber, Mayer I. "The Tragedy of Cain and Abel: A Case of Depression." *JQR* 69 (1978): 95–97.

Gunkel, Hermann, and Heinrich Zimmern. *Schöpfung und Chaos in Urzeit und Endzeit: Eine religionsgeschichtliche Untersuchungüber Gen 1 und Ap. Joh 12.* 2d ed. Göttingen: Vandenhoeck und Ruprecht, 1921.

Habel, Norman C. "Geophany: The Earth Story in Genesis 1." In *The Earth Story in Genesis*, ed. Norman C. Habel and Shirley Wurst. The Earth Bible, vol. 2, 34–48. Sheffield: Sheffield Academic Press, 2000.

Hamilton, Victor P. *The Book of Genesis: Chapters 1–17.* NICOT, ed. R. K. Harrison. Grand Rapids: Eerdmans, 1990.

Hanson, K. C. "Alphabetical Acrostics: A Form Critical Study." Ph.D. diss., Claremont Graduate School, 1984.

Harris, R. Laird, Gleason Leonard Archer, and Bruce K. Waltke, eds. *TWOT.* Chicago: Moody, 1980.

Hart, Ian. "Genesis 1:1–2:3 as a Prologue to the Book of Genesis." *TynBul* 46 (1995): 315–36.

Hauser, Alan J. "Genesis 2–3: The Theme of Intimacy and Alienation." In *Art and Meaning: Rhetoric in Biblical Literature, Art, and Meaning*, ed. David J. A. Clines, 23–36. Sheffield: JSOT Press, 1982.

———. "Linguistic and Thematic Links Between Genesis 4:1–16 and Genesis 2–3." *JETS* 23 (1980): 297–305.

Hendel, Ronald S. *The Text of Genesis 1–11: Textual Studies and Critical Edition.* New York: Oxford University Press, 1998.

Herion, Gary A. "Why God Rejected Cain's Offering: The Obvious Answer." In *Fortunate the Eyes that See: Essays in Honor of David Noel Freedman in Celebration of His Seventieth Birthday*, ed. Astrid B. Beck, et al., 52–55. Grand Rapids: Eerdmans, 1995.

Hess, Richard S. "The Genealogies of Genesis 1–11 and Comparative Literature." *Bib* 70 (1989): 241–54.

———. "Genesis 1–2 in its Literary Context." *TynBul* 41 (1990): 143–53.

———. "Genesis and Ancient Near Eastern Stories of Creation and Flood: An Introduction." In *I Studied Inscriptions from before the Flood: Ancient Near Eastern, Literary, and Linguistic Approaches to Genesis 1–11*, ed. Richard S. Hess and David

Bibliography

Toshio Tsumura. Sources for Biblical and Theological Studies, ed. David W. Baker, 27-57. Winona Lake, IN: Eisenbrauns, 1994.

———. "Splitting the Adam: The usage of *'adam* in Genesis i-v." In *Studies in the Pentateuch*, ed. J. A. Emerton. VTSup, ed. J. A. Emerton, et al., vol. 41, 1-16. New York: Brill, 1990.

———. *Studies in the Personal Names of Genesis 1-11*. AOAT, ed. Manfried Dietrich and Oswald Loretz, vol. 234.Neukirchen-Vluyn: Neukirchener, 1993.

Holladay, William L. *A Concise Hebrew and Aramaic Lexicon of the Old Testament*. Grand Rapids: Eerdmans, 1971.

House, Paul R. *Old Testament Theology*. Downers Grove, IL: InterVarsity, 1998.

Huey, F. B. Jr. "Are the 'Sons of God' in Genesis 6 Angels? Yes." In *The Genesis Debate: Persistent Questions About Creation and the Flood*, ed. Ronald Youngblood, 184-211. Grand Rapids: Baker, 1990.

Johnson, Marshall D. *The Purpose of the Biblical Genealogies with Special Reference to the Setting of the Genealogies of Jesus*.2d ed. SNTSMS, ed. G. N. Stanton, vol. 8. New York: Cambridge University Press, 1988.

Joines, Karen Randolph. "The Serpent in Gen 3." *ZAW* 87 (1975): 1-11.

Jónsson, Gunnlaugur A. *The Image of God: Genesis 1:26-28 in a Century of Old Testament Research*. Translated by Lorraine Svendsen. ConBOT, ed. Tryggve N. D. Mettinger and Magnus Y. Ottosson, vol. 26. Lund: Almqvist & Wiksell International, 1988.

Kaiser, Walter C. *Toward an Old Testament Theology*. Grand Rapids: Zondervan, 1978.

Kempf, Stephen. "Introducing the Garden of Eden: The Structure and Function of Genesis 2:4B-7."*JOTT* 7 (1996): 33-53.

Kikawada, Isaac M., and Arthur Quinn. *Before Abraham Was: The Unity of Genesis 1-11*. Nashville, TN: Abingdon, 1985.

Kline, Meredith. "Because It Had Not Rained." *WTJ* 20 (1958): 146-57.

———. "Divine Kingship and Genesis 6:1-4." *WTJ* 24 (1962): 187-204.

Koehler, Ludwig, and Walter Baumgartner. *HALOT*. Translated by M. E. J. Richardson. 2 vols., ed. M. E. J. Richardson. Leiden: Brill, 2001.

Levenson, Jon D. *Creation and the Persistence of Evil: The Jewish Drama of Divine Omnipotence*. San Francisco: Harper & Row, 1988.

Lim, Johnson T. K. "Explication of an Exegetical Enigma in Genesis 1:1-3." *AJT* 16 (2002): 301-14.

———. *Grace in the Midst of Judgment: Grappling with Genesis 1-11*. BZAW, ed. Otto Kaiser, vol. 314. New York: Walter de Gruyter, 2002.

Lode, Lars. "The Two Creation Stories in Genesis Chapters 1 to 3." *JOTT* 14 (2001): 1-52.

Longacre, Robert E. "The Discourse of the Flood Narrative." *JAAR* 47 (1979): 89-133.

Löning, Karl, and Erich Zenger. *To Begin with, God Created . . . Biblical Theologies of Creation*. Translated by Omar Kaste. Collegeville, MN: Liturgical Press, 2000.

Maier, John. "The Flood Story: Four Literary Approaches." In *Approaches to Teaching the Hebrew Bible as Literature in Translation*, ed. Barry N. Olshen and Yael S. Feldman, 106-09. New York: The Modern Language Association, 1989.

Malamat, Abraham. "King Lists of the Old Babylonian Period and Biblical Genealogies." *JAOS* 88 (1968): 163-73.

Mann, Thomas W. *The Book of the Torah: The Narrative Integrity of the Pentateuch*. Atlanta: John Knox Press, 1988.

Martens, Elmer A. *God's Design: A Focus on Old Testament Theology*. Grand Rapids: Baker, 1981.

Martin, Francis. "Male and Female He Created Them: A Summary of the Teaching of Genesis Chapter One." *Comm* 20 (1993): 240–65.
Mathews, Kenneth A. *Genesis 1–11:26*. NAC, ed. E. Ray Clendenen, vol. 1A. Nashville, TN: Broadman & Holman, 1996.
McBride Jr., S. Dean. "Divine Protocol: Genesis 1:1–2:3 as Prologue to the Pentateuch." In *God Who Creates: Essays in Honor of W. Sibley Towner*, ed. William P. Brown and S. Dean McBride Jr., 3–41. Grand Rapids: Eerdmans, 2000.
McCabe, Robert V. "A Defense of Literal Days in the Creation Week." *Detroit Baptist Seminary Journal* 5 (2000): 97–123.
Merrill, Eugene H. "A Theology of the Pentateuch." In *A Biblical Theology of the Old Testament*, 7–87. Chicago: Moody Press, 1991.
Millar, J. Gary. *Now Choose Life: Theology and Ethics in Deuteronomy*. New Studies in Biblical Theology, ed. D. A. Carson. Grand Rapids: Eerdmans, 1998.
Miller, Patrick D. *Genesis 1–11: Studies in Structure and Theme*. JSOTSup, ed. David J. A. Clines, Philip R. Davies, and David M. Gunn, vol. 8. Sheffield: University of Sheffield, 1978.
Moran, William L. "The Ancient Near Eastern Background of the Love of God in Deuteronomy." *CBQ* 25 (1963): 77–87.
Morris, Henry Madison. *The Genesis Record: A Scientific and Devotional Commentary on the Book of Beginnings*. Grand Rapids: Baker, 1976.
Mulzac, Kenneth. "Genesis 9:1–7: Its Theological Connections with the Creation Motif." *JATS* 12 (2001): 65–77.
Ouro, Roberto. "The Earth of Genesis 1:2: Abiotic or Chaotic? Part 1." *AUSS* 35 (1998): 259–76.
―――. "The Earth of Genesis 1:2: Abiotic or Chaotic? Part 3." *AUSS* 38 (1998): 59–67.
―――. "The Garden of Eden Account: The Chiastic Structure of Genesis 2–3." *AUSS* 40 (2002): 219–43.
―――. "Linguistic and Thematic Parallels Between Genesis 1 and 3." *JATS* 13 (2002): 44–54.
Patte, Daniel, and Judson F. Parker. "A Structural Exegesis of Genesis 2 and 3." SBLSP 13 (1978): 141–59.
Perry, T. A. "A Poetics of Absence: The Structure and Meaning of Genesis 1:2." *JSOT* 58 (1993): 3–11.
Postell, Seth D. *Adam as Israel: Genesis 1―3 as the Introduction to the Torah and Tanakh*. Eugene, OR: Pickwick, 2011.
Pritchard, James B., ed. *Ancient Near Eastern Texts Relating to the Old Testament*, 3d ed. Princeton, NJ: Princeton University Press, 1969.
Provan, Iain. "Creation and Holistic Ministry: A Study of Genesis 1:1 to 2:3." *ERT* 25 (2001): 292–303.
Radday, Yehuda T., and Haim Shore. *Genesis: An Authorship Study in Computer-Assisted Statistical Linguistics*. AnBib, vol. 103. Rome: Biblical Institute Press, 1985.
Ramsey, George W. "Is Name-Giving an Act of Domination in Genesis 2:23 and Elsewhere?" *CBQ* 50 (1988): 24–35.
Renaud, B. "Les généalogies et la structure de l'histoire sacerdotal dans le livre de la Genèse." *RB* 97 (1990): 5–30.
Rendsburg, Gary. *The Redaction of Genesis*. Winona Lake, IN: Eisenbrauns, 1986.
Robinson, H. Wheeler. *Corporate Personality in Ancient Israel*, rev. ed. Philadelphia: Fortress, 1980.

Bibliography

Robinson, Robert B. "Literary Functions of the Genealogies of Genesis." *CBQ* 48 (1986): 595–608.

Rooker, Mark F. "Genesis 1:1–3: Creation or Re-Creation?" In *Vital Old Testament Issues: Examining Textual and Topical Questions*, ed. Roy Zuck. Vital Issues Series, vol. 7, 11–27. Grand Rapids: Kregel, 1996.

Ross, Allen P. *Creation and Blessing: A Guide to the Study and Exposition of Genesis*. Grand Rapids: Baker, 1996.

Rudman, D. "A Little Knowledge is a Dangerous Thing: Forbidden Boundaries in Gen 3–4." In *Studies in the Book of Genesis: Literature, Redaction and History*, ed. A. Wénin. Bibliotheca Ephemeridum Theologicarum Lovaniensium, vol. 155, 461–66. Leuven: Leuven University Press, 2001.

Ruppert, Lothar. *Genesis: Einkritischer und theologischer Kommentar*. Vol. 1.FB, ed. Rudolf Schnackenburg and Josef Schreiner, vol. 70.Würzburg: Echter, 1992.

Sailhamer, John H. *Genesis Unbound: A Provocative New Look at the Creation Account*. Sisters, OR: Multnomah, 1996.

———. *The Pentateuch as Narrative: A Biblical-Theological Commentary*. Grand Rapids: Zondervan, 1992.

Sarna, Nahum M. "The Anticipatory Use of Information as a Literary Feature of the Genesis Narratives." In *The Creation of Sacred Literature: Composition and Redaction of the Biblical Text*, ed. Richard Elliott Friedman. University of California Publications: Near Eastern Studies, vol. 22, 76–82. Berkeley, CA: University of California Press, 1981.

———. *Genesis*. The JPS Torah Commentary, ed. Nahum M. Sarna. Philadelphia: Jewish Publication Society, 1989.

Sasson, Jack M. "The 'Tower of Babel' as a Clue to the Redactional Structuring of the Primeval History." In *The Bible World: Essays in Honor of Cyrus H. Gordon*, ed. Gary Rendsburg, et al., 211–20. New York: Ktav and the Institute of Hebrew Culture and Education of New York University, 1980.

Schmitt, Hans-Christoph. "Redaktion des Pentateuch im Geiste der Prophetie." *VT* 32 (1982): 170–89.

Schwarz, Hans. *Die biblische Urgeschichte: Gottes Traum von Mensch und Welt*. Breisgau: Herder Taschenbuch, 1989.

Scobie, Charles H. H. *The Ways of Our God: An Approach to Biblical Theology*. Grand Rapids: Eerdmans, 2003.

Shea, William H. "The Unity of the Creation Account." *Origins* 5 (1978): 9–38.

Smelik, K. A. D. "The Creation of the Sabbath (Gen. 1:1–2:3)." In *Unless Some One Guide Me . . . Festschrift for Karel A. Deurloo*, ed. J. W. Dyk, et al. Amsterdamse Cahiers voor Exegese van de Bijbel en zijn Tradities: Supplement Series vol. 2, 9–12. Maastricht: Uitgeverij Shaker, 2001.

Smith, Gary V. "Structure and Purpose in Genesis 1–11." *JETS* 20 (1977): 307–19.

Smith, Ralph L. *Old Testament Theology: Its History, Method, and Message*. Nashville: Broadman & Holman, 1993.

Speiser, E. A. *Genesis*. AB, ed. William F. Albright and David N. Freedman. Garden City, NY: Doubleday, 1964.

Steinmann, Andrew E. "אחד as an Ordinal Number and the Meaning of Genesis 1:5." *JETS* 45 (2002): 577–84.

Steinmetz, Devora. "Vineyard, Farm, and Garden: The Drunkenness of Noah in the Context of the Primeval History." *JBL* 113 (1994): 193–207.

Sterchi, David A. "Does Genesis 1 Provide a Chronological Sequence?" *JETS* 39 (1996): 529–36.
Sternberg, Meir. *The Poetics of Biblical Narrative*. Bloomington: Indiana University Press, 1985.
Stordalen, Terje. *Echoes of Eden: Genesis 2–3 and Symbolism of the Eden Garden in Biblical Hebrew Literature*. Leuven: Peeters, 2000.
———. "Man, Soil, Garden: Basic Plot in Genesis 2–3 Reconsidered." *JSOT* 53 (1992): 3–26.
Strecker, Georg. *Theology of the New Testament*. Translated by M. Eugene Boring, ed. Friedrich Wilhelm Horn. New York: Walter de Gruyter, 2000.
Strus, A. "Gn 2,4b–3,24. Structure et décodage du message." In *Studies in the Book of Genesis: Literature, Redaction and History*, ed. A. Wénin. BELT, vol. 155, 449–60. Leuven: Leuven University Press, 2001.
Thompson, Thomas L. *The Origin Tradition of Ancient Israel: The Literary Formation of Genesis and Exodus 1–23*. JSOTSup, ed. David J. A. Clines and Philip R. Davies, vol. 55. Sheffield: JSOT Press, 1987.
Toews, Brian G. "Genesis 1–4: The Genesis of Old Testament Instruction." In *Biblical Theology: Retrospect and Prospect*, ed. Scott J. Hafemann, 38–52. Downers Grove, IL: InterVarsity, 2002.
Tomasino, Anthony J. "History Repeats Itself: The 'Fall' and Noah's Drunkenness." *VT* 42 (1992): 128–30.
Trible, Phyllis. *God and the Rhetoric of Sexuality*. OBT, ed. Walter Brueggemann and John R. Donahue. Philadelphia: Fortress, 1978.
Trimpe, Birgit. *Von der Schöpfung bis zur Zerstreuung: Intertextuelle Interpretationen der biblischen Urgeschichte (Gen 1–11)*. Osnabrücker Studien zur jüdischen und christlichen Bibel, ed. Christoph Dohmen and Helmut Merkel, vol. 1.Osnabrück: Universität verlag Rasch, 2000.
Tsevat, M. "שני העץים אשר בתוך הגן."In *Nelson Glueck Memorial Volume*, ed. B. Mazar. Eretz-Israel: Archaeological, Historical and Geographical Studies, vol. 12, Hebrew Section, 40–43. Jerusalem: Israel Exploration Society, 1975.
Tsumura, David Toshio. *The Earth and the Waters in Genesis 1 and 2: A Linguistic Investigation*. JSOTSup, ed. David J. A. Clines and Philip R. Davies, vol. 83. Sheffield: JSOT Press, 1989.
Turner, Laurence A. *Genesis*. Readings: A New Biblical Commentary, ed. John Jarick. Sheffield: Sheffield Academic Press, 2000.
Valiquette, Hilaire Paul. "Exodus–Deuteronomy as Discourse: Models, Distancing, Provocation, Paraenesis." *JSOT* 85 (1999): 47–70.
VanGemeren, Willem A., ed. *NIDOTTE*. 5 vols. Grand Rapids: Zondervan, 1997.
van Wolde, Ellen. "The Earth Story as Presented by the Tower of Babel Narrative." In *The Earth Story in Genesis*, ed. Norman C. Habel and Shirley Wurst. The Earth Bible, vol. 2, 147–57. Sheffield: Sheffield Academic Press, 2000.
———. "Profiling Creation as Grace." In *The Bright Side of Life*, ed. Ellen van Wolde. Concilium, vol. 2000/4, 17–25. London: SCM, 2000.
———. *A Semiotic Analysis of Genesis 2–3: A Semiotic Theory and Method of Analysis Applied to the Story of the Garden of Eden*. Assen: van Gorcum, 1989.
———. *Stories of the Beginning: Genesis 1–11 and Other Creation Stories*. Translated by John Bowden. Ridgefield, CT: Morehouse Publishing, 1997.
———. "The Story of Cain and Abel: A Narrative Study." *JSOT* 52 (1991): 25–41.

Bibliography

———. "A Text-Semantic Study." *JBL* 113 (1994): 19-35.

———. *Words Become Worlds: Semantic Studies of Genesis 1-11.* Biblical Interpretation Series, ed. R. Alan Culpepper and Rolf Rendtorff, vol. 6. New York: Brill, 1994.

Vervenne, Mark. "All They Need is Love: Once More Genesis 6.1-4." In *Words Remembered, Texts Renewed: Essays in Honour of John F. A. Sawyer*, ed. Jon Davies, et al. JSOTSup, ed. David J. A. Clines and Philip R. Davies, vol. 195, 19-40. Sheffield: Sheffield Academic Press, 1995.

von Rad, Gerhard. *Genesis: A Commentary.* Translated by John H. Marks. Philadelphia: Westminster Press, 1961.

Wallace, Howard N. *The Eden Narrative.* HSM, ed. Frank Moore Cross, vol. 32. Atlanta: Scholars, 1985.

———. "Rest for the Earth: Another Look at Genesis 2:1-3." In *The Earth Story in Genesis*, ed. Norman C. Habel and Shirley Wurst. The Earth Bible, vol. 2, 49-59. Sheffield: Sheffield Academic Press, 2000

———. "The Toledot of Adam." In *Studies in the Pentateuch*, ed. J. A. Emerton. VTSup, ed. J. A. Emerton, et al., vol. 41, 17-34. New York: Brill, 1990

Walsh, Jerome T. "Genesis 2:4b-3:24: A Synchronic Approach." *JBL* 96 (1977): 161-77.

———. *Style and Structure in Biblical Hebrew Narrative.* Collegeville, MN: Liturgical Press, 2001.

Waltke, Bruce K., and Cathi J. Fredricks. *Genesis: A Commentary.* Grand Rapids: Zondervan, 2001.

Waltke, Bruce K. "Creation Account in Gen 1:1-3." *BibSac* 132 (1975): 136-44, 222-28.

Waltke, Bruce K., and M. O'Connor. *An Introduction to Biblical Hebrew Syntax.* Winona Lake, IN: Eisenbrauns, 1990.

Walton, John H. *Genesis 1 as Ancient Cosmology.* Winona Lake: Eisenbrauns, 2011.

———. *Genesis: From Biblical Text to Contemporary Life.* Grand Rapids: Zondervan, 2001.

———. *The Lost World of Genesis One: Ancient Cosmology and the Origins Debate.* Downers Grove: IVP Academic, 2009.

Wells, M. Jay. "Figural Representation and Canonical Unity." In *Biblical Theology: Retrospect and Prospect*, ed. Scott J. Hafemann, 111-25. Downers Grove, IL: InterVarsity, 2002

Wenham, Gordon J. "The Coherence of the Flood Narrative." *VT* 28 (1978): 336-48.

———. *Genesis 1-15.* WBC, ed. David A. Hubbard and Glenn W. Barker, vol. 1. Waco, TX: Word, 1987.

———. *Genesis 16-50.* WBC, ed. David A. Hubbard and Glenn W. Barker, vol. 2. Waco, TX: Word, 1994.

———. "Sanctuary Symbolism in the Garden of Eden Story." In *Proceedings of the Ninth World Congress of Jewish Studies: Jerusalem, August 4-12, 1985. Division A. The Period of the Bible*, 19-26. Jerusalem: World Union of Jewish Studies, 1986

Westermann, Claus. *Genesis 1-11: A Commentary.* Translated by John J. Scullion. Vol. 1. Minneapolis, MN: Augsburg, 1984.

White, Hugh C. *Narration and Discourse in the Book of Genesis.* Cambridge: Cambridge University Press, 1991.

Whybray, R. Norman. *Introduction to the Pentateuch.* Grand Rapids: Eerdmans, 1995.

Williams, A. J. "The Relationship of Genesis 3:20 to the Serpent." *ZAW* 89 (1977): 357-74.

Wilson, Robert R. "Between 'Azel' and 'Azel': Interpreting the Biblical Genealogies." *BA* 42 (1979): 11-22.

———. *Genealogy and History in the Biblical World.* Yale Near Eastern Researches, ed. William W. Hallo, vol. 7. New Haven, CT: Yale University Press, 1977.

———. "The Old Testament Genealogies in Recent Research." *JBL* 94 (1975): 169–89.

Witte, Markus. *Die biblische Urgeschichte.* BZAW, ed. Otto Kaiser, vol. 265. Berlin: Walter de Gruyter, 1998.

Wittenberg, Gunther. "Alienation and 'Emancipation' from the Earth: The Earth Story in Genesis 4." In *The Earth Story in Genesis*, ed. Norman C. Habel and Shirley Wurst. The Earth Bible, vol. 2, 105–16. Sheffield: Sheffield Academic Press, 2000

Woudstra, Martin H. "The *Toledot* of the Book of Genesis and their Redemptive-Historical Significance." *CTJ* 5 (1970): 184–89.

Wyatt, Nicolas. "The Darkness of Genesis I.2." *VT* 43 (1993): 543–54.

Youngblood, Ronald F. *The Book of Genesis: An Introductory Commentary.* 2d ed. Grand Rapids: Baker, 1991.

———. *The Genesis Debate: Persistent Questions About Creation and the Flood.* Grand Rapids: Baker, 1990.

www.ingramcontent.com/pod-product-compliance
Lightning Source LLC
Chambersburg PA
CBHW050807160426
43192CB00010B/1674